Richmond, Fredericksburg & Potomac Railroad
The Capital Cities Route

by
William E. Griffin, Jr.

R. F&P. R.R.

T L C
PUBLISHING

1994
TLC Publishing, Inc.
Route 4 - Box 154
Lynchburg, Virginia 24503-9711

Front Cover Ilustration: Two of RF&P's "Governor Class" passenger 4-8-4 type locomotives, No. 601, *Governor Patrick Henry*, and No. 602, *Governor Thomas Jefferson*, prepare to leave Richmond for the North, while a set of E8s, precursor of things to come, waits for its train. Broad Street Station's elegant classical dome looms in the background. RF&P revived the practice of naming locomotives that had been dropped in the 1870s, when its 4-8-4 types began to arrive. The first group was named for Confederate generals, the next for Virginia Governors, and the last for other famous Virginia statesmen. *This painting was commissioned especially for this book and is by noted railroad artist Andrew Harmantas.*

Library of Congress Catalog Card Number 94-60863
ISBN 1-883089-12-3

Typography and layout
by
Tom & Carolyn Dixon

Printed by
Walsworth Publishing Co.
Marceline, Missouri 64658

Contents

Introduction - 1

Chapter 1 — A Brief History of the RF&P - 3

Chapter 2 — The Glory Days of Steam - 25

Chapter 3 — The Diesel Era - 57

Chapter 4 — Passenger Service - 83

Chapter 5 — Special Trains - 109

Chapter 6 — Freight Service - 117

Chapter 7 — Passenger Train Equipment - 143

Chapter 8 — Freight Train Equipment - 167

Chpater 9 — An RF&P Color Album - 190

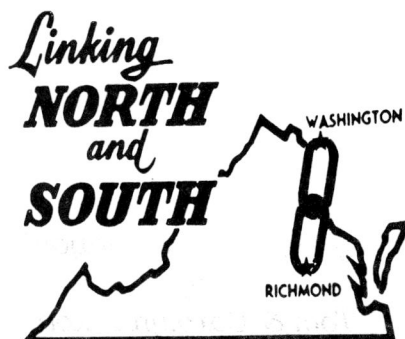

Linking
NORTH
and
SOUTH

WASHINGTON

RICHMOND

Richmond, Fredericksburg and Potomac Railroad

In the time-honored tradition of railroading, an RF&P conductor and engineer review their train orders before leaving Broad Street Station in Richmond with their northbound train to Washington. Their locomotive is 4-8-4 No. 602, one of the RF&P's named locomotives, *Governor Thomas Jefferson.* RF&P revived the ancient practice of naming locomotives (passe since the 1870s) with its 4-8-4s, naming them for famous Virginia statesmen, governors, and Civil War generals.

Introduction and Acknowledgements

In the early morning hours of October 10, 1991, documents were signed, bank drafts cleared, and the deal was struck to end the 157-year independent operation of the Richmond, Fredericksburg and Potomac Railroad Company. Born during the earliest stage of railroad development, its unique arrangement of stock ownership had enabled the RF&P to retain independent status long after other railroad companies succumbed to the rail industry's modern merger movement.

This is my second book on the RF&P. The first—*A Hundred and Fifty Years of History Along the RF&P*—was published by the Company in 1983 to commemorate the 150th anniversary of its corporate existence. That work, actually a compilation of articles that had previously appeared in the Company's employee magazine, focused on the RF&P's history as it related to the communities along its right-of-way.

With the demise of the Company, I resolved to tell the story of the RF&P in a more comprehensive manner. This book has been written to fulfill that goal. Herein, we'll review the RF&P's corporate history from birth to merger; the Company's motive power and rolling stock; its passenger and freight operations; and, the special train operations that won so many friends for the RF&P in the Commonwealth of Virginia.

I am indebted to many for their assistance in the production of this work. The following photographers and collectors graciously made photographs available from their collections: August A Thieme, Homer R. Hill, J. R. Quinn, H. B. McBride, J. I. Kelly, E. D. Siler, Frank Dementi, Charles A. Brown, H. K. Vollrath, Wiley M. Bryan, C. K. Marsh, Jr., Herbert H. Harwood, Jr., L. W. Rice, Jim Shaw, Margaret Cornell, D. Wallace Johnson, Anthony Dementi, Jeff Morfit, David E. George, Howard W. Ameling, Paul B. Wright, Warren Calloway, Doug Koontz, Alex M. Mayes, E. L. Thompson, H. W. Pontin, Joseph A. Rose, C. L. Goolsby, Tom Dixon, Ted Gay, H. Reid, Bruce Fales, Joseph M. Welsh, E. P. Willis, John C. LaRue, William B. Gwaltney, the Library of Congress, and the National Archives.

This book is dedicated with love to my wife Janice, who has made my life complete. Without her patience and understanding this book would not have been possible.

William E. Griffin, Jr.
Orange Park, Florida
July 1994

RICHMOND, FREDERICKSBURG and POTOMAC R.R. with CONNECTIONS

Scale of Miles

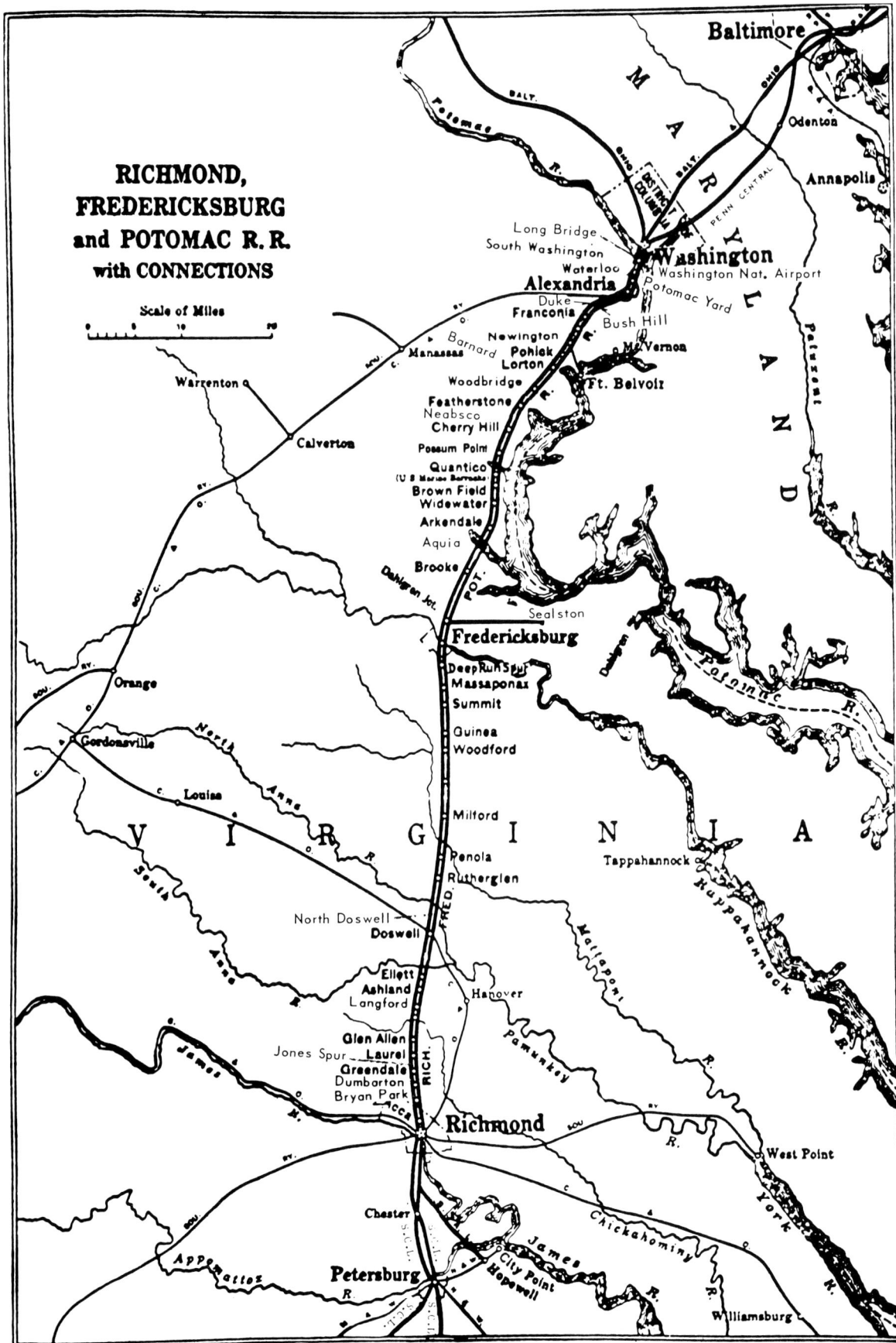

This 1970-era map of the RF&P's 113-mile straight railroad from Richmond to Washington shows its relationship to connecting lines. Note the C&O's parallel line from Doswell to Richmond, the matter of a legal fight in the 1840s.

Chapter 1
A Brief History of the Richmond, Fredericksburg & Potomac Railroad Company

Until its demise in October 1991, the Richmond, Fredericksburg and Potomac Railroad Company had the distinction of being the oldest American railroad still operating under its original name and charter. Formed when rail transportation was still in its earliest stage of development, the RF&P was the sixth railroad to be chartered in Virginia and only the third to operate its trains in the state with steam motive power. When CSX Corporation and its affiliates acquired the railroad assets and operations of the RF&P Railroad in a 1991 transaction, it brought to an end the RF&P's remarkable achievement of continuously operating its rail property with its own organization during the 157 years of its corporate existence.

The RF&P was also notable as one of our country's most successful short line railroads. With only 113 miles of main line track, it was one of the shortest railroads in the nation. However, the RF&P's importance resulted from its strategic location, which formed the principal route through which the commerce of the northern and southern cities of the Atlantic seaboard region could flow.

Throughout its long and illustrious history, the RF&P was truly "the connecting link between North and South". It was a role the founders of the RF&P had visualized for their railroad. In 1833 the Petersburg Railroad Company, Virginia's first steam railway and the earliest predecessor of the Atlantic Coast Line Railroad, had demonstrated the practicality of railroad construction and operation by opening a line between the Appomattox and Roanoke Rivers. To the north, the Baltimore and Ohio Railroad had just announced its intention to extend a line south to Washington. The RF&P would provide the important link between these developing rail lines. Moncure Robinson, the civil engineer who surveyed the RF&P, wrote: "The proposed work will have the effect of affording to the districts of the Commonwealth through which it will pass, as well as to the towns of Richmond and Fredericksburg, all the benefits which must necessarily result from positions on the great line of national thoroughfare; no work which has been projected in Virginia can be, in proportion to the expenditure which will be required for its completion, of more importance to the Commonwealth."

On February 25, 1834, the Richmond, Fredericksburg and Potomac Railroad Company was granted a charter by Act of the General Assembly of Virginia. That charter provided for the construction of a railroad from some point in the City of Richmond to some point within the corporate limits of Fredericksburg, with the authority to extend the railroad "should it be deemed advisable, to the Potomac River or some creek thereof."

The history of the RF&P is likewise notable as a result of the Commonwealth of Virginia's direct interest in the railroad throughout its existence. This interest was initiated in the Company's charter which contained certain unique features. Under its charter, the RF&P was exempt from city, county and State taxation. Even more unique was the provision that "... the General Assembly will not, for the period of thirty years (later extended) from the completion of the said railroad, allow any other railroad to be constructed between the City of Richmond and the City of Washington, or for any portion of the said distance, the probable effect of which would be to diminish the number of passengers traveling between the one city and the other ... or to compel the company, in order to retain such passengers, to reduce the money passage." (These provisions remained in effect until an Act of the General Assembly on March 14, 1912, whereby the tax exemption and other privileges were revoked and the RF&P became subject to the general railroad laws of Virginia.)

The pledge of the State to protect the RF&P

With the exception of one purchased from the Petersburg Railroad, the first RF&P steam locomotives were acquired in England. They rode on strap rail nailed to wooden stringers that were wedged into the cross ties. This artist's rendering shows an enthusiastic crowd greeting an RF&P train in the streets of Richmond in the 1830s, its coaches of the early type using bodies of stage coaches. In this early period of railroad development lines such as the RF&P were sometimes given public financial support because of the widespread interest in the new technology and its potential. In this case the Commonwealth of Virginia (Board of Public Works) purchasing 2/5ths of the stock. This stock ownership by the state would persist to modern times and influenced the final disposition of the railroad's assets in 1991.

William E. Griffin Coll.

Artist's concept of an 1830s RF&P train, carrying both passengers and cargo.

from competition in passenger traffic between Richmond and Washington became even more positive after the State became a stockholder. The Act that incorporated the RF&P did not provide or contemplate that the Commonwealth of Virginia would be a stockholder of the railroad. However, since 1784 it had been the policy of the Commonwealth to encourage transportation enterprises and by a subsequent Act, passed on January 23, 1835, the Board of Public Works was authorized to subscribe on behalf of the State to two-fifths of the RF&P's capital stock after three-fifths had been taken by the public. The final result was that the private subscriptions accounted for more than three-fifths and the Commonwealth actually acquired 2,752 shares, something less than it had contracted to purchase.

The Commonwealth retained ownership of RF&P stock and it proved to be a most valuable investment. As a result of the remarkable earning capacity of the RF&P throughout its existence, the Company never defaulted on the payment of interest or principal and maintained an unbroken dividend record from 1881 until its demise in 1991.

The RF&P stockholders held their first meeting on June 20, 1834 to elect officers. Among those elected to the Company's first Board of Directors was Conway Robinson, a prominent Philadelphia attorney. His brother Moncure Robinson was appointed Chief Engineer. The three Robinson brothers would each serve as President of the RF&P: Conway (1836 to 1838); Moncure (1840 to 1847); and, Edwin (1847 to 1860). Moncure's son, John M. Robinson, served as President from 1871 to 1878. Long-time stockholders, the Robinson family of Philadelphia, would exercise influence and control over the opera-

Moncure Robinson, RF&P's Chief Engineer (1834-39) and fourth President (1840-47). Two of his brothers and his son were all presidents of the RF&P over a 42-year period.

tion of the RF&P until 1885.

Construction of the RF&P began in December of 1834 and an agent was promptly dispatched to England to purchase two locomotives and tenders. The Company's offices, shops and passenger station were located 8th and H (now Broad) Streets in downtown Richmond. By 1836 the line had been completed a distance of twenty miles north of Richmond to the South Anna River. On Saturday, February 13, 1836, the RF&P operated the first train ever to depart the City of Richmond with the engine "Liverpool" and six coaches. On board for the hour and a half trip to the South Anna were some one hundred fifty passengers including the Governor of Virginia and members of the General Assembly. Regular service between Richmond and the South Anna was established the next day.

The line was opened to Fredericksburg, 61 miles, on January 23, 1837. A stage line from there to the mouth of the Potomac Creek connected the railroad with a line of steamers to Washington via the Potomac River.

As the Company began its operations, other railroads were being constructed in Virginia that promised increased travel over the RF&P. The Richmond and Petersburg (another ACL predecessor company) was chartered in 1836 and opened its line from Richmond to the Appomattox River early in 1838. Rail lines now extended into North Carolina and between Baltimore and Philadelphia but transfers from road to road would be necessary for many years. Another new railroad was the Louisa Railroad Company, the earliest predecessor company of the Chesapeake and Ohio Railway. Its charter of February 18, 1836 provided that the road would be constructed from Hanover Junction (now Doswell) on the RF&P to Orange County, Virginia. Pursuant to a contract between the Louisa and the RF&P, the Louisa would build and maintain its line and the RF&P would perform all transportation service on the line of the Louisa for a period of nearly ten years.

Soon after the RF&P line had been opened to Fredericksburg, it was decided to extend it across the Rappahannock River to reach one of the steamboat landings on the Potomac River. Surveys convinced the RF&P that the best route and deeper water could be obtained by going to a landing on Aquia Creek, located some fourteen miles from Fredericksburg. The line was opened to Aquia in November of 1842.

To assure the coordination of rail and steamboat operations, the RF&P acquired a controlling interest in the Washington and Fredericksburg Steam-

boat Company (later renamed the Potomac Steamboat Company) and in 1845 the Officers and Directors of the railroad also took over the management of the steamboat company. The RF&P had now established its line as an important link in a through route of travel from the South to Baltimore, passengers being handled by rail on the RF&P from Richmond to Aquia Creek, thence by steamboats to Washington, thence by rail (the Baltimore and Ohio Railroad) to Baltimore.

The first challenge to the RF&P's charter occurred during a dispute with the Louisa Railroad Company. For nearly ten years the RF&P had performed all transportation service on the line of the Louisa pursuant to a contract between the two companies. As the termination date for that contract approached, the Louisa advised the RF&P that it desired to begin the operation of its own railroad. A new agreement between the railroads was reached for a two year period ending July 30, 1849, which provided for the freight traffic on the Louisa to be handled through by the RF&P to and from Richmond to avoid the transfer of lading at Hanover Junction. The RF&P was reimbursed by the Louisa for certain operating expenses and guaranteed a minimum annual revenue on through freight traffic.

The Louisa soon became dissatisfied with its access to Richmond via the RF&P and in 1848 obtained authority from the Virginia General Assembly to extend its line from Hanover Junction to the Dock in the City of Richmond. The RF&P was unsuccessful in an attempt to negotiate another operating agreement, the Louisa's President announcing that it was his Company's intention to build to Richmond "... no matter what terms might be offered."

When the Louisa's operating agreement with the RF&P terminated on June 30, 1849, it arranged for a stage coach line to transport passengers between Richmond and Hanover Junction. The Louisa, renamed the Virginia Central Railroad in 1850, then commenced construction of its Richmond extension, opening the new line for service in January, 1851. The Virginia Central became a competitor of the RF&P when it arranged with the Orange and Alexandria Railroad (a predecessor of the Southern Railway operating between Gordonsville and Alexandria) for the joint transportation of passenger and freight traffic between Richmond and the North.

The RF&P argued that the legislation authorizing the extension of the Louisa Railroad to Richmond was a manifest violation of its charter and in direct conflict with the General Assembly's guaranty that the RF&P could not for a period of 30 years be paralleled by any other railroad. It resorted to the Courts for the protection of its rights and in February, 1860, the Virginia Supreme Court of Appeals decided the case in favor of the RF&P. However, by this time the Virginia Central's extension to Richmond had been built and the existence of war and the operation of the so-called "Stay Laws" delayed even the RF&P's recovery of damages from the Virginia Central and the Orange and

Alexandria until October of 1863.

The RF&P had originally been laid with strap rails weighing about twelve pounds per yard and spiked down to wooden stringers. During the 1850's, the RF&P began to replace this strap rail with "T" rail purchased from the Tredegar Iron Works in Richmond. The line of road from Richmond to the north bank of the Rappahannock at Fredericksburg was laid with "T" rail by June, 1858, but work north of Fredericksburg as well as the Company's plans to build an a rail connection to Washington were abruptly halted by the start of the Civil War.

Located directly in the theater of the war, both of the warring factions were anxious to hold or get control of as much of the RF&P as possible. As early as 1862, the northern portion of the RF&P was seized by the Union army. Thereafter, portions of the railroad were alternately in possession of the Union and/or Confederate forces, giving service to both causes. All of the property of the RF&P was finally taken over by Union military authorities in March, 1865, following the complete destruction of the line between Fredericksburg and Richmond.

Thus, the Company faced appalling conditions at the end of the war. The Aquia Creek steamboat wharf and most of its bridges had to be replaced, much of the track had been torn up and the locomotives and rolling stock were all in need of repair or replacement. To make matters worse, the Company's treasury contained only worthless Confederate bonds and currency.

To finance reconstruction of the railroad, $100,000 worth of bonds were sold in Philadelphia to be redeemable July 1, 1867. No doubt the RF&P's ability to acquire this financing in the North so promptly after the war was due to the influence of its Philadelphia stockholders. Additional financing to discharge accumulated debts was provided by legislative action of the Virginia General Assembly authorizing the Company to increase its capital stock.

The task of rebuilding the railroad was given to Major E. T. D. Myers, who had served in the Engineer Corps of General Lee's Army of Northern Virginia during the war. An able engineer, he would become the RF&P's General

RF&P

A man who had great influence on the RF&P was Major E. D. T. Myers, General Superintendent from 1870 to 1889 and President 1889-1905.

Superintendent in 1870 and later served with distinction as the Company's President from 1889 until his death in 1905. To rebuild the line of road and bridges, Major Myers arranged a contract for purchase of rails, cross ties, bridge timbers and countless other supplies from the War Department of the United States. By September of 1865, the bridges had been rebuilt and the main line was reopened from Richmond to the Aquia Creek wharf.

In the aftermath of the war, the operations of the RF&P, as did those of all Southern railroads, changed dramatically. In the antebellum days, railroads in the South had been regarded as mere connections between cities and the localities that had invested funds for their construction had generally resisted any physical unification of the lines. Thus the early railroads had looked to local traffic for their revenues. But the war left the Southern economy in disarray. Now Southern communities and their railroads realized that they would have to look to commerce with the North if they were to overcome the post-war paralysis of business and social conditions that existed throughout the South.

The time had come to join the railroads operating between Weldon, North Carolina and the Potomac River. The tracks of the Petersburg Railroad were joined with those of the Richmond and Petersburg in August of 1867 when the companies completed the construction of a bridge over the Appomattox River. Connection through Richmond was achieved by construction of the Richmond, Fredericksburg and Potomac and Richmond and Petersburg Railroad Connection Company. Chartered on March 3, 1866, the Connection Railroad, as it was called, opened for service in April of 1867 and was operated under lease by the RF&P. Only one and a fourth miles long, the Connection Railroad joined the Richmond and Petersburg by a trestle at 5th and Byrd Streets, necessitating a tunnel 900 feet long at Gamble's Hill and its track extended as far as a trestle at Second and Belvidere Streets. The track was laid along Byrd Street to Grace Street to a connection with the RF&P at Broad and Pine Streets. For a distance of one fourth mile, the grade of the line was nearly 2.2%, quite steep for railroad operation in a city. Cary, Main, Franklin and Grace Streets—all important city streets—were crossed at grade. The RF&P did not abandon its operations on Broad Street at this time, but all through trains were handled over the Connection Railroad until 1919.

Connections with northern lines came more slowly and involved one of the most tumultuous periods of RF&P history. The owners and managers of the RF&P feared that with the expiration in 1868 of the thirty year monopoly granted by its charter, a large rail system might lay a parallel line through Virginia to take away the RF&P's business or force the sale of its line. Those fears were soon realized.

In 1868 the Baltimore and Ohio Railroad tried to secure a charter to build a parallel line through King George and Caroline Counties to Richmond. Then in 1871 the Richmond and Danville, another Southern Railway predecessor, proposed the construction of a direct line between Richmond and Washington. The RF&P and its supporters were able to defeat both proposals in the Virginia General Assembly.

The Pennsylvania Railroad was more successful in its efforts to extend a rail line into Virginia. In 1870 the Pennsylvania took over the 1864 charter of the Alexandria and Fredericksburg Railway and began construction of a line southward from Alexandria, Virginia, with the intention of making connection at some point with the RF&P. At the same time, the Pennsylvania acquired control of the Alexandria and Washington Railroad that had been organized in 1854 to build a railroad from Alexandria to the City of Washington in the District of Columbia. That railroad opened its line from Duke Street in Alexandria to the south end of the "Long Bridge" over the Potomac River in 1858 and later constructed a line from the north end of the bridge to the station of the Baltimore and Ohio Railroad in Washington. No tracks were laid over the Long Bridge at this time, traffic being transferred by omnibus.

To compete with the Baltimore and Ohio Railroad, the Pennsylvania extended its subsidiary, the Baltimore and Potomac Railroad, into Washington and procured authority from Congress to run its line down Maryland Avenue to the north end of the Long Bridge. Congress also granted the Pennsylvania the authority to take possession of the Long Bridge with the condition that it maintain the bridge.

By July of 1872 the Pennsylvania had completed its line from Baltimore to Washington, gained control of the rail line from Washington to Alexandria, built a rail line south to connect with the RF&P and, by acquisition of the Long Bridge had gained control of the only railroad crossing over the Potomac River south of Harpers Ferry, effectively shutting the Baltimore and Ohio Railroad off from the railroads leading to the South, whose traffic the B&O had previously enjoyed through its connection with the Alexandria and Washington Railroad in the District of Columbia.

When the Pennsylvania Railroad commenced construction of the new rail line between Alexandria and Quantico, the RF&P promptly moved to extend its line north to establish an all-rail connection at Quantico before the Pennsylvania could apply to the Virginia General Assembly for authority to bring the new rail line all the way to Richmond. At a special meeting of the RF&P stockholders on October 11, 1870, construction was authorized under the Company's charter of a 10 mile extension from Brooke for the purpose of making connection near Quantico with the Alexandria and Fredericksburg Railroad. As this extension was 1.7 miles short of the desired connection, the RF&P arranged for the additional mileage to be provided by the Potomac Railroad Company, which had been incorporated in 1867 to build a railroad from some point on the RF&P north to the City of Alexandria.

Except Sunday. No. 7.	Except Saturday P. M. No 87.	Except Sunday. No. 81.	Daily. No. 47.	Except Sunday. No. 45.	Daily. No. 43.	Time Card No. 7, '81. Whole No. 89.	Distances between Stations. Miles.	Daily. No. 40.	Except Sunday. No. 42.	Daily. No. 48.	Except Sunday. No. 82.	Except Sunday A. M. No. 88.	Except Sunday No. 8.
	Ar. 12.30 a.m.	1.33 p.m.	Ar.8.00 p.m.	Ar 11.56 a.m.	Ar 7.54* a.m.	Quantico,	0.83	Le.12.20 p.m.	Le.6.29 p.m.	Le 7.55* a.m.	Le. 2.30 p.m.	Le.1.45 a.m.	
	12.15 a.m.	1.11 / 1.06	F 7.50 p.m.	F 11.43	7.42	Blue Wing,	4.27		F 6.39	8.08	2.45 / 2.50	2.07	
	11.48 p.m.	12.39* / 12.30*	F 7.36	F 11.30	7.30	BROOKE,	6.43	12.39*	F 6.54	F 8.25	3.21 / 3.26	2.45	
	11.38	·12.18 p.m.	7.30		7.25	POT'C RUN,	2.65	12.44	7.01		3.38		
	11.17 / 11.02	11.48 a.m. / 11.25	7.16* / 7.14*	11.06 / 11.03	F 7.14	FREDK'SBURG,	6.16	F 12.55	7.16* / 7.22*	8.48 / 8.52	4.00 / 4.35	3.26 / 3.41	
	10.38	11.02 / 10.58	F 6.59	F 10.46	7.00	Summit,	7.97	1.11	F 7.47	F 9.12	5.10 / 5.15	4.21	
	10.24	10.40* / 10.25*	F 6.51	F 10.36*	6.52	GUINEA,	4.49	1.19	F 7.58	F 9.21	5.3 / 5.40	4.37	
	10.16	10.17 / 10.12	F 6.46	F 10.30	6.47	Woodford,	2.40	1.24	F 8.03	F 9.27	5.50 / 5.55	4.47	
	9.54 / 9.48	9.45* / 9.26*	6.33* / 6.29*	10.14 / 10.10	6.35 / 6.30	MILFORD,	6.75	1.34 / 1.38	8.17 / 8.22	9.42* / 9.47*	6.18* / 6.33*	5.09 / 5.14	
	9.33	9.08 / 8.58	F 6.20	10.00* / 9.54*	6.21	PENOLA,	4.75	1.45	F 8.32	F 9.57*	6.53 / 7.02	5.30	
	9.12	8.33 / 8.24	F 6.08	F 9.42	6.10*	RUTH'RGLEN,	5.94	1.55	F 8.45	F 10.12	7.30 / 7.42	5.55* / 6.10*	
	8.57* / 8.38*	8.00 / 7.32	F 5.56	F 9.30	6.00	JUNCTION,	5.18	2.03	F 8.57*	F 10.23	8.04* / 8.38*	6.30 / 7.00	
	8.30	7.21*	F 5.51	F 9.25		TAYLORSV'LE,	2.23		F 9.02*	F 10.28	8.50* / 9.07*	7.12* / 7.21*	
5.04 p.m.	8.11 / 8.08	6.54 / 6.39	F 5.39	9.15 / 9.13	5.46	Ashland,	4.96	2.14	F 9.12	F 10.39	9.33 / 9.43	7.43 / 7.48	Le.7.35 a.m.
F 4.52	7.56	6.24				Kilby,	3.25						F 7.45
F 4.39	7.39	6.00	5.22	8.59		Hungary,	5.12	2.27	9.30	10.57 a.m.	10.20	8.17	F 7.58
4.20	7.15	Le. 5.28 a.m.	5.08	8.48	5.18	Boulton,	6.32	2.37	9.45	11.12	Ar.10.50 p.m.	Ar.8.38 a.m.	8.18
4.14	Le.6.48 p.m.			8.42		Elba,	0.75						Ar. 8.24
			Le. 4.52 p.m.	Le.8.32 a.m.	Le 5.02 a.m.	Byrd Street,	1.25	Ar.2.51 p.m.	Ar.10.00 p.m.	Ar.11.30 a.m.			
Le.4.02 p.m.						Broad Street,							Ar. 8.36 a.m.

SUNDAY, NOVEMBER 27, 1881.   T. L. COURTNEY, Asst. Supt.   E. T. D. MYERS, General Superintendent.

This 1881 employee timetable shows passenger trains operating between Quantico and Richmond, with 17 stations in between.

The RF&P's extension to Quantico was opened to a new connection with the Potomac Steamboat Company at the mouth of Quantico Creek on May 1, 1872. Thereafter, the RF&P's line from Brooke down to the mouth of Aquia Creek was abandoned and steamboat service via the Aquia Creek wharf was discontinued. The Alexandria and Fredericksburg Railway was completed to Quantico on July 2, 1872, and on July 18th through train operation on a night schedule was established between Baltimore, Maryland and Weldon, North Carolina. However, the RF&P day train terminated at Quantico with connecting steamboat service via the Potomac Steamboat Company to Washington where the exclusive rail service to Baltimore was provided by the B&O Railroad.

Even though it soon became evident that the public preferred the quicker and more convenient all-rail route between Richmond and Washington, the management of the RF&P resisted the discontinuance of the daylight steamboat connection with the Richmond trains. This was due to the fact that the Philadelphia stockholders, who held a substantial majority of the railroad's common stock and nearly 50% of the guaranteed stock, also controlled the Potomac Steamboat Company. To protect their financial interest in the steamboat company they insisted on retention of the water connection at Quantico.

It was a policy that angered the Pennsylvania Railroad. Having just established all-rail service via its Alexandria and Fredericksburg subsidiary, the Pennsylvania was in no mood to see any of its business lost to the B&O at Washington as a result of the RF&P's operation of a day train to perpetuate the business of the Potomac Steamboat Company.

A feud over the rail connection at Quantico persisted from 1872 until 1882, eventually resulting in the resignation of two RF&P Presidents and the investigation of the financial relationship of the RF&P and the Potomac Steamboat Company by the Virginia General Assembly. To impress upon the RF&P the advisability of discontinuing its steamboat connection between Quantico and Washington in favor of the all-rail route, the Pennsylvania acquired an interest in the Virginia Midland Railroad (former Orange and Alexandria) and diverted all of its traffic for Richmond and south over the Virginia Midland and Chesapeake and Ohio roads between Alexandria and Richmond via Gordonsville. The Post Office Department also notified the RF&P that it greatly preferred the all-rail route and threatened "... to send the great southern mails by some route or routes other than yours."

Faced with the potential loss of substantial rail revenues and the burdensome costs of subsidizing a diminishing boat traffic, the RF&P sold its steamboat company holdings and abandoned the operation of daylight trains for the exclusive connection with the steamboats. Thereafter, both day and night trains were operated between Richmond and Washington

A northbound RF&P passenger train on the Connection Railroad in Richmond, is handled by 4-6-2 No. 63 en route to Elba Station from Byrd Street Station on October 3, 1907. The train is shown on the trestle alongside the wall of the State Penitentiary. The 1-1/2-mile Connection Railroad joined RF&P and the Petersburg Railroad in 1867 and remained in use for through trains to the ACL until 1919.

A. A. Thieme Coll.

over the all-rail route and the Pennsylvania Railroad restored the routing of its through traffic over the RF&P.

During this period of the RF&P's feud with the Pennsylvania Railroad over the rail connection at Quantico, the Company was also engaged in a legal battle with the City of Richmond over the city's right to prohibit the use of steam locomotives on Broad Street. The city argued that the steam emitted was objectionable and the trains both blocked and scared horse-drawn vehicles. In response to an adverse decision by the Virginia Supreme Court of Appeals in April, 1875, the RF&P substituted horse power on Broad Street east of Belvidere Street to its depot at 8th Street and erected a new shop facility at Boulton off Broad Street near the Belvidere connection.

Early in 1880 the RF&P established a new passenger station in the vicinity of Broad and Pine Streets at its junction with the Connection Railroad. Known as Elba, this station continued in operation until the opening of Broad Street Station in 1919 and was much used by the residents of Richmond's West End. With the opening of Elba Station, the RF&P leased its tracks on Broad Street to the city's street railway company and thereafter streetcars handled the transportation of passengers between the RF&P stations at Elba and 8th Street. The Company's general offices remained at 8th and Broad but the Richmond freight depot was relocated from that point to Broad and Hancock.

In the 1880's, Baltimore produce merchant William T. Walters and his banking associate, Benjamin F. Newcomer, acquired control of the Richmond and Petersburg Railroad, the Petersburg Railroad, the Wilmington and Weldon Railroad, and a number of other southern railroads, later consolidating them to form the Atlantic Coast Line Railroad. In 1885, control of the RF&P also passed to Walters and Newcomer,

who purchased large blocks of the Company's stock from the RF&P's Philadelphia stockholders.

Until 1901, the RF&P was operated as a part of the Walters system of railroads and participated in a number of new through freight and passenger operations. In 1887 the RF&P and the Richmond and Petersburg Railroad built a new passenger station at the corner of Byrd and 7th streets in Richmond as a joint facility of the two railroads. The new Byrd Street Station also provided space for the general offices of the two companies. The following year the RF&P participated in the operation of the new *New York and Florida Special*, a Pullman passenger train that ran three times a week between New York and Jacksonville. Also in 1888, a new through fast freight service known as the "Atlantic Coast Dispatch" was established for the movement of fresh fruits and vegetables in train loads from the south to northern markets.

Soon the RF&P found itself in another fight with the City of Richmond over the operation of trains across those streets between the Byrd Street and Elba stations. Having been successful in forcing the RF&P to abandon operations on Broad Street, the city passed an ordinance in 1888 prohibiting the use of steam locomotives on the Connection Railroad after April 9, 1890. To avoid another confrontation with the City and to provide for the better operation of through trains, in November of 1888 the RF&P and the Richmond and Petersburg Railroad agreed to jointly construct a belt line from Branch's Crossing (Acca) on the RF&P to Clopton on the R&P RR to accommodate the freight trains then operating over the Connection Railroad. This belt line, known as the James River Branch, skirted to the west of Richmond and to the west and south of Manchester. It was opened for freight service only on February 2, 1891 and was operated by the RF&P for the joint account of both railroads.

By the turn of the century, RF&P freight trains were no longer operating through the city streets in Richmond; the entire main line had been laid with steel "T" rail; all of the locomotives had been converted to burn coal; and, most of the wooden bridges had been replaced with substantial steel structures. Three daily passenger schedules were operated and the RF&P joined with its connections in the shared ownership of sleeping cars operated over their lines.

During the period from 1885 to 1900, when the RF&P was operated as a component of the Walters system of railroads - known after 1898 as the Atlantic Coast Line Railroad - the Company's revenues more than doubled and net income tripled. The year 1900 was notable as it marked the first time in the RF&P's history that revenues from freight trains exceeded the revenue produced by passenger service.

The remarkable increase in the traffic handled by the RF&P was an outgrowth of its role as a connection for the ACL's through service. In fact, the RF&P was the ACL's direct link to the Northern markets and, had it not been for the entry of a new player on the rail scene, it is possible that the RF&P might eventually have been absorbed into the ACL system. However, everything changed in 1900 with the formation of the Seaboard Air Line Railway.

The SAL was assembled under the direction of Richmond banker John Skelton Williams over the five year period between 1895 and 1900. During that period, Mr. Williams and his banking associates purchased the control of a number of separately organized railroads that operated through six Southeastern states from Virginia to Florida.

Mr. Williams realized that direct rail service through the Washington gateway was essential if the SAL was to compete with the ACL and Southern rail systems. It was his desire to bring the SAL northward to Richmond, and possibly to Washington, if arrangements could not be reached with the RF&P to handle SAL through traffic. At first, the ACL-controlled management of the RF&P refused to work out satisfactory arrangements to handle SAL traffic north of Richmond. However, when the Virginia General Assembly passed an Act on March 3, 1900 granting John Skelton Williams a charter to build a new railroad between Richmond and Washington and coupled to this franchise the condition that the incorporators of the new railroad could purchase the Commonwealth's interest in the RF&P's common stock, the RF&P and its controlling interests quickly acquiesced in an agreement for the interchange of SAL traffic at Richmond. This agreement provided that the facilities of the RF&P would be enlarged and that SAL traffic would be handled by the RF&P on the same terms and conditions applied to the traffic of the ACL. The tracks of the SAL

and RF&P were joined at a point known as Hermitage on July 1, 1900.

To implement the RF&P's commitment to handle the SAL's traffic on the same terms and conditions as those of the ACL, it was essential that the control of the RF&P be removed from the ACL and divided equally among the various connecting lines. In an agreement dated July 31, 1901, the Pennsylvania Railroad, Atlantic Coast Line Railroad, Southern Railway, Chesapeake and Ohio Railway, Seaboard Air Line Railway, and the Baltimore and Ohio Railroad created a proprietary company under New Jersey law, the stock of which would be held one-sixth by each of the parties to the agreement. This new company would be known as the "Richmond-Washington Company".

The Richmond-Washington Company acquired all of the stock of the Pennsylvania Railroad-controlled Washington Southern Railway, which had been formed on April 10, 1890 by merger of the Alexandria and Washington Railway and the Alexandria and Fredericksburg Railway and the majority of the voting stock of the RF&P. Under the terms of the agreement, the two railroads would be operated under one management as a single unit called the "Richmond-Washington Line". The traffic of the six railroads would be handled with "equal promptness" and upon equal terms. No corporate consolidation or merger of the property rights of the Washington Southern and RF&P were effected, but the desired result of unity of interest and operation was accomplished by putting the two railroads under the common management of the RF&P with headquarters in Richmond. On November 1, 1901, the operation of the Washington Southern was taken over by the RF&P and thereafter the two roads were operated as one unit.

The six railroads also agreed that none of them would construct, or promote the construction of, any other railroad forming a line in whole, or in part, between Richmond and Washington or use, operate or forward traffic over any such line as long as the July

A northbound freight crosses the Potomac Creek bridge in the late 1940s. To the left are stone bridge abutments of the Civil War bridge erected by the U. S. military that President Lincoln described as being built of nothing but "beanpoles and cornstalks."

William E. Griffin Coll.

Washington Union Terminal's magnificent station opened on November 17, 1907, and became the northern terminus for RF&P's trains.

William E. Griffin Coll.

31, 1901 agreement remained in effect. Thereafter the Virginia Legislature revoked the charter of the new railroad and the authority to sell the Commonwealth's holdings in the RF&P expired. Interestingly, when the new State Constitution of 1902 created the State Corporation Commission to take over the duties of the old Board of Public Works, the Constitution specifically reserved to the General Assembly the right to prevent by statute any railroad from being built parallel to the RF&P. Legislation to that effect was passed by the General Assembly in 1903.

Traffic over the Richmond-Washington Line rapidly increased to such an extent that the single track operated at the turn of the century was soon found to be inadequate. For this reason, the entire line was double tracked between Richmond and Washington during the years 1902 to 1907, with many sections of track relocated, sharp curves eliminated and grades reduced. Most of the Washington Southern line between Quantico and Washington was put on a new location.

The plans to upgrade the Richmond-Washington Line included plans for a new passenger station just west of the Alexandria city limits to be used jointly by the C&O, Southern and Washington Southern; and, the construction of extensive facilities between Alexandria and the Long Bridge to be known as "Potomac Yard". This facility was designed to serve as the major clearinghouse for the freight traffic of the Pennsylvania and B&O railroads on the north and the C&O, Southern and Washington Southern railroads on the south. The Washington Southern constructed Potomac Yard between the south end of the Long Bridge and Seminary Junction. The six interested railroads adopted a plan of operation for the facilities on December 5, 1905 and the yard was opened for service on August 1, 1906.

With so many railroads using the facility, Potomac Yard became the major gateway for traffic handled between North and South. The huge facility included tracks for the receipt and dispatch of northbound and southbound trains, northbound and southbound classification facilities operated by grav-

ity (humps), an engine terminal, facilities for making running repairs to locomotives and freight cars, pens for feeding and resting livestock in transit, icing facilities for perishable freight, and tracks upon which fruits and vegetables could be held for reconsignment to Northern markets. There were also shop tracks for Fruit Growers Express (removed in 1926 to a location near "AF" Tower) and extensive facilities for the handling and transfer of less-than-carload (LCL) freight.

The connection with the Southern Railway was established about a mile south of Alexandria at "AF" Tower and both the Southern and the C&O railroads were granted trackage rights over the Washington Southern to Potomac Yard for freight traffic and to the Long Bridge for passenger traffic. At the same time, the B&O was granted trackage rights over the Pennsylvania between Anacostia Junction in Washington and the south end of the Long Bridge for freight service. The Pennsylvania then rebuilt the Long Bridge as a new double track steel bridge to accommodate the rapidly increasing traffic handled over the Richmond-Washington Line.

The six railroads also entered into an agreement to organize the Washington Terminal Company for the purpose of building and operating a joint passenger facility to accommodate the Washington traffic of all the tenant lines. This agreement was reached in 1907 and granted trackage rights to the Washington Southern, C&O and Southern railroads over the Pennsylvania from the south end of the Long Bridge to the tracks of the Washington Terminal Company. The new Union Station was opened on November 17, 1907.

During this period when the RF&P was finalizing arrangements with its connections for the cooperative handling of traffic over the Richmond-Washington Line, one last attempt was made by a company, not party to the 1901 agreement, to build a railroad parallel to the RF&P. Frank Jay Gould and his associates controlled the electric power facilities in the cities of Richmond and Fredericksburg. In January of 1905, they obtained a charter for the Richmond and Chesapeake Bay Railroad Company, ostensibly to build a railroad from Richmond to the Rappahannock River in the vicinity of Tappahannock. Under this charter an electric railroad was built from Richmond to Ashland and began operations in 1907. However, when Gould and his associates later applied for a charter between Doswell and Fredericksburg, it became apparent that their real plans contemplated an electrically operated railroad between Richmond and Washington. After a determined legislative contest, in 1908, the Virginia General Assembly repealed the Act of May 21, 1903 that had prohibited the paralleling of the RF&P. However, efforts to extend the electric line beyond Ashland were abandoned. Even though there no longer existed any legislative prohibition, there would never again be an effort to build another railroad parallel to the RF&P.

Having outgrown its office space in Byrd Street Station, the RF&P joined with the First National Bank and the C&O Railway as stockholders in the First National Bank Building Corporation for the construction of a modern bank and office building at Ninth and Main Streets in Richmond. In 1912 the RF&P relocated its general offices from Byrd Street Station to the new building and remained there until Broad Street Station was opened in January of 1919.

The plans for the construction of Broad Street Station were reached in an agreement between the RF&P and the ACL in 1916. Under this agreement, the two railroads chartered the Richmond Terminal Railway Company to erect and operate the new station. Construction began early in 1917 and the magnificent new station of the jointly owned terminal company was opened for service at noon on January 6, 1919. The

RF&P had relocated its general offices from the First National Bank Building to its new quarters in Broad Street Station in December of 1918.

Other provisions of the RF&P/ACL agreement provided for the rebuilding and double tracking the tracks on the James River Branch; operation by the ACL on the RF&P's line from Pier 5 of the James River Bridge to Acca Yard for freight service; enlargement of the RF&P locomotive facilities to accommodate ACL engines; the use of the respective freight facilities of the RF&P and ACL for traffic of the other company; and the transfer of the RF&P interest in the Byrd Street Station facilities to the ACL. With the abandonment of operations on the Connection Railroad and the depression of the double tracks on the James River Branch to eliminate grade crossings, the RF&P had finally completed the removal of all train operations from the streets of Richmond.

Construction of the new station and improvements to the James River Branch were hampered by the scarcity of labor and materials due to the war conditions. Although the RF&P had played an important part in the movement of troops during the short Spanish-American War of 1898, the importance of the Richmond-Washington Line's strategic location to the national defense and its ability to handle large volumes of traffic were not fully realized until the United States' participation in World War I. Indicative of the enormous war traffic, the passenger mileage in 1918 increased 175% over 1916 and the revenue ton-miles of freight traffic in 1919 increased 52% over that handled in 1916.

During World War I the Federal government

William E. Griffin Coll.

Completed in 1919, Broad Street Station served RF&P passenger trains until Amtrak moved to its new station on November 15, 1975. RF&P's general offices were in the station from 1919 until 1976. Today the magnificent neo-classical building houses the Virginia Science Museum.

took control of the nation's railroads, placing them under a Railroad Administration and its Director General. The contracts with the Director General of the Railroads determined the annual compensation to be paid by the Government for the use of the railroad properties. This operation of the railroads by the Government resulted in the loss of several hundred million dollars, but the net Federal revenue of the RF&P and Washington Southern was nearly three times the "standard return" (the payment by the Government to the companies during Federal control) and exceeded the proportion of profit to the Government from the operation of any other railroad.

With a revenue producing main line of only 32 miles in freight service and 35 miles in passenger service, the cost of using the passenger terminal facilities in Washington and interchanging freight among its connections at Potomac Yard bore heavily on the Washington Southern. Therefore, on February 24, 1920, the Washington Southern Railway was merged into the RF&P Railroad.

Pursuant to the 1916 agreement between the RF&P and the ACL, the RF&P opened its new Acca Locomotive Terminal in Richmond in January of 1924. Located adjacent to the Acca freight yard, this large and modern locomotive terminal serviced and maintained all steam locomotives of the RF&P. It also handled the servicing and running repairs on the road locomotives of the ACL, which jointly used the Acca freight yard with the RF&P. Only the passenger car shops and the offices of the Mechanical Department remained at the old Boulton location.

Meanwhile, the Southern Railway had become dissatisfied with the operation of Potomac Yard and commenced construction of its own freight yard in November of 1923 at Cameron Run just south of Alexandria. The Southern gave notice that it would withdraw from Potomac Yard on September 1, 1924 and commenced operations at Cameron Yard on November 20, 1924. After further negotiations, and pursuant to an agreement between the Southern and the RF&P providing for the handling of the former's freight traffic, the Southern reentered Potomac Yard on October 1, 1925. The December 5, 1905 Plan of Operation was then superseded by a long term contract dated December 31, 1927 between the RF&P, B&O, Pennsylvania, C&O and Southern, which provided for the operation of Potomac Yard under the supervision of a Board of Managers consisting of one representative of each of the five lines. The actual day-to-day administration and operation of the yard was the responsibility of the RF&P. The RF&P appointed the Superintendent of the yard, subject to the approval of the Board. Though the different railroads used the yard, the RF&P owned and operated the locomotives and provided the crews that carried out the interchange of traffic and other duties. The operating and maintenance expenses of the joint facility were charged to the

Many railroads established bus lines in the 1920s and 1930s to replace local service. RF&P Transportation Company was established in 1929 to cut the cost of local steam train passenger service between Richmond and Washington. In this scene one of the company's buses is loading at Broad Street Station.

tenants on the basis of use. The agreement was for a term of years expiring on October 31, 2001, and thereafter until terminated on five years notice.

Responding to an order of the Interstate Commerce Commission, a system of automatic two speed train control of the continuous inductive type was installed on the RF&P in 1927. The cabs of locomotives were also equipped with green, yellow and red light signals to indicate conditions on the track ahead. Electrically operated wayside color lights were substituted for the automatic semaphore signals in the period 1926 to 1929. The new elevated tracks through Fredericksburg and the handsome new bridge over the Rappahannock River were put in service during 1927.

The following year the RF&P got into the passenger bus business. For many years the commuter travel between Richmond and Ashland had been handled by steam powered accommodation trains. With commuter travel dwindling due to competition from the electric railway and automobiles, in 1928 the RF&P organized the Suburban Motor Coach Company to operate passenger buses between Richmond and Ashland. The bus service began on November 12, 1928, at which time the accommodation trains were withdrawn.

In January of 1929, the RF&P chartered the RF&P Transportation Company as a wholly owned subsidiary of the railroad and established interstate bus service over the Richmond-Washington Highway. The operation proved most satisfactory and soon the Suburban Motor Coach Company was merged into RF&P Transportation Company. Then, in August of that year, the RF&P Transportation Company was merged with The Greyhound Corporation to form the Richmond-Greyhound Lines, a bus line owned 49% by RF&P and 51% by the Greyhound Corporation.

The changing of the guard. New F7A diesel No. 1101 sits beside 4-8-4 "Statesman" No. 622, the *Carter Braxton*, at Ivy City engine terminal in Washington. Road diesel locomotives were placed in service on the RF&P in 1949. The *Carter Braxton* made the last regular service steam run on the RF&P on January 3, 1954.

In an effort to continue the reduction in the expense of operating steam powered local passenger trains, the RF&P purchased an all steel gas-electric train in 1928 consisting of a motor unit with passenger and baggage compartments and a trailer coach. The train proved so successful that a duplicate gas-electric train was acquired early in 1929.

The Great Depression began in 1930 and alarmingly reduced the RF&P's business. The lowest level of passenger travel was in 1933. Freight traffic bottomed out in 1934. However, even in the depth of the depression, the RF&P still found time to celebrate its centennial in 1934 and to stimulate passenger business, it drastically reduced fares, installed modern comfortable coach seats and introduced the air-conditioning of cars. Other improvements during the decade included the electrification of tracks at Potomac Yard in 1935 to permit operation of electric locomotives by the Pennsylvania Railroad; the purchase in 1937 of the 4-8-4 "Generals" for fast freight service, followed in 1938 by the 4-8-4 "Governors" for both passenger and fast freight service; and, beginning in 1939, the operation by SAL and ACL of New York to Florida diesel-powered stainless steel streamlined passenger trains.

World War II provided a thorough test of railroading ability throughout the nation as passenger and freight volume hit new highs. Beginning late in 1941 the withdrawal of all Atlantic coastal steamship service, because of attacks by German submarines and the Government's requirement for the ships for military purposes, threw to the railroads, and particularly to the RF&P, an enormous tonnage of freight which ordinarily would have moved entirely by water. In 1943 RF&P traffic and revenue records were set as more than 8 1/2 million passengers and more than 14 million tons of freight were carried. The daily average of trains operated was 103 (the equivalent to a train every 14 minutes), of which 57 were in passenger service and 46 in freight service. On April 21st a maximum of 131 trains were operated. On April 23rd some 33,324 passengers were carried, the most in a single day during the Company's history.

The RF&P's first diesels, two 1000 HP diesel-electric switch engines were placed in service in March of 1942 at Acca Yard in Richmond. The first diesel switchers were placed in service at Potomac Yard in August of 1946. During the war years, it was necessary for the RF&P to rent locomotives from other lines both for road freight service and for switching service at Potomac Yard.

From 1941 to 1947 the RF&P invested more than $6 million in yard additions, improvements to roadway, signals and other fixed properties, and $7 million in locomotives, cars and other equipment. The Company began making the transition from steam to diesel road power in 1949 with the purchase of 30 diesel locomotives costing more than $5 million. The change was completed with the operation of the last steam locomotive in 1953.

At the end of the war the RF&P naturally experienced a substantial decrease in traffic volumes and revenues. The decline in passenger traffic was the most pronounced. With a large post-war inventory of surplus passenger equipment, a program of special trips and tours, designed to stimulate passenger travel, was launched in 1955. The result was an overwhelming public response to such activities as theater trips to Washington and New York; baseball and football trains to Washington; little folks trains for the children; and, father-son caboose trains to Quantico. The popular Santa Claus Specials became a Richmond tradition and by the 1960's were being offered to various communities on the railroad.

In 1958 arrangements were made to accommodate the trains of the SAL at Broad Street Station when an agreement was reached between the SAL, ACL and RF&P for the Seaboard to acquire 1/3 ownership in the Richmond Terminal Company. Prior to its move to Broad Street Station, the SAL had shared use of Main Street Station with the C&O and its through passenger trains were interchanged with the RF&P at Hermitage.

13

The decade of the 1960's marked the beginning of momentous change for the RF&P. Travel on passenger trains continued the perennial decrease that had begun with the conclusion of the Second World War and, in 1969, the number of passengers carried by the RF&P dropped below the one million mark for the first time since the Depression years. On May 1, 1970 the Company's long history in the passenger business came to an end as the National Railroad Passenger Corporation (Amtrak) assumed responsibility for the provision of intercity rail passenger service over the RF&P and on most other remaining rail passenger routes throughout the United States.

It was also during the 1960's that the RF&P began to make substantial investments in the acquisition of land for development as commercial or industrial sites. Initially, the objective was to grow the railroad business by acquiring land for future development of rail-served industries. However, the Company soon moved into commercial development of its property, of which the Crystal City Complex in Arlington County was the foremost example. Begun as a office-apartment project on less than 2 acres of land in 1964, Crystal City evolved into a multi-million dollar complex on 70+ acres of land. In the years ahead, real estate activities conducted by the RF&P and its subsidiaries would be an increasingly significant contributor to the Company's earnings.

Significant changes were likewise occurring on the RF&P's owner and connecting lines during this period. On December 31, 1962, the Chesapeake and Ohio Railway acquired control of the Baltimore and Ohio Railroad. Five years later, in 1967, the Seaboard Air Line Railway merged with the Atlantic Coast Line Railroad to form the Seaboard Coast Line Railroad. Within ten years the Chessie System Railroads would be adopted as the new corporate identity for what had previously been the B&O, C&O and Western Maryland railroads; and, the Seaboard System Railroad was formed through the consolidation of the Seaboard Coast Line, Louisville and Nashville, Clinchfield, and the Georgia railroads. The 113-mile RF&P connected the Chessie System on the north to the Seaboard System on the south.

A notable improvement to RF&P facilities during the 1960's was the construction of a new consolidated shop in Richmond. Known as Bryan Park Terminal, this $1.8 million facility, which housed the Company's mechanical, engineering, purchasing, and stores departments, was completed in 1962. In 1964 the RF&P acquired the Dahlgren Railroad line that had been put up for sale by the federal government. This line had been built during World War II to serve the old Naval Proving Grounds at Dahlgren and had been idle for about seven years. During the 1960's, the RF&P refurbished a portion of the line and promoted industrial development along the adjacent trackage.

In 1969 an agreement was reached with the Seaboard Coast Line Railroad providing for the SCL and RF&P to jointly use the RF&P's Acca Yard and Bryan Park Terminal for all operations previously performed at the former SAL's Hermitage Yard. SCL operations were transferred to the RF&P on January 1, 1970.

The renovation and improvement of the RF&P's existing office building at Acca Yard made it possible to move the Transportation Department, including the Train Dispatcher's Office, from Broad Street Station to the refurbished facility. The move coincided with the installation of a new Centralized Traffic Control machine and, by 1971, the RF&P had completed consolidation of all main line train dispatching, supervision and control at the new Acca Transportation Center.

One of the highlights of the 1970's was the relocation of the RF&P's general headquarters to a new General Office Building on Laburnum Avenue in Richmond, adjacent to Acca Yard. The new building was occupied in October of 1976 and accommodated all of the departments and functions formerly located at Broad Street Station, which had served as the RF&P's corporate headquarters for over fifty-seven years. The relocation was occasioned by the liquidation of Richmond Terminal Railway Company and the sale by the Terminal Company of fifty-two acres of land, including the Broad Street Station building, to the Commonwealth of Virginia. Passenger operations had ceased in October of 1975 when Amtrak opened its new station facility in Henrico County adjacent to the RF&P main line at Greendale. Today, Broad Street Station continues of serve the citizens of the Virginia as a science

The refurbished Acca Transportation Center in Richmond housed RF&P's Transportation Department and the Train Disptacher's office.

museum.

During this period, the Nation's attention was focused on the Northeastern rail situation. Historically, the preponderance of traffic interchanged between the RF&P and its northern connections through the Potomac Yard gateway was via the Pennsylvania Railroad. In 1968 the Pennsylvania merged with the New York Central to form the Penn Central Transportation Company. Within two years the Penn Central filed for bankruptcy. This followed the bankruptcy of seven other railroads operating in the Northeast and Midwest. The RF&P management closely watched this situation because of its potential impact on the traffic handled through the Potomac Yard gateway.

In 1973 the United States Railway Association was established to formulate a proposed system plan for revitalizing these financially troubled lines. Enactment of the Railroad Revitalization and Regulatory Reform Act ("the 4-R Act") by Congress in 1976 facilitated the takeover by the Consolidated Rail Corporation on April 1, 1976 of most of the properties of six bankrupt railroads. It was during the period of the Penn Central bankruptcy and the formation of Conrail that the ownership of the Richmond-Washington Company's stock by the former Pennsylvania Railroad came to an end. Hence, by the late 1970's, the capital stock of the Richmond-Washington Company was owned by the Chessie System Railroad, Seaboard Coast Line Railroad, Southern Railway and the Commonwealth of Virginia. Conrail owned no stock in the RF&P but did remain a tenant of Potomac Yard and continued to be a major connection for RF&P traffic handled through that gateway.

The "4-R Act" also brought a new tenant into Potomac Yard. Through trackage rights arrangements provided under the Regional Rail Reorganization Act of 1973 and implemented by the "4-R Act" of 1976, the Delaware and Hudson Railway gained access to Potomac Yard via Conrail trackage. These rights were granted to the D&H pursuant to a Congressional mandate to provide competition to Conrail.

Of particular significance to the RF&P was the provision of the "4-R Act" that enabled Amtrak to purchase and operate the former Pennsylvania Railroad's mainline between Washington and New York. The Act also provided government financing to upgrade this line, known as the "Northeast Corridor", for high-speed passenger operations. The increased passenger orientation and the mix of Conrail freights with Amtrak's high-speed passenger trains soon proved to have a serious negative impact on rail freight service. While the Pennsylvania Railroad's access to Potomac Yard had derived from its ownership of the Northeast Corridor trackage, Conrail was in essence a tenant of Amtrak and had to pay ton-mile charges to the passenger corporation for the operation of its freight trains on the Amtrak-owned line. Amtrak justified the charges on the basis that the operation of freight trains on a section of railroad engineered for high-speed passenger operations caused excessive wear and tear on the track.

When Amtrak imposed an additional charge in 1981 for electrical power used on the Corridor by the Conrail electric locomotives, the electrics were quickly replaced with diesels. However, when Amtrak continued to increase the ton-mile charges for all freights and then restricted the operation of freight trains on the Corridor to a window between 8 p.m. and 5 a.m., the freight carriers sought a diversion of Conrail freights from the Corridor to a route better suited to the accommodation of freight service. To protect the interchange of freight with its northern connections through

The last train to use RF&P's Broad Street Station was No. 88, Amtrak's northbound *Meteor/Champion* on the morning of November 15, 1975, arriving at 4:39 a.m. and departing 19 minutes later. SDP40 No. 608 is on No. 88 as it makes its last departure from the venerable Broad Street Station.

Potomac Yard was opened August 1, 1906 for classification and interchange of freight among the Pennsylvania and Baltimore & Ohio Railroads on the north and the Chesapeake & Ohio, Southern, and Washington Southern Railroads on the south. This view is looking north in the 1920s.

the Potomac Yard gateway, the RF&P advocated an arrangement whereby Conrail freights would be operated over the parallel Chessie route (old B&O freight line) between Washington and Philadelphia.

To enhance operational efficiency and thus halt the decline in traffic handled through the Potomac Yard gateway, the RF&P began a $7.6 million capital improvement project at the facility in 1982. Known as the PY Reconfiguration and Improvement Project, it involved retirement of the Southbound Hump, the installation of a computerized process control humping system, and certain track and facility changes in the northbound classification yard. Effective November 19, 1986, humping over the Southbound Hump ceased and all hump-type classification of freight was combined over the modernized Northbound Hump.

The RF&P rolled past some historical milestones during the decade of the 1980's. On August 1, 1981, Potomac Yard celebrated its 75th anniversary. Then, on February 25, 1984, the RF&P celebrated the 150th anniversary of its incorporation. The year 1985 was also notable as it marked the first time in the RF&P's history that non-transportation earnings exceeded the profits generated by the Company's railroad operations. Most of the non-transportation revenue was produced by the real estate activities.

In recognition of the increasing contribution to the Company's net earnings from its real estate activities, the RF&P changed its corporate structure in 1988 from that of a railroad with real estate interests to a holding company where equal attention would be given to the running of trains and the management of land. Under the organizational restructuring, RF&P Corporation was created as a Virginia holding company to control the wholly owned subsidiaries of RF&P Railroad and RF&P Properties.

However, even as these milestones were being reached, the end was drawing near for both Potomac Yard and the RF&P Railroad. On September 23, 1980, the Interstate Commerce Commission approved the 1978 application of Chessie System, Inc. and Seaboard Coast Line Industries, Inc. to merge the two holding companies into a new holding company to be known as CSX Corporation. The former Chessie and SCL each owned 40% of the Richmond-Washington Company, which in turn, owned 65.9% of the RF&P's voting stock. Hence, as a result of the Chessie-Seaboard merger, CSX gained control of 80% of the common stock of the Richmond-Washington Company and received ICC approval to control RF&P. However, the RF&P continued to operate as a separate, independent railroad and retained its own management. This was due to the fact that while CSX controlled the voting stock of the RF&P by virtue of its ownership of a majority of the Richmond-Washington Company, CSX only owned approximately 43% of all classes of outstanding RF&P stock. There remained a substantial minority stockholder interest in the RF&P including 20% of the voting stock of Richmond-Washington Company still held by the Southern Railway.

Another factor influencing the retention of RF&P's autonomous management was the Commonwealth of Virginia's continued interest in the railroad. The State owned nearly 20% of the RF&P's stock, which was held in the investment fund of the Virginia Supplemental Retirement System. Moreover, legislation passed by the Virginia General Assembly provided that the Virginia Supplemental Retirement System could sell its RF&P stock, but only back to the State at the State's demand. Another Act of the Virginia Legislature required legislative approval of any merger of a transportation company in which the state owned stock. Hence, the Commonwealth was in a position to block any attempt by CSX to gain full control of the RF&P.

The creation of CSX had little immediate effect upon Potomac Yard. The creation of Norfolk Southern was another matter. In 1982 the Interstate Commerce Commission approved the common control of the Southern Railway and the Norfolk and Western Railway by Norfolk Southern Corporation. This merger enabled Southern to divert traffic from Potomac Yard by effecting an interchange with Conrail at Hagerstown either via its sister road, the N&W, or directly by obtaining trackage rights over N&W's line. Conrail had wanted to divert traffic from Potomac Yard to Hagerstown to avoid the operational restrictions and escalating charges imposed by Amtrak for Conrail's use of the Northeast Corridor. When an Agreement was reached between NS and Conrail in June of 1988 to provide for a diversion of their interchange traffic to Hagerstown, it doomed Potomac Yard. Sometime after the Conrail/NS diversion of traffic from Potomac Yard, CSX Transportation began to operate pre-blocked run-through trains. Soon there was no longer any requirement for the services that Potomac Yard had to offer. As a result, the RF&P began to dismantle the facility. Almost incredibly, within four years of the Conrail/NS diversion of traffic to Hagerstown, the mighty expanse that was once Potomac Yard had disappeared. The rail yard that once served as the "the Gateway between North and South" had become an anachronism.

The creation of CSX did bring about a fundamental change in the historical role of the RF&P. Prior to 1980, the RF&P had served as a bridge line for the traffic of its various owner lines and it was in the interest of those roads that the RF&P be independently managed to ensure that all traffic was handled upon equal terms. That was the basis for the creation of the Richmond-Washington Company. However, after the creation of CSX, more than 80% of RF&P's rail busi-ness was overhead traffic and in excess of 85% of its revenues were generated from traffic in which it participated with CSX. While RF&P was largely dependent on CSX for its business, CSX regarded the existence of a separate operating railroad between its northern (former Chessie) and southern (former Seaboard) properties as an impediment to its operating and marketing efficiencies.

Beginning in 1985, CSX and RF&P began to discuss methods of combining the two companies' operations. The several years of discussions culminated in a definitive merger agreement that was announced on February 20, 1990. Under the terms of the agreement, the RF&P was to be merged into CSX and RF&P shareholders were given the option of exchanging their RF&P shares, one for one, for shares in CSX or for $34.50 cash. The public announcement of the merger set off a storm of controversy. Critics, including financial analysts and shareholders alike, immediately argued that RF&P was undervalued at that price. The merger proposal was also politically controversial as a result of the Commonwealth of Virginia's ownership of more than 20% of all outstanding RF&P shares through the Virginia Supplemental Retirement System. Under Virginia law, the pension fund could not sell its RF&P stock without approval of the General Assembly. When the VSRS replaced its appointees on the RF&P's Board of Directors who had negotiated and endorsed the proposed transaction and, the Governor of Virginia accepted the resignation of the VSRS Chairman and ordered an intensive study of the transaction, CSX and RF&P mutually agreed to terminate the merger agreement.

Within months of the failed merger attempt, a new proposal was announced - this time initiated by the Virginia Retirement System.

The pension fund had been in the process of reviewing its investment strategies and had determined that it wanted a portion of its money invested in real estate. With hundreds of acres of prime real estate in the Washington suburbs of Arlington and Alexandria (including Potomac Yard), the pension fund found the RF&P to be quite attractive. In August of 1990, the Virginia Retirement System disclosed that it had been purchasing RF&P stock on the open market since May of that year, including the RF&P stock owned by Norfolk Southern Corporation. With the shares purchased from NS and private investors, the retirement system had increased its total ownership of RF&P stock from approximately 20% to approximately 28%. In September, the Virginia Retirement System came forward with its own proposal.

VRS and CSX jointly proposed to RF&P a transaction in which CSX would acquire RF&P's railroad operations in exchange for its shares of RF&P stock and the VRS would buy the remaining RF&P shares held by CSX. The proposal also included a self-tender offer by RF&P for the outstanding shares not held by CSX or VRS. Upon consummation of the proposal, it was contemplated that the RF&P would become a real estate company, with VRS as its majority stockholder, and only the railroad operations would be transferred to CSX. Significantly, while the proposed transaction would require certain favorable governmental rulings and approval by the Trustees of VRS and the Board of Directors of the two companies, it would not require approval by the Virginia General Assembly. The RF&P's Board of Directors promptly established a Special Committee of independent directors to evaluate the proposal and negotiate the related terms.

Following months of negotiations, the long-running drama over the sale of the RF&P finally came to an end in August of 1991 when the RF&P's Board of Directors gave their final approval to the multimillion dollar transaction. The complicated deal was accomplished in a series of interrelated and inseparable transactions detailed in three definitive agreements between the parties. Under a tender agreement, RF&P's public stockholders were to be given the opportunity to sell any and all of their RF&P shares to Systems Holdings, Inc., a new wholly owned subsidiary of VRS specially constituted for the sole purpose of completing the transaction. Under an asset purchase agreement, the RF&P would sell all of its railroad assets (excluding the Potomac Yard real estate) to RF&P Railway, a new wholly owned subsidiary of CSX, in return for the RF&P stock owned by CSX. Under a stock purchase agreement, VRS would purchase the remaining RF&P stock held by CSX. Upon the consummation of the three agreements, the 157 year old RF&P would go out of the railroad business and become a real estate company controlled by the Virginia Retirement System.

In the final transaction, which closed after the expiration of the tender offer for all outstanding shares of stock, CSX took the rail assets and cash in return for its shares of RF&P stock. The retirement system purchased nearly 3 million shares from CSX and 5.9 million shares from public shareholders, gaining control of over 99% of the outstanding RF&P stock. The agonizing 21 month takeover tug of was over. RF&P's business was now the ownership, operation, development and management of real estate.

On the morning of October 10, 1991, the long and proud history of the Richmond, Fredericksburg and Potomac Railroad Company quietly came to an end. For 157 years the little railroad that had been built to link the North and South had been continuous in the purpose for which it was originally organized, while at the same time serving in the development of the Commonwealth and the Nation. Today, the tracks its 113-mile rail line still serve as a vital link between the northern and southern properties of CSX Transportation's 18,800 route mile network.

William E. Griffin Coll.

Looking down from the coaling station onto the roundhouse and turntable at the Acca locomotive terminal. Opened on January 1, 1924, the facility served as the Richmond engine terminal for both RF&P and ACL.

Concurrent with the construction of Broad Street Station (1919), RF&P built this new concrete arch bridge over the James River. RF&P extended to the center of the bridge (pier 5) and south of that point the line was owned by ACL. Southern Railway's Richmond-Danville line is in the foreground.

In July 1962 RF&P opened its new consolidated shop facility in Richmond. Known as "Bryan Park Terminal," this $1.8 million shop housed the company's mechanical, engineering, and purchasing and stores departments. In 1993 CSX Transportation, having no need for a locomotive shop at Richmond after its merger of the RF&P into its system, recycled this modern facility as a shop for repair of maintenance-of-way equipment.

This RF&P Advertisement from *Traffic World* magazine announced the arrival of its new Berkshire (2-8-4) type steam locomotives— just in time to assist with the war effort. Like all railroads during the war, RF&P handled record levels of freight and passenger traffic. RF&P received a huge volume of freight traffic that would normally have gone by coastwise shipping because of the German U-boat raids along the Atlantic Coast. The daily average of trains operated over RF&P during 1943 was 103, or one every 14 minutes.

RICHMOND, FREDERICKSBURG AND POTOMAC RAILROAD COMPANY

PRESIDENTS

As with any company the person who heads it as president usually has a marked influence on the company's daily and long term operations. This list depicts the Presidents of the RF&P from its chartering in 1834 until its absorption into the CSX Transportation System in 1991. Moncure Robinson, whose name is closely associated with the early development of the railroad appears as President from 1840-47 after having served since the railroad's creation as its Chief Engineer. His brothers Conway and Edwin also served as the company's President and as well as his son John. Another person who had profound influence on the road was Major E.T.D. Myers, who served as the line's General Manager from just after the Civil War until he became President in 1889, serving in that capacity until his death in 1905.

John A. Lancaster	(1834-1836)
Conway Robinson	(1836-1838)
Joseph M. Sheppard	(1838-1840)
Moncure Robinson	(1840-1847)
Edwin Robinson	(1847-1860)
Peter V. Daniel, Jr.	(1860-1871)
John M. Robinson	(1871-1878)
Robert Ould	(1878-1881)
Joseph P. Brinton	(1881-1889)
Edmund T. D. Myers	(1889-1905)
William J. Leake	(1905-1906)
William H. White	(1907-1920)
Eppa Hunton, Jr.	(1920-1932)
Norman Call	(1932-1955)
W. Thomas Rice	(1955-1957)
Wirt P. Marks, Jr.	(1957-1960)
Stuart Shumate	(1961-1981)
John J. Newbauer, Jr.	(1981-1985)
Richard L. Beadles	(1985-1986)
Frank A. Crovo, Jr.	(1986-1991)

William E. Griffin Coll.

The magnificent waiting room under the dome of Broad Street Station.

The RF&P Railroad in the Civil War

On April 19, 1861, just seven days after Confederate forces bombarded Fort Sumter, the four vessels of the Potomac Steamboat Company were seized at Washington, D. C. by the United States Government. Shortly thereafter, the Commonwealth of Virginia took possession of the RF&P's property at Aquia Creek and dispatched military engineers to fortify the area against attack. Suddenly, the railroad that had been built to link the North with the South was deprived of all connection with the North. Situated between the capital cities of two warring factions, the RF&P was about to enter upon the most trying and disastrous period of its existence.

The Company's position during the war was also complicated due to the fact that while the RF&P was a Southern railroad, the majority of its stockholders resided in the North. During the 25 years of its existence before the start of the Civil War, the RF&P had been controlled by the Robinson family. Moncure Robinson, the Company's former Chief Engineer and President, was a native Richmonder who had relocated his engineering business to Philadelphia. He was also the President of the Potomac Steamboat Company and the leader of the RF&P's Philadelphia stockholders who owned a majority of the common stock in both the railroad and its steamboat connection. When the Company paid dividends during the war, as it did each year except 1865, a majority of those dividends were paid to its Northern owners.

The Northern stockholders' interest in the RF&P aided the Company's financial position throughout the war. In 1861, Moncure Robinson was successful in securing reimbursement from the United States for the steamboats seized from the Potomac Steamboat Company. In 1864, when the RF&P was straining to keep its worn and battered railroad going, Robinson made payment to the RF&P for its share of his settlement with the Federal Government for the seized steamboats. Also, in 1862, an agent of the RF&P was able to collect from the United States Post Office monies which were due the Company for U. S. Mail transported before the outbreak of the war.

Interestingly, the man elected by the RF&P stockholders to serve as the Company's President during the war years – and who was re-elected each year - was Peter V. Daniel, Jr. A staunch secessionist, Daniel's father had been a member of the Supreme Court of the United States and an ardent defender of state rights. However, he was also an able manager and under his direction the RF&P was kept open for business until the last several months of the war.

Certainly, the most controversial figure during this period was Samuel Ruth, the RF&P's Superintendent of Transportation. A Northerner by birth, he moved to Virginia in 1839 and was employed by the RF&P. By 1858 he was the Company's Superintendent in charge of actual operation of the railroad. Whether he was a true Union man or an opportunist who changed sides when he foresaw the ultimate defeat of the Confederacy, there can be no doubt that Ruth conveyed both military and economic intelligence to the Union Army and there is strong possibility, even probability, that he deliberately mismanaged the RF&P to the detriment of the Confederate cause.

Both sides realized the value of the RF&P from the very outset of the war. Besides providing an essential north-south approach between the capitals of the opposing forces, the RF&P also afforded the means of carrying troops and supplies as the ebb and flow of battle swept across Virginia. Early in 1862, RF&P trackage north of Fredericksburg was seized by the Union forces under the command of General Irvin McDowell as General George B. McClellan launched his Peninsula Cam-

National Archives

RF&P's bridge over the Rappahannock River was destroyed by both the Federal and Confederate armies in 1862, Union troops view the damaged bridge in this Civil War photograph.

paign to capture Richmond. The line of the RF&P south of Fredericksburg remained in the possession of its owner and was used to carry men and supplies to the Confederate forces in that area until late in 1865. The northern terminus of the RF&P during this period was at Hamilton's Crossing, about four miles south of Fredericksburg.

Trains ran at the government's convenience and schedules were a military secret. Troop movements were directed by the Superintendent's Office of Transportation and it was always questionable as to whether either men or supplies would reach any certain destination.

RF&P trackage north of Fredericksburg was subsequently rebuilt and operated by the United States Military Railroad, which had been created by Congress to control the operation of captured Southern railroads. This section of the railroad also supplied the Army of the Potomac while it was camped on Falmouth Heights during the winter of 1862-63 and during the battles of Fredericksburg and Chancellorsville.

Throughout the fray, the combatants contested every mile of the RF&P. The Company's many bridges were an especially attractive target for Union calvary. As McClellan approached Richmond, the Sixth U. S. Cavalry of Brigadier General George Stoneman burned the bridge across the South Anna River in May 1862, preventing rail movements north of the river for about five months. Bridges over both the South and North Anna Rivers were destroyed in May 1864, suspending rail service for over three months. The final destruction of the line occurred in March 1865, when Union forces burned the four principal bridges south of Fredericksburg along with a train of twenty-eight freight cars.

At the end of the war the RF&P faced appalling conditions. Most of its bridges were down, much of its track, locomotives, and rolling stock were either destroyed or worn out. The Company's records relate that "No dividends were paid in 1865."

This temporary bridge over Potomac Creek was built by Engineers of the United States Military Railroads in nine days in May 1862. Abraham Lincoln remarked about the bridge that it seemed to be made of "beanpoles and cornstalks." But as can be seen, it certainly supported trains.

Library of Congress

National Archives

The high bridge over Potomac Creek was replaced by U. S. Military Railroads with this more substantial truss structure, most of which had been prefabricated, in the spring of 1863.

RF&P 4-8-4 No. 602, *Governor Thomas Jefferson* blows off steam at Acca engine terminal in 1947. Among the RF&P's most powerful and certainly most beautiful locomotives, the 4-8-4s were the archetypical "Georgian Locomotive" with the aristocratic face and graceful proportions that associated well with Virginia's Colonial history. *(Anthony Dementi photo, William E. Griffin Coll.)*

Chapter 2

The Glory Days of Steam

Steam power was still in the experimental stage when the RF&P Railroad was chartered in 1834. As an indication of the public's uncertainty of steam locomotion, no mention was made of locomotives or engines in the Company's charter. The President and Directors were authorized to purchase "all machines, wagons, vehicles, carriages and teams of any description whatsoever, which they deem necessary or proper for the purposes of transportation".

With the exception of the *Roanoke*, that was purchased from the Petersburg Railroad, the first RF&P steam engines were all bought in England. These engines bore the names *Richmond, Fredericksburg, Washington, Potomac, American, Jefferson, Virginia,* and *Florida.* They weighed about five tons with engine and tender, burned wood, and were known as the 2-2-0 type with a large pony wheel and drive wheel on each side.

Later locomotives were named for officers and directors of the company, for southern states and for local points on the line. In 1850, a locomotive was built in the company's shops in Richmond and named *Thomas Sharp* for the RF&P's Superintendent. Within three years, two more locomotives were built by the Company's shop forces.

In 1840 the Norris Works of Philadelphia built the first American or 4-4-0 type locomotive for the RF&P, named the *John A. Lancaster* in honor of the Company's first president. When the Civil War began the RF&P owned eleven locomotives which were named *John A. Lancaster, Thomas Sharp, George W. Munford,* *James Bosher, North Star, Eclipse, G. A. Myers, Nicholas Mills, Tecumseh, Henry Clay,* and *G. P. R. James.* The RF&P's practice of naming locomotives was discontinued in 1875 and thereafter until the late-1930's engines were designated by number only.

The American type of locomotive was the RF&P's standard for both freight and passenger service until the 1880's. These locomotives, as well as all other RF&P engines, were converted to burn coal by 1883. While the trains operated through between Richmond and Washington after 1872, the RF&P's locomotives ran only to Quantico where they were fueled, watered, and turned for operation back to Richmond. The practice of changing locomotives at Quantico continued until the creation of the Richmond-Washington Line in 1901.

The increase in traffic over the RF&P following the establishment of the all-rail route in 1872 resulted in the need for more powerful locomotives and, during the 1880's and 1890's, twenty-one locomotives (Nos. 1-21) of the Mogul or 2-6-0 type were acquired by the Company. Thirteen of these moguls were equipped with 62" drivers that made them suitable for either fast freight or heavy passenger service.

This policy of favoring dual-service motive power would prevail on the RF&P throughout the steam era. The company's traffic density, time sensitive perishable traffic, and heavy seasonal freight and passenger business made it desirable to use locomotives that were suitable for either fast freight or heavy passenger service. Drag freight operations would have resulted in

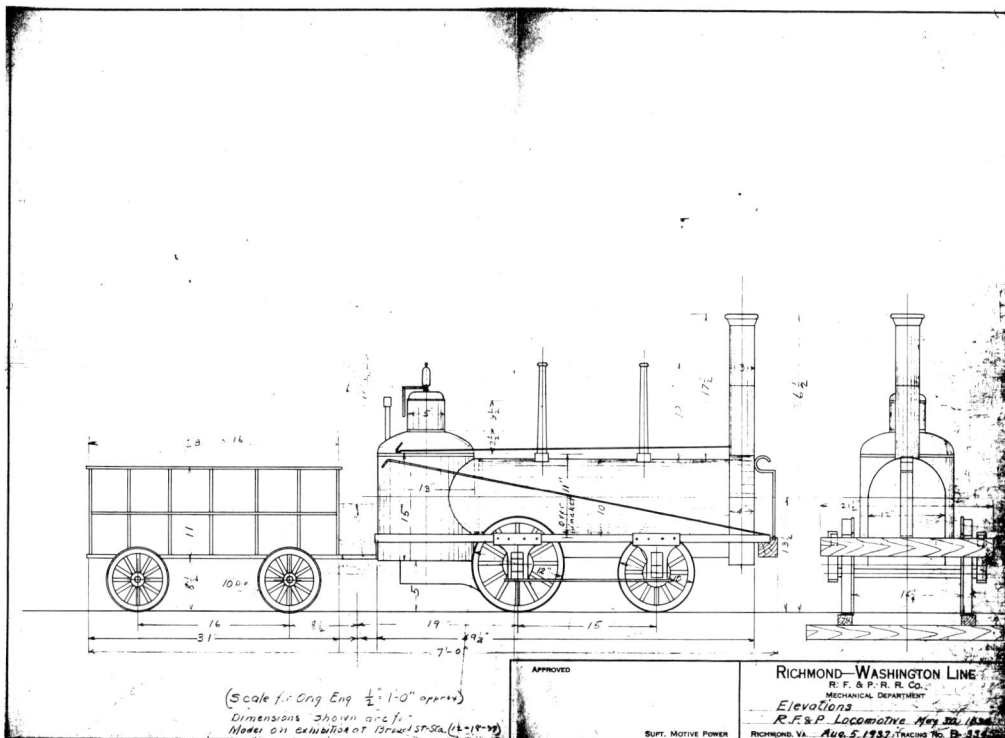

This drawing of one of RF&P's first steam locomotives, of the 2-2-0 type, built in England, probably near the specifications of *Richmond* was constructed in 1834 by Robert Stevenson in Liverpool. A model of this locomotive was on display at Broad Street Station for many years, and this drawing is scaled from that model. These early 2-2-0s had horsepower ratings of 11 or 14!

William E. Griffin Coll.

25

train delays that could not be tolerated given the traffic and operating conditions on the RF&P.

When RF&P locomotives began to operate through between Richmond and Washington after the turn of the century, the Tenwheeler or 4-6-0 type was acquired the Company for both freight and passenger service. Eight locomotives (Nos. 30-37) of this type were purchased in 1900. Fourteen more (Nos. 38-46) were built by the Richmond Locomotive Works between 1901 and 1903. In 1926 those Tenwheelers that remained on the roster were renumbered 101 to 113.

The Tenwheelers were eventually relegated to local freight service with the arrival of the Pacifics or 4-6-2 type locomotives. Between 1904 and 1927 the RF&P and Washington Southern purchased over sixty of this type of locomotive. Until the late 1930's, the majority of the RF&P's road engines would be the Pacific type locomotive.

The first Pacifics were delivered by Baldwin in 1904 for the Washington Southern (Nos. 60-69), followed by RF&P Nos. 70-74 from Alco's Richmond Locomotive Works in 1905. They became Nos. 151-165 in the 1926 renumbering of locomotives. Used in both passenger and freight service, they spent their last days in local freight service until scrapped between the years 1929 and 1940.

Over a two-decade period, heavier Pacifics were added to the RF&P roster. The next group of Pacifics arrived in 1907. Built by Baldwin, they were numbered 80-85 (later renumbered 201-206), and with their 73-inch drivers they were primarily used in passenger service. Similar Pacifics in the number series WS 51-59, RF&P 86-94 (renumbered 251-268) arrived in three subsequent orders between 1911 and 1913.

In 1915-16, Baldwin delivered six heavy Pacifics with 69-inch drivers for primary used in freight service. Originally numbered Nos. 1-6, they were renumbered 401-406 and substantially rebuilt in 1927. Elesco Feedwater Heaters were installed and the air pumps were mounted on the upper portion of the smokebox. Stokers were also installed along with a trailer booster that created an additional 11,000 lbs of tractive effort.

Twelve similar sized Pacifics were delivered by Alco's Richmond Locomotive Works between 1918 and 1925, but these engines had 75-inch drivers that made them particularly suited for passenger service. Originally numbered Nos. 10-21, they were renumbered in the 301-312 series and were also rebuilt and modernized in the late 1920's to increase their capacity and efficiency.

The final group of RF&P Pacifics were among the most powerful of their type ever built. They were delivered by Baldwin in 1927 and numbered 325-328. With 75-inch drivers and steam pressure that gave them a starting tractive force of 52,050 lbs., they were capable of handling either fast freight or heavy passenger service. These locomotives were sold to the Chesapeake and Ohio Railway in 1947 after the RF&P took delivery of its last group of the 600 series locomotives.

In 1924-1925, the RF&P purchased four locomotives (Nos. 201-203) from Alco of the Mountain (4-8-2) type. Later renumbered the 501-503, they developed a tractive force of 61,620 lbs. While intended for freight service, they were also used extensively in passenger service during the heavy tourist seasons.

Both the Mountain and Pacific type locomotives had tender tanks of 10,000 gallons capacity. On a through run in freight service the water consumption was about twice that amount, and when it was desired to cut out intermediate stops, a tank car of 10,000 gallons capacity was used in addition to the regular tender. With this arrangement the run between Acca and Potomac Yards was made without stopping for water.

The RF&P greatly improved its motive power with the purchase in 1937 of five powerful 4-8-4 locomotives for fast freight service, followed in 1938 by six heavy 4-8-4 locomotives suitable for both passenger and fast freight service. In addition to numbering these locomotives, the RF&P revived the practice of naming each engine. The freight locomotives (Nos. 551-555) bore the names of Confederate Generals Robert E. Lee, T. J. Jackson, J. E. B. Stuart, A. P. Hill and J. E. Johnston. The passenger locomotives (Nos. 601-606) were named for the first six Virginia Governors—Patrick Henry, Thomas Jefferson, Thomas Nelson, Benjamin Harrison, James Monroe and John Tyler.

Tenwheeler No. 39 with a local RF&P train leaving Washington (at 7th Street Subway) March 8, 1912. No. 39 was built by Richmond Locomotive Works in 1901 and served RF&P until it was sold to a shortline in 1923.

26

T. W. Dixon, Jr. Coll.

With the outbreak of World War II and the requirement for additional motive power, the RF&P ordered six more "Governors" (Nos. 607-612) from Baldwin in 1941. These 4-8-4 locomotives were named for Virginia Governors Edmund Randolph, Henry A. Wise, John Letcher, Fitzhugh Lee, Claude A. Swanson and William Smith.

Such were the traffic demands on the RF&P that it was necessary to rent steam locomotives from other lines both for road freight service and for handling trains in Potomac Yard during the years 1942-1943. The leased locomotives were returned to their owners in February and March, 1943 when the RF&P received ten powerful 2-8-4 locomotives (Nos. 571-580) for fast freight service that had been ordered in 1942 from the Lima Locomotive Works. During the year, the RF&P also purchased three secondhand 2-6-6-2 Mallet locomotives (Nos. 1-3) from the C&O Railway for handling trains on the humps at Potomac Yard.

In 1944 the RF&P also purchased six secondhand 4-8-2 locomotives (Nos. 515-520) from the Norfolk and Western Railway to assist in handling the wartime traffic. Their 68,880 lbs. of tractive effort was the greatest of any RF&P road locomotive but their 63-inch drivers made them unsuitable for fast freight service. In 1948, the RF&P sold these locomotives to the Wheeling and Lake Erie Railroad.

The final RF&P road locomotives were acquired in 1945. Known as the "Statesmen", these ten 4-8-4 Baldwin locomotives (Nos. 613-622) were named for famous Virginians - John Marshall, George Washington, Henry Clay, George Mason, John Randolph, James Madison, William Byrd, George Wythe, Richard Henry Lee and Carter Braxton. With a tonnage rating identical to that of the "Governors", they were equipped with roller bearings on all axles and were used in passenger and freight service. Retired in 1953 and 1954, several were retained for emergency service and were then leased to the C&O Railway for a brief period in 1955.

Due to the RF&P's extensive switching operations at Acca and Potomac Yards, the Company owned a large number of yard engines. Several series of 0-6-0 yard switchers were assigned switching duties at both of the facilities. Fifteen 0-6-0's with 50-inch drivers (variously numbered between 100 and 117) were built by Baldwin for the RF&P and Washington Southern. They were renumbered to the series 1-36 in 1926. The RF&P also owned ten 0-6-0's with 51-inch drivers (variously numbered between 107 and 128). These locomotives were renumbered in the series 41-47.

For service as hump engines at Potomac Yard, the RF&P purchased four heavy 0-8-0 switchers (WS No. 126 and RF&P Nos. 118-120) with 51-inch drive

wheels between 1914 and 1918. They were renumbered in the series 71-74 and remained in service until the early 1950's. Two even larger 0-8-0's with 53-inch drivers (Nos. 130-131 that were renumbered the 90 and 91) were acquired for service at Potomac Yard in 1923. They were retired at Potomac Yard in 1953.

At the end of World War II, the RF&P was well equipped with a roster of up-to-date and highly efficient steam locomotives. In 1940, there were 24 steam yard locomotives and 58 steam road locomotives, of which only 15 of the road locomotives were of the heavy, fast 4-8-2 and 4-8-4 types. Of the 72 steam road engines owned by the RF&P in 1947, 14 were modern 4-8-2 and 2-8-4 types and 27 were of the highly efficient 4-8-4 type adapted to fast service with heavy passenger trains. The tractive power of the 72 road engines was nearly 50% greater than that of the 58 road engines running in 1940. At the end of 1947 the yard power consisted of 20 steam and 12 diesel-electric locomotives with tractive force about 90% higher than that of the 1940 yard power.

Nevertheless, diesels would rapidly replace the RF&P's magnificent stable of steam locomotives. Dieselization of yard operations began in 1942 at Acca Yard and in 1946 at Potomac Yard. The RF&P's first road diesels went into service in 1949. Steam locomotives were removed from yard and then road service. The last RF&P-owned steam locomotive to operate in regular service over the line was the Statesman 4-8-4 No. 622, the "Carter Braxton", passing "RO" Tower at 1:50 p.m. with a southbound passenger train, arriving "AY" Tower, Richmond, at 4:39 p.m. on January 3, 1954.

L. W. Rice, T. W. Dixon, Jr. Coll.

Two RF&P 4-8-4s at Washington Terminal's Ivy City engine facility June 23, 1949. No. 619 (Baldwin 1938) on the left was "Statesman" *William Byrd*, and No. 601 on the right was "Governor" class *Governor Patrick Henry*, from the last batch of 4-8-4s, built by Baldwin in 1945.

Representative Locomotive Rosters

RF&P Locomotives as of Sept. 30, 1870 - [Last Year When Locomotives Were Named]					
Name	No.	Builder	Date	Driver size	Cylinder/stroke
Lancaster	1	RF&P	1855	54-in.	11-1/2x20-in.
Munford	2	Norris	1852	54-in.	10-1/2x22-in.
Sharp	3	RF&P	1848	54-in.	12x18-in.
Bosher	4	RF&P	1849	54-in.	11x-18-in.
Occoquan	5	Danforth	1870	60-in.	14x24-in.
Quantico	6	Danforth	1870	60-in.	14x24-in.
Myers	7	N. J. Loco.	1857	60-in.	12x22-in.
Mt. Vernon	8	Danforth	1865	60-in.	13x22-in.
Haxall	9	N. J. Loco.	1861	42-in.	11x22-in.
Clay	10	RF&P	1843	48-in.	10-1/2x22-in.
Ashland	11	RF&P	1868	60-in.	13x22-in.
Fredericksburg	12	Danforth	1865	60-in.	13x22-in.

INVENTORY OF LOCOMOTIVE EQUIPMENT — December 31, 1925

Old Locomotive Numbers	New Locomotive Numbers	Type	Size of Cylinders (Inches)	Diameter of Driving Wheels (Inches)	Weight on Drivers (Pounds)	Total Weight of Engine (Pounds)	Total Weight of Engine and Tender (Pounds)	Capacity of Tank (Gallons)	Year Built	Builder	Tractive Power (Pounds)
100	1	0-6-0	19x24	50	110,000	110,000	165,000	2,500	1903	Baldwin	29,460
110	2	0-6-0	18x24	50	100,000	100,000	163,760	2,500	1903	Baldwin	24,450
101	3	0-6-0	19x24	50	110,000	110,000	170,000	3,000	1905	Baldwin	29,460
111–112	4–5	0-6-0	19x24	50	110,000	110,000	170,000	3,000	1905	Baldwin	29,460
102–103–104	11–13	0-6-0	20x26	50	150,226	150,226	252,226	5,000	1905	Baldwin	35,360
113–114	14–15	0-6-0	20x26	50	150,226	150,226	252,226	5,000	1906	Baldwin	35,360
105–106	21–22	0-6-0	20x26	50	150,226	150,226	252,226	5,000	1912	Baldwin	35,360
115–116–117	25–27	0-6-0	20x26	50	145,975	145,975	235,175	5,000	1908	A. L. Co.	35,360
107–108	31–32	0-6-0	20x26	51	131,500	131,500	246,500	5,000	1919	Baldwin	34,900
121–122	35–36	0-6-0	22x26	51	160,000	160,000	250,000	4,500	1918	Baldwin	37,750
109	41	0-6-0	21x26	51	172,000	172,000	309,000	7,000	1918	A. L. Co.	41,200
123–124	42–43	0-6-0	21x28	51	169,000	169,000	289,000	6,000	1921	A. L. Co.	41,200
125	44	0-6-0	21x28	51	169,000	169,000	289,000	6,000	1923	A. L. Co.	41,200
127–128	45–46	0-6-0	21x28	51	169,000	169,000	289,000	6,000	1925	A. L. Co.	41,200
118–119	71–72	0-8-0	24x28	51	229,000	229,000	412,000	10,000	1914	A. L. Co.	53,770
120	73	0-8-0	24x28	51	229,000	229,000	412,000	10,000	1918	A. L. Co.	53,770
126	74	0-8-0	24x28	51	229,000	229,000	412,000	10,000	1923	A. L. Co.	53,770
130–131	91–92	0-8-0	26x28	53	257,050	257,050	439,400	10,000	1923	A. L. Co.	60,800
25–29	101–105	4-6-0	19x26	62	107,000	141,700	221,100	4,500	1903	A. L. Co.	25,700
38–40–41	106–108	4-6-0	19x26	68	107,000	141,700	221,100	4,500	1901	A. L. Co.	23,460
42–46	109–113	4-6-0	19x26	68	107,000	141,700	221,100	4,500	1903	A. L. Co.	23,460
60–69	151–160	4-6-2	20x26	68	116,620	180,560	280,560	5,500	1904	Baldwin	26,000
70–74	161–165	4-6-2	20x26	68	116,620	180,560	280,560	5,500	1905	A. L. Co.	26,000
80–85	201–206	4-6-2	22x28	73	159,000	238,000	375,900	7,000	1907	Baldwin	31,560
51–55	251–255	4-6-2	23x28	73	151,200	240,000	370,000	7,000	1913	Baldwin	34,500
56–59	256–259	4-6-2	23x28	73	161,500	241,000	379,200	7,000	1911	A. L. Co.	34,500
86–89	260–263	4-6-2	23x28	73	161,500	241,000	379,200	7,000	1912	A. L. Co.	34,500
90–94	264–268	4-6-2	23x28	73	161,500	244,000	398,200	8,000	1913	A. L. Co.	34,500
10–15	301–306	4-6-2	26x28	75	199,000	293,300	488,400	10,000	1918	A. L. Co.	42,800
16–17	307–308	4-6-2	26x28	75	199,000	293,300	488,400	10,000	1920	A. L. Co.	42,800
18–19	309–310	4-6-2	26x28	75	199,000	293,300	488,400	10,000	1924	Baldwin	42,800
20–21	311–312	4-6-2	26x28	75	195,290	303,530	505,210	10,000	1925	Baldwin	42,800
1–6	401–406	4-6-2	26x28	68	191,500	291,500	464,900	10,000	1915	Baldwin	47,320
200–201	501–502	4-8-2	28x30	73	262,000	381,000	582,600	10,000	1924	A. L. Co.	57,510
202–204	503–504	4-8-2	28x30	73	276,500	384,000	583,300	10,000	1925	A. L. Co.	57,510

SUMMARY—Five 4-6-0 locomotives with 62-inch wheels; Eight 4-6-0 locomotives with 68-inch wheels; Twenty-one 4-6-2 locomotives with 68-inch wheels; Twenty-four 4-6-2 locomotives with 73-inch wheels; Fifteen 0-6-0 locomotives with 50-inch wheels; Twelve 4-6-2 locomotives with 75-inch wheels; Ten 0-6-0 locomotives with 51-inch wheels; Four 0-8-0 locomotives with 51-inch wheels; Two 0-8-0 locomotives with 53-inch wheels; Four 4-8-2 locomotives with 73-inch wheels.

EXTRA TENDERS—Three 8,000 gallons capacity—not numbered.

Number locomotives on hand December 31, 1924............................ 99
Number sold since last report.. 0
Number locomotives on hand December 31, 1925............................ 105
Number purchased since last report.. 6

LOCOMOTIVE NOS.	TYPE	SIZE OF CYLINDERS (INCHES)	DIAMETER OF DRIVING WHEELS	WEIGHT ON DRIVERS (POUNDS)	TOTAL WEIGHT OF ENGINE (POUNDS)	TOTAL WEIGHT OF ENGINE AND TENDER (POUNDS)	CAPACITY OF TANK (GALLONS)	YEAR BUILT	BUILDER	TRACTIVE POWER (POUNDS)
1,2,3	2-8-8-2	23x32	57"	493,070	567,500	777,700	12,000	1924	A.L.CO.	108,550
31,32	0-6-0	20x26	51"	131,500	131,500	246,500	5,000	1910	BALDWIN	34,900
35,36	0-6-0	22x26	51"	156,700	156,700	246,700	4,500	1918	BALDWIN	37,750
41	0-6-0	21x28	51"	170,000	170,000	300,500	7,000	1918	A.L.CO.	41,200
42,43	0-6-0	21x28	51"	170,000	170,000	295,700	6,000	1921	A.L.CO.	41,200
44	0-6-0	21x28	51"	170,000	170,000	295,700	6,000	1923	A.L.CO.	41,200
45,46	0-6-0	21x28	51"	170,000	170,000	295,700	6,000	1925	A.L.CO.	41,200
47,48	0-6-0	21x28	51"	170,000	170,000	295,700	6,000	1927	BALDWIN	41,200
71,72	0-8-0	24x28	51"	229,000	229,000	412,000	10,000	1914	A.L.CO.	55,460
73	0-8-0	24x28	51"	229,000	229,000	412,000	10,000	1918	A.L.CO.	55,460
74	0-8-0	24x28	51"	229,000	229,000	412,000	10,000	1923	A.L.CO.	55,460
91,92	0-8-0	26x28	53"	259,000	259,000	441,350	10,000	1923	A.L.CO.	65,360
102	4-6-0	19x26	62"	107,000	141,700	221,100	4,500	1903	A.L.CO.	25,700
151,153,156	4-6-2	21x26	69"	142,500	210,000	365,500	7,000	1904	BALDWIN	28,200
201,205	4-6-2	23x28	73"	161,500	249,420	387,320	7,000	1907	BALDWIN	34,500
255	4-6-2	23x28	73"	161,500	240,000	370,000	7,000	1913	BALDWIN	34,500
256-259	4-6-2	23x28	73"	161,500	252,100	390,300	7,000	1911	A.L.CO.	34,500
260-262	4-6-2	23x28	73"	161,500	252,100	390,300	7,000	1912	A.L.CO.	34,500
264,265	4-6-2	23x28	73"	161,500	258,340	412,540	8,000	1913	A.L.CO.	34,500
267,268	4-6-2	23x28	73"	161,500	258,340	412,540	8,000	1913	A.L.CO.	34,500
301-305	4-6-2	26x28	75"	207,000	319,600	537,200	11,000	1918	A.L.CO.	42,800
306	4-6-2	26x28	75"	207,000	319,600	537,200	10,000	1918	A.L.CO.	48,266
307,308	4-6-2	26x28	75"	207,000	319,600	537,200	11,000	1920	A.L.CO.	42,800
309,310	4-6-2	26x28	75"	207,000	319,600	537,200	11,000	1924	BALDWIN	42,800
311,312	4-6-2	26x28	75"	207,000	319,600	537,200	11,000	1925	BALDWIN	42,800
325-328	4-6-2	26x28	75"	208,000	342,600	552,800	10,000	1927	BALDWIN	48,266
401,402	4-6-2	26¼x28	69"	207,000	319,800	503,900	10,000	1915	BALDWIN	48,450
403	4-6-2	26x28	69"	207,000	319,800	503,900	10,000	1915	BALDWIN	52,456
404-406	4-6-2	26¼x28	69"	207,000	319,800	503,900	10,000	1915	BALDWIN	48,450
501,502	4-8-2	27x30	73"	262,000	381,000	582,600	10,000	1924	A.L.CO.	57,296
503,504	4-8-2	27x30	73"	262,000	381,000	582,600	10,000	1925	A.L.CO.	57,296
515-520	4-8-2	28x30	63"	275,400	401,900	688,433	16,000	1926	N.& W.	68,880
551-555	4-8-4	27x30	77"	277,245	466,040	842,940	20,000	1937	BALDWIN	62,800
571-580	2-8-4	25x34	69"	271,000	434,000	815,850	22,000	1943	LIMA	64,100
601-606	4-8-4	27x30	77"	261,486	407,810	689,810	16,000	1938	BALDWIN	62,800
607-612	4-8-4	27x30	77"	262,800	409,400	723,000	18,000	1942	BALDWIN	62,800
613-622	4-8-4	27x30	77"	266,500	415,000	802,500	20,000	1945	BALDWIN	62,800

In 1870 RF&P needed 12 locomotives to handle its business, all but two of which were built before or during the Civil War. By 1925 when the second roster in this series is shown business had grown, the railroad systems both north and south of RF&P had become major networks, and the line needed just over a hundred locomotives to do its work, ranging in size from 0-6-0 switchers to 4-8-2 Mountains. By far the most common type in 1925 was the Pacific. Indeed all RF&P's business was handled by five locomotive types, the oldest were about 25 years and the newest just acquired, with an average age of about 10 years.

At the peak of the steam era at the end of 1945 as depicted in the roster on this page RF&P had eight wheel arrangements ranging from the 0-6-0 to the 4-8-4, but the roster was still dominated by the Pacifics, which were used for both freight and passenger service on RF&P, whereas on most railroads they were almost always excusively passenger haulers.

During most of the 20th Century RF&P purchased its locomotives from Baldwin Locomotive Works and American Locomotive Company. The ALCOs were all from that company's Richmond plant. A single exception to this was the group of 10 Lima superpower 2-8-4s that were built during the World War II.

A study of RF&P steam locomotives is fairly complicated since they often changed numbers or re-used numbers. The best work dealing with this subject is Richard E. Prince's *The Richmond — Washington Line and Related Railroads*, Millard, Nebraska, 1973 and 1975 The reader is commended to this book for accurate and highly detailed steam locomotive data.

Switchers

RF&P 0-6-0 switcher No. 1 was originally delivered as No. 100 by Baldwin in 1903. This photo was taken at Acca engine terminal in Richmond in July 1927.

Due to its extensive switching operations for its tenants at both Acca Yard and Potomac Yard, RF&P rostered a large group of yard switchers. No. 25, an 0-6-0 with its sloped tender, was photographed at Acca in 1941

0-6-0 No. 41 switches perishable traffic at Potomac Yard in 1946. It was built in 1918 for the Washington Southern as No. 109 by ALCO's Richmond Works, and was finally retired in 1949, about 3 years after this photo was made.

For service as hump engines at Potomac Yard, the Washington Southern purchased two heavy 0-8-0 switchers in 1914. Delivered as Nos. 118 and 119, they were renumbered as RF&P Nos. 71 and 72 in 1926. No. 72 is at the Potomac Yard roundhouse turntable in this June 6, 1940 photo.

(both) L. W. Rice photo, T. W. Dixon Coll.

(Right) Hefty-looking 0-8-0 No. 9 at Potomac Yard in 1928, was fairly new, having been built by Richmond Works in 1923. It exerted 65,360 pounds tractive effort, and was in service until 1953.

L. W. Rice photo, H. H. Harwood, Jr. Coll.

No. 71 was the other heavy 0-8-0 from 1914 mentioned above, shown here at Potomac Yard roundhouse in March 1937.

American Types and Ten Wheelers

H. K. Vollrath Coll.

RF&P 4-4-0 American type No. 18 was built by Baldwin in 1886. It was among the last 4-4-0s to be acquired by the Company and remained in service into the the second decade of the 20th Century. It was renumbered to 53 in 1898. Typical of its era it had 66-inch drivers and a tractive effort of 85,000 pounds.

J. R. Quinn Coll.

Ten Wheeler No. 103 entered the service of RF&P as No. 27 in 1903 from ALCO's Richmond plant. It was equipped with 62-inch drivers and was used primarily in freight service. No. 103 was one of four 4-6-0s used in switching passenger trains at Broad Street Station, hence the decorative striping. It is shown at Richmond in this January 1937 photo.

Pacific Types (4-6-2)

The Pacific type was developed in 1902 by C&O and Missouri Pacific, and RF&P was early to acquire locomotives of the new wheel arrangement. Pacific No. 69 was originally built by Baldwin in 1904 for the Washington Southern and became RF&P No. 160 in 1926. The 4-6-2 is shown at Milford with a passenger train in a 1920s-era photo, its classic lines a carry-over from the 19th Century days.

(both) William E. Griffin Coll.

One of RF&P's Number 1-6-series heavy Pacifics (later numbered in the 401-406 series) is shown with a passenger train near Alexandria in a 1920s-era photo. Note the "fish-belly" type baggage car behind the locomotive, and the engine's large off-center headlight.

Pacific No. 403 (originally No. 3) arrives at Potomac Yard in 1926 with a perishable train. Renumbered in 1926, this locomotive was rebuilt with an Elesco tank type feedwater heater and its air pumps would be relocated to the front of the smokebox in 1927.

A builder photo of 4-6-2 No. 2 at Baldwin in 1915. Built for dual service, these heavy Pacifics were used primarily in freight service. It became 402 in the 1926 renumbering, and was rebuilt in 1927.

New at Baldwin in 1907, No. 84 was renumbered to 205 in 1926. With 73-inch drivers it was designed for high-speed passenger service.

In 1927 RF&P purchased four Pacifics in series 325-328 from Baldwin Locomotive Works. They were the largest of the line's 4-6-2s, and until the arrival of the 600-series 4-8-4s, they were the largest and most powerful passenger locomotives. This builder photo of No. 325 was made at Baldwin in 1927.

(Above) Built between 1919 and 1925, the 300-series Pacifics were the standard RF&P passenger locomotives until the 600-series 4-8-4s arrived in 1938. Originally numbered in the series 10-21, they were renumbered to 301-312 in 1926. No. 307 is seen at Acca Engine Terminal in 1926 in its original condition.

This February 18, 1946 view at the Ivy City engine terminal in Washington shows the "flying pumps" face on No. 311, as well as the high Elesco feedwater heater behind the headlight.

Homer R. Hill

(Above) RF&P Pacifics in the 251-268 series were considered freight engines and were frequently doubleheaded. Nos. 256 and 268 were especially suited for freight work because they were equipped with mechanical stokers. Here No. 268 has a northbound local freight at Franconia in 1943.

(Above) No. 264 is seen at the Ivy City terminal in Washington on July 11, 1937. It was built as RF&P No. 90 by ALCO-Richmond in 1913 and sold for scrap in 1950. It had 73-inch drivers and was rated at 34,500 pounds of tractive effort.

(Right) Another of the class, No. 263 (ex-89) also at Ivy City, on May 7, 1927. It was constructed at Richmond in 1912, and was sold in 1937 to a Railroad Equipment dealer.

36

(Above) 4-6-2 No. 258 was originally built for the Washington Southern by ALCO-Richmond in 1911 as WS No. 55. It was one of the last Pacifics to come to the road from the builder with D-slide valves that controlled saturated steam. It is shown here at Richmond on August 22, 1947.

(Right) The 300-series Pacifics could also handle freight assignments as evidenced by this photo of No. 308 at Fredericksburg on June 22, 1947.

Homer R. Hill

When used in freight service the 325-328-series Pacifics were rated at 2,300 tons northbound and 1,800 tons southbound. No. 325 gets under way from Potomac Yard with a southbound box-car freight in 1943.

The 300-series Pacifics were modernized with mechanical stokers, Elesco feedwater heaters, and their air pumps were relocated from the side to the smokebox front. With 75-inch drivers, they could handle passenger trains of 12-to-15 heavyweight cars on the 2-1/2-hour run between Richmond and Washington. This classic portrait of No. 310 was taken at Richmond on September 5, 1936.

J. R. Quinn Coll.

Bruce Fales

L. W. Rice photo, T. W. Dixon Coll.

(Above) No. 304 is hustling the *Atlanta-Washington Fast Mail* at high speed in this 1930 photo.

(Right) The cluttered face of No. 310 at Ivy City terminal on January 19, 1941. With its "flying pumps" and high Elesco heater, it looks very similar to one of its contemporary Pacifics on the C&O, the headlight positioning being the major difference.

L. W. Rice photo, T. W. Dixon Coll.

No. 306 in a classic portrait view at Washington in 1940, shining, with its bold RF&P emblem centered on the tender.

No. 327 leaves Broad Street Station with a northbound passenger train on August 27, 1946. These locomotives could handle 16 heavyweight cars northbound and 14 southbound between the capital cities. On the slower schedules even more cars could be accommodated.

No. 401 charges south with a freight of 48 cars around "Eastern View Curve" at Mile Post 54, south of Fredericksburg, on July 2, 1946.

400-series Pacific No. 402, as rebuilt, is at Acca Engine Terminal on February 22, 1932. Attached is 10,000-gallon auxiliary tank car to eliminate water stops between Richmond and Potomac Yard. The 401-406-series 4-6-2s were built by Baldwin in 1915 and 1916, and were in service until 1950. They were designed primarily for freight service.

No. 403 has a 60-car freight in tow on Franconia Hill, south of Alexandria on January 8, 1939. Although the Pacific type was most often used in passenger service on American railroads, some did see freight service or dual-service work, especially on lines without long, heavy ruling grades to worry about.

Mountain Type (4-8-2)

In 1924-25 RF&P purchased four locomotives of the Mountain (4-8-2) wheel-arrangement from ALCO's Richmond Works. Numbered 200-203, these locomotives developed a tractive effort of 57,500 pounds. No. 200 is show here new at Acca Engine Terminal in Richmond in 1924. The total weight of the engine and tender was 582,850 pounds, with tenders having 10,000-gallon/16-ton capacity. Boiler pressure was 210 psi, and they had 73-inch drivers.

In 1926 RF&P's Mountains were renumbered 501-504. No. 502 is shown here at Potomac Yard on October 2, 1937. The four 4-8-2s were sold for scrap in 1950.

Homer R. Hill

Mountain No. 503 climbs Franconia grade (the ruling grade southbound on the RF&P) with a southbound freight in 1942. These locomotives were rated to handle freight trains of 2,970 tons northbound and 2,310 tons southbound. Their tenders held 16 tons of coal and 10,000 gallons of water. No. 503 has an auxiliary tank coupled to its tender on this trip to eliminate stops for water en route to Richmond.

C. A. Brown photo, W. E. Griffin Coll.

The RF&P 4-8-2s had 73-inch drivers and although intended for freight service, they were used extensively in passenger service as well. In this photo, No. 503 is handling the northbound Mail and Express Train at Alexandria on June 22, 1947.

Mountain type No. 503 rests at Potomac Yard in 1935, its graphite smokebox in contrast with the black boiler jacket.

(both) Bruce D. Fales photo, T. W. Dixon Coll.

Again at Franconia with a heavy freight train on May 4, 1930, Mountain No. 502 is using another type of auxiliary tender.

H. W. Pontin photo, T. W. Dixon Coll.

No. 503 with an auxiliary tender for water is near Alexandria on May 31, 1930. Note that an engineman is on his hands and knees looking under the front truck. Undoubtedly there is some minor problem, or he's just checking over the locomotive during a stop.

43

Berkshire Type (2-8-4)

The two builder photos on this page illustrate RF&P 2-8-4 No. 574 new at the Lima Locomotive Works in early 1943. The ten Berkshire types ordered in 1942 and delivered in the first three months of 1943, were needed to relieve the tremendous pressure on RF&P motive power occasioned by unprecedented war-time traffic. Similar in appearance and general characteristics with those on other railroads which used this wheel-arrangement extensively (NKP, W&LE, Erie, Pere Marquette and C&O especially), they had 69-inch drivers (intended exclusively for freight service) and 245 psi boiler pressure. The large rectangular tenders held 22,000 gallons and 25 tons. They were rated at 3,200 tons northbound and 2,500 tons southbound. After the war they handled much of the heavy freight traffic.

(both) T. W. Dixon Coll.

Anthony Dementi photo, W. E. Griffin Coll.

When the Berkshires arrived the RF&P was able to terminate the lease of several foreign-line locomotives that had been brought in to accommodate the burden of traffic. Here No. 574 is on an extra freight near Acca soon after its delivery. A superbly handsome locomotive by any standard, it fit perfectly the Lima "Superpower" image with its centered headlight, clean face and shielded air pumps located on the pilot beam. Placed next to a Pere Marquette or Nickel Plate Road Berkshire one would be hard pressed to discern differences at first glance.

William E. Griffin Coll.

Berkshire No. 572 rolls a southbound extra freight near AF Tower, south of Alexandria on June 22, 1947.

Berkshire No. 578 storms around the Cameron Run Curve south of Alexandria in November of 1948 with a southbound extra freight.

No. 571 at Potomac Yard March 20, 1948. This angle emphasizes the compact, massive appearance of these locomotives.

Berkshires Nos. 576 and 577 sit together on the radial tracks at the Potomac Yard Roundhouse March 20, 1948.

RF&P's 4-8-4 Type Locomotives - The "Generals," "Governors," and "Statesmen."

RF&P purchased three classes of 4-8-4 type locomotives, naming the first series after Confederate generals, the second after Virginia governors, and the third after great statesmen from Virginia. The "Generals," Nos. 551-555 were primarily for freight service, while the "Governors" were for passenger service, and the "Statesmen" were dual service. In 1937 Nos. 551-555 arrived from Baldwin Locomotiove Works. They had 27x30-inch cylinders, 77-inch drivers, 275 psi boiler pressure, and exerted 66,500 pounds of tractive force. The "Governors" (Nos. 601-612) were lighter and exerted only 62,800 pounds of tractive force. They were lightened to accommodate bridge clearances into Washington. The "Statesmen" (Nos. 613-622) had basically the same dimensions as the "Governors."

No.	Name	Acquired/Retired	No.	Name	Acquired/Retired
551	General Robert E. Lee	4/37-3/52	613	John Marshall	3/45-5/53
552	General T. J. Jackson	4/37-4/52	614	George Washington	3/45-5/53
553	General J. E. B. Stuart	4/37-4/52	615	Henry Clay	3/45-5/53
554	General A. P. Hill	4/37-4/52	616	George Mason	3/45-5/53
555	General J. E. Johnston	5/37-4/52	617	John Randolph	3/45-12/54
			618	James Madison	3/45-12/54
601	Governor Patrick Henry	10/38-3/53	619	William Byrd	4/45-5/53
602	Governor Thomas Jefferson	10/38-3/53	620	George Wythe	4/45-5/53
603	Governor Thomas Nelson	10/38-3/53	621	Richard Henry Lee	4/45-5/53
604	Governor Benjamin Harrison	10/38-3/53	622	Carter Braxton	4/45-12/54
605	Governor James Monroe	10/38-3/53			
606	Governor John Tyler	10/38-3/53			
607	Governor Edmund Randolph	9/42-3/53			
608	Governor Henry A. Wise	9/42-3/53			
610	Governor Fitzhugh Lee	9/42-3/53			
611	Governor William Smith	1/43-3/53			
612	Governor Claude A. Swanson	10/42-3/53			

Baldwin photo, T. W. Dixon Coll.

Builder photo shows left side of No. 610, *Governor Fitzhugh Lee*, new at Baldwin in 1942. The name appears below the number under the cab window. The tradition of naming locomotives which had passed by the 1870s was revived by two Virginia railroads during the 1930s-40s, RF&P and C&O, both on 4-8-4 types.

No. 552, General T. J. Jackson, is shown at Acca Engine Terminal in Richmond on July 19, 1951.

J. R. Quinn Coll.

47

The "Generals" were restricted to freight service as they were too wide and heavy for operation across the Long Bridge and through the First Street Tunnel into Washington Union Station. Here No. 551, *General Robert E. Lee*, passes between Alexandria Union Station on the left and the old freight station on the right as it gets under way from Potomac Yard with a southbound freight in 1947.

H. H. Harwood, Jr.

Baldwin Loco. Works, T. W. Dixon Coll.

No. 551, again, new at Baldwin, shined up for the official photographer. The very image of the superpower steam locomotive, its face looking very much like the Berkshires. The 842,940 pounds of this huge locomotive and tender prohibited its operation on the Long Bridge over the Potomac and relegated the "Generals" to freight service between Potomac Yard and Richmond.

Homer R. Hill

Baldwin Loco. Works, T. W. Dixon Coll.

(Above) With 27x30-inch cylinders, 77-inch drivers and a tractive effort rating of 62,800 pounds and 260 psi of steam pressure, the "Governors" could handle 18-car passenger trains both north and southbound on 2-1/2-hour schedules. This photo is a clasic view of No. 601, *Governor Patrick Henry*, rolling a southbound train past Franconia in 1943.

(Left) This Baldwin builder photo of No. 610, *Governor Fitzhugh Lee*, shows a front-end arrangement almost exactly similar to the "Generals."

Another builder photo of No. 610 shows its stylish striping, and the decorative Vanderbilt Tender. Its clean lines and sleek appearance mark it as among the most aesthetically pleasing steam locomotives in the RF&P's history. Their total weight in working order was 689,810 pounds for engine and tender. The engine alone weighed nearly 30 tons less than the "Generals," which helped with bridge loading restrictions at Washington. The Vanderbilt style tenders held only 17 tons of coal and 15,500 gallons of water, and weighed 45 tons less than those of the "Generals" with their 20,000-gallon/22-ton capacity.

The second group of 4-8-4s, beginning with No. 601 and ending with 612 were named for famous Virginia Governors and arrived from Baldwin in 1938. They were truly dual-service locomotives, equally at home on heavy passenger or freight trains, but their primary use was in passenger service. No. 603, *Governor Thomas Nelson*, was photographed at Acca Yard on May 10, 1947.

Baldwin Loco. Works, H. L. Broadbelt Coll.

Right and left broadside views of No. 613, John Marshall, taken at Baldwin Locomotive Works show the "Statesmen" type with its rectangular tender, but looking basically very much like the "Generals" and "Governors." The 613-622 came in 1945 at the end of the war-time traffic, and had a fairly short service life, being retired in 1953-54. The tenders carried 22 tons and 20,000 gallons. They were slightly heavier than the "Governors" but still much lighter than the "Generals" and capable of serving Washington Union Station. The decorations, including striped cylinder chests and sand box were tasteful, yet unusual in steam locomotive design even in this late period.

No. 617, *John Randolph*, speeds southbound with Train No. 375 past signal No. 126, near Ashland on October 2, 1949.

D. Wallace Johnson

(Above) This slightly low angle gives No. 617, *John Randolph*, a massive appearance. Taken at Washington's Ivy City Terminal in the late 1940s.

(Below) John Cannon hostler at the Ivy City Terminal moves No. 619, *William Byrd*, around the servicing facility in 1948, sitting on the fireman's side in this close-up view.

(all) L. W. Rice photo, T. W. Dixon Coll.

(Above) The clean, some would say "Patrician" face of No. 622 at Ivy City in the late 1940s.

No. 614, *George Washington*, passes SAL's Hermitage Yard as it is being hostled from Acca Engine Terminal to Broad Street Station on September 22, 1949. The "Statesmen" had large rectangular tenders similar to the "Generals," but retained the overall dimensions of the "Governors." The increased weight of the "Statesmen" created no problems for operation into Washington as the Long Bridge had been rebuilt in 1942 to accommodate heavier locomotives.

D. Wallace Johnson

From July 1955 to July 1956 613-622 were leased to the motive power-short Chesapeake & Ohio to help it cope with an increase in coal traffic. Here No. 622, *Carter Braxton,* rolls a C&O freight west past BS Cabin at Cattlettsburg, Kentucky. Immediately after their return to the RF&P they were scrapped.

C&O Railway photo, C&O Hist. Soc. Coll.

Because C&O had retired so many of its steam locomotives before diesel replacements were available, it had to lease the RF&P 4-8-4s. Here No. 619, *William Byrd,* is westbound near Ashland, Kentucky, in April 1955.

R. E. Tobey

53

In 1943 RF&P purchased three H-7 class 2-8-8-2 simple articulated locomotives from C&O and renumbered them RF&P No. 1, 2 and 3 (formerly C&O 1558, 1564, and 1552). They were used as hump engines at Potomac Yard. No. 2 was photographed there on May 8, 1946.

Almost at the apex of the northbound hump, just imagine the symphony of sound as No. 2 shoves its cut of cars on this winter day in 1945.

Such was the traffic on the RF&P during World War II that it was necessary to lease locomotives from other lines for both yard and road freight work. That's C&O F-15 class 4-6-2 No. 455 flying white flags of an extra and doubleheading with a 200-series RF&P 4-6-2 on a southbound freight at Accotink in 1943. Note the distinctive train control box located between the pilot and smokebox of 455, indicating the C&O engine has been equipped for mainline RF&P service.

Homer R. Hill

Another train control-equipped C&O locomotive, J-2 class 4-8-2 No. 546, leased by RF&P in 1942, passes Accotink with a freight in 1943. Other C&O locomotives leased by RF&P at the time included 2-6-6-2 No. 1499, 4-8-2 No. 547, and 2-8-2 Nos. 2326, 2327. RF&P was so impressed with the performace of the C&O's H-6 class 2-6-6-2s in hump service at Potomac Yard that it bought three H-7 2-8-8-2s from C&O for that purpose.

(Left) RF&P also purchased six Norfolk & Western K-3 class Mountain type 4-8-2s in 1944. While these locomotives provided valuable service during the war, they were rough riding and too slow for suitable operation on the RF&P. After the war they were re-sold to Wheeling & Lake Erie Railway. In this photo, 4-8-2 No. 515 is shown arriving at Acca Yard in 1945.

The former N&W 4-8-2s had 28x30-inch cylinders, weighed 401,000 pounds without tenders and exerted 68,800 pounds of tractive force. Another view of 515 entering Acca Yard in 1945.

RF&P supplied the medallion which was applied to the nose of the locomotive by EMD. Styling and design of RF&P E- and F-units was similar to that of Atlantic Coast Line, but with a blue-gray paint scheme. - *(William E. Griffin Coll.)*

Chapter 3

The Diesel Era

The first diesel-electric locomotives to operate over the RF&P were units owned by the Seaboard Air Line Railway. In 1938 the SAL purchased several diesel-electrics to power its "Orange Blossom Special" winter train operating between New York and Florida. Under agreements with the SAL, the RF&P hired the SAL diesel locomotives for service between Richmond and Washington in charge of RF&P crews. Similar arrangements were also made to operate diesel power over the RF&P to handle the SAL's "Silver Meteor" and the ACL's "Champion".

The first diesel-electric yard engine to work on the RF&P's property was Richmond Terminal Company's SW-1 No. 1. This 660 horsepower diesel was built by EMD in 1939 and was placed in service on March 15, 1940 at Broad Street Station. However, during the early years of World War II it was found that the engine was not heavy enough for the increased passenger work at the station. Hence, it was decided to transfer the diesel to the RF&P, substituting in its place one of the 1000 horsepower Alco diesel switchers that the RF&P then had on order. On April 1, 1944, Richmond Terminal No. 1 was purchased by the RF&P from the Terminal Company and renumbered No. 50. The diesel was used by the RF&P on Boulton Yard in the vicinity of the Richmond freight station until sold to the Canton Railroad in 1956.

Dieselization of the RF&P began at Acca Yard in March, 1942 with the delivery by Alco of two S-2 1000 horsepower switchers (Nos. 51 and 52). The diesels were so successful that five additional switchers (Nos. 53-57) were delivered between 1943 and 1944.

On March 25, 1946, following a comprehensive study by a tenant line committee, Potomac Yard placed its order with Alco for the purchase of four diesel-electric switching locomotives (Nos. 58-61). They were also S-2 1000 horsepower units and the first S-2 (No. 58) was received at Potomac Yard on August 4, 1946 and was placed in service two days later on yard assignment 15-C working at Four Mile Run.

To assure that sufficient power could be generated to perform hump service, two of the first four diesel units (Nos. 58 and 59) came equipped with devices which allowed them to be coupled and operated in multiple. The diesels were an immediate success and in 1948 ten additional S-2's were ordered and the full conversion to full diesel use at Potomac Yard was achieved on September 30, 1948. These diesels had an electrical traction motor geared to each of their four axles to supply the required power to shove the heavy tonnage trains over the humps. Normally, one unit could safely handle a draft of cars not exceeding 3000 tons.

The Alco S-2's remained in service at both Acca

and Potomac Yards until the late-1960's. Three of these diesels (Nos. 62, 70 and 71) were converted to auxiliary power booster units (Slugs A, B and C) for use in hump service at Potomac Yard. The slug's diesel motor had been inactivated but its traction motors were operated by electrical current supplied by the main generator of the SW-1500 diesel to which it was coupled.

The RF&Ps' first road diesel locomotives were built and delivered by the Electro-Motive Division of General Motors in 1949.

The Company received five (Nos. 1001-1005) E-8-A lead units and five (Nos. 1051-1055) E-8-B booster units. The model E-8 lead and booster diesels were six-axle 2250 horsepower units that respectively generated 54,087 and 50738 lbs. of tractive effort. Ten additional E-8-A lead units (Nos. 1006-1015) were acquired in 1952-1953. Each of the lead units was equipped with two independent 1125 horsepower, V-12 GM diesel engines. The styling and design of all RF&P passenger, as well as freight, units was similar to the Atlantic Coast Line Railroad locomotives but with an RF&P blue-grey paint scheme. An RF&P decal medallion provided by the railroad was applied by

William E. Griffin Coll.

This F7 nose looks different from the E8 on the opposite page only in the numberboards. RF&P's F7s were equipped with one 16-cylinder, V-type, 2-cycle GM diesel engine rated at 1,500 horsepower. The units were purchased in 1949-50, when road freight diesels were still an important segment of the market, before road switchers became the norm.

EMD to the nose of the locomotives.

The first E-8 to operate over the road of the RF&P was No. 1002 which handled Train No. 14 to Washington on December 2, 1949. The EMD E-8's were the standard passenger locomotive on the RF&P and were so successful that the railroad was completely dieselized by 1952. In the final years of their service, the E-8's were used in freight service in multiple with new GP-diesels. All of the RF&P E-8-B units and E-8-A units 1002, 1003, 1004 and 1009 were traded in to EMD in 1972 on the purchase of the new GP-40-2's. The remaining RF&P E-8-A's were sold to Amtrak in 1972 and continued to be used in passenger service by the new passenger corporation.

The first standard RF&P freight locomotives were the model F-7 diesel designed and built by EMD. The RF&P owned ten "A", or lead units, numbered 1101-1110; and, ten "B", or booster units, numbered 1151-1160. Each unit was equipped with one 16-cylinder, V-type, 2-cycle, GM diesel engine. The diesels were rated a full 1500 horsepower and each engine was coupled to a DC-AC generator with alternating current powering auxiliary equipment. The F-7's were purchased in 1949-1950. The first service trip was made by F-7-A No. 1106 with an extra freight north on December 12, 1949.

The RF&P also owned four first generation Geeps, or General Purpose, diesels. They were GP-7 1500 horsepower units numbered 101-104. The 101-102 were built by EMD in 1951; the 103-104 in 1953. These four axle diesels had 16-cylinder 567B GM engines and had a tractive effort of 61,351 lbs. The RF&P GP-7's were passenger variations and equipped with a steam generator and the expanded underbelly tank partitioned for a 1100 gallon water tank and fuel tank forced the air reservoirs to the top of the long hood.

The initial service trip by a GP-7 on the RF&P was made by No. 101 in local freight service on January 4, 1951. These diesels were used in both through freight and local freight service and remained on the RF&P roster until put into storage in 1980. In June, 1977 the RF&P leased GP-7 No. 102 to Amtrak for use between Richmond and Petersburg, Virginia on Trains 34 and 35, the "Hilltopper". The unit was returned to the RF&P in October of that year after construction of a direct connection track from the SCL to the N&W at Petersburg.

In 1986 the RF&P recommissioned GP-7 No. 101 to service after a painstaking restoration by the Company's mechanical forces at Bryan Park Terminal. Using parts taken from four locomotives, the "new 101" was restored as nearly as possible to its original appearance. It was recommissioned in ceremonies at Acca Yard on June 19, 1986 and was then used in freight service for one year before donation to the Old Dominion Chapter, National Railroad Historical Society. In recent years, the locomotive has been leased by the chapter to the Buckingham Branch Railroad and has been used in both freight and passenger excursion service.

In November 1950 the RF&P purchased three FP-7-A diesels from EMD. These diesels were four feet longer than the F-7's and were equipped with steam generators for operation in both passenger and freight service. Numbered 1201-1203, the 1500 horsepower locomotives were also heavier and possessed more tractive power than the freight-only F-7's. Equipped with a Nathan 5 chime whistle, they were rated for a maximum speed of 83 m.p.h.

EMD F-5-A diesel locomotive No. 1111 was notable as it was not originally purchased by the RF&P from the manufacturer. This diesel was built for the Aberdeen and Rockfish Railroad in 1948 and was sold to the RF&P in October, 1952. The 1500 horsepower diesel was repainted to RF&P colors and made its first service trip as Extra 1111-1158 on December 12, 1952.

The RF&P began to replace its first generation diesels with a fleet of modern and efficient road and

Slug unit "A" and SW-1500 switcher No. 5 move over the northbound hump at Potomac Yard. Immediately below the diesels from left to right are the mechanical shop, superintendent's office builidng and bunkhouse. Just beyond the buildings are the locomotive ready tracks with Conrail diesels and electric units waiting assignments. The SW-1500 unit came as part of a group of eight received in October 1967. The Slug is rebuilt from ALCO S-2 switcher No. 62 originally received in 1948.

William E. Griffin

GP-35 No. 134 leads Train No. 406 across the new single-track Quantico Creek Bridge in February 1982.

Doug Koontz

yard diesels in 1965. Eight new GP-35 2500 horsepower general purpose diesels (Nos. 111-118) and three SW-1200 1200 horsepower switcher diesels (Nos. 81-83) were delivered by EMD in July, 1965. The initial service trip made by a GP-35 was handled by No. 112 on August 19, 1965. The three SW-1200 switchers were all placed in service at Acca Yard.

The GP-35's were later renumbered to number series 131-138 in 1969. These diesels were equipped with dual cab controls and were frequently operated with either the short hood or long hood end of the locomotive in the lead of the motive power consist.

In September 1965, two additional SW-1200's (Nos. 84-85) were purchased by the RF&P for switching service at Acca Yard. All of the SW-1200's had dual cab controls and Nos. 81-83 were equipped with automatic train control, coded cab signals and speed control in order that they could be operated in road train service. While they spent most of their career on Acca Yard, these units were used in road service on occasion, making the RF&P one of the few railroads in the country to SW-type switcher diesels in high-speed road service.

Another RF&P switcher that was used frequently in road service was SW-1500 No. 91. Built by EMD in 1966, this 1500 horsepower diesel also had dual cab controls and was equipped for road service. With a gear ratio of 61:16 it could attain a maximum speed of 71 m.p.h. and was used in both local and through freight service.

In October 1967 eight new EMD SW-1500 switchers (Nos. 1-8) were purchased and assigned to Potomac Yard. These diesels had a 12-cylinder diesel motor, V-type, as opposed to the 6-cylinders of the Alco S-2's formerly used at Potomac Yard. The new SW-1200's had 4 traction motors, one geared to each of their four axles and produced a horsepower output rated at 1500 lbs. These diesels when used in hump

service at Potomac Yard were coupled to an auxiliary power booster unit ("Slug").

In conjunction with a Potomac Yard modernization project in 1984-1985, four of the SW-1200 diesels (Nos. 4, 5, 6 and 7) were completely remanufactured for the RF&P by Chrome Locomotive. On March 13, 1986, a ceremony was held at Potomac Yard at which time one of the remanufactured locomotives, the No. 7, was formally dedicated and named the "Wilbur S. Morris", in honor of Potomac Yard's recently retired master mechanic.

In addition to the remanufactured locomotives, the RF&P also purchased two new power booster units (S-1 and S-2), which were designed and constructed by Chrome Locomotive for use at Potomac Yard.

The RF&P completely replaced its first generation diesels with the purchase in 1966-1967 of seven GP-40 3000 horsepower diesels (Nos. 121-127) and in 1972 of seven GP-40-2 3000 horsepower diesels (Nos. 141-147). While the GP-40's were equipped with dual cab controls, the GP-40-2's were not so equipped. GP-40's, like the GP-35's, were frequently operated long hood forward. Without dual controls, the GP-40-2's were only operated with the short hood forward. These were exceptional diesels, giving excellent service to the RF&P. Each of these units were still in service on the RF&P when the Company was acquired by CSXT in 1991.

59

Richmond, Fredericksburg, and Potomac Railroad
Diesel Locomotive Roster

Road No.	Qty.	Builder	Model	Horsepower	Date Delivered	Notes
S-1,S-2	2	Chrome Loco	[Slug]	NA	2/1985	19
A, B, C	3	RF&P	[Slug]	1000	11-12/1967	7, 20
1-8	8	EMD	SW1500	1500	10/1967	18
50	1	EMD	SW1	600	2/1939	1
55	1	ALCO	S-2	1000	3/1944	5
91	1	EMD	SW1500	1500	10/1966	21
1111	1	EMD	F5A	1500	11/1948	13
51-52	2	ALCO	S-2	1000	3/1942	2
53-54	2	ALCO	S-2	1000	8/1943	3, 4
56-57	2	ALCO	S-2	1000	9/1944	4
58-59	2	ALCO	S-2	1000	7-8/1955	6
60-61	2	ALCO	S-2	1000	8/1948	6
62-71	10	ALCO	S-2	1000	9-10/1948	6, 7
81-83	3	EMD	SW1200	1200	8/1965	22
84-85	2	EMD	SW1200	1200	7/1965	22
101-102	2	EMD	GP7	1500	12/1950	8, 16
103-104	2	EMD	GP7	1500	6/1953	8, 16
111-118	8	EMD	GP35	2500	8/1965	9, 17
121-127	7	EMD	GP40	3000	10/1966 and 3/1967	23
131-138	8	EMD	GP35	2500	8/1965	17
141-147	7	EMD	GP40-2	3000	9/1972	24
1001-1005	5	EMD	E8A	2250	11/1949	10
1006-1009	4	EMD	E8A	2250	2/1952	10
1010-1011	2	EMD	E8A	2250	8/1952	10
1012-1015	4	EMD	E8A	2250	9-10/1953	10
1051-1055	5	EMD	E8B	2250	12/1949	11
1101-1108	8	EMD	F7A	1500	11/1949	12
1109-1110	2	EMD	F7A	1500	2/1950	12
1151-1158	8	EMD	F7B	1500	11/1949	14
1159-1160	2	EMD	F7B	1500	2/1950	14
1201-1203	3	EMD	FP7A	1500	11/1950	15

General Notes

A - Numbers 1001-1015 and 1201-1203 equipped with steam generators.

B - Numbers 1-8, 81-85, 91, 101-104, 121-127 and 131-138 had dual cab control.

C - Numbers 81-83 and 91 equipped with flexicoil trucks and were suitable for application of radio equipment with mainline frequencies.

D - Numbers 81-83 equipped with automatic train control and used in road service as well as at Acca Yard.

E - Numbers 1-8, A, B and C assigned to Potomac Yard.

F - Numbers 81-85 and 91 assigned to Acca Yard in Richmond. Numbers 81-83 and 91 used in road service when needed.

Specific Notes

1 - Number 50, ex-Richmond Terminal No. 1, acquired by RF&P 4/1/1944. Was in service 3/15/1940. Sold by RF&P in March 1956 to Canton Railroad and renumbered to No. 56. Sold by Canton in August 1963 to Jersey Contracting as No. 26. Sold to McCormic Sand of South Amboy, N. J., as No. 26 in 1970. Sold to Morristown & Erie Railroad, then leased to Towanda-Monroeton Shippers Lifeline as No. 26 in 1977.

2 - Number 51 to Richmond Terminal as No. 51 in 12/1964; retired and soild to dealer David J. Joseph. No. 52 retired in 12/1972 and sold to Precision National Corp. 8./1974.

3 - Number 53 retired 12/1966 and scrapped.

4 - Numbers 54, 56, and 57 sold to ACL in 5/1966. Renumbered to ACL 44, 45, 46. Became SCL 98, 96, and 97. SCl 96 retired 12/31/1979 and sold to Republic Locomotive of Greenville, S.C. (possibly scrapped). SCL 98 retired 4/1/9181 and sold to General Power Systems in late 1981, then leased to Fruit Growers Express at Lakeland, Fla.

5 - Number 55 retired 3/1972 and sold to Precision National Corp. in 8/1974.

6 - Numbers 59, 61, 63, and 67 sold to Steelton and Highspire in 12/1967. Renumbered 62, 61, 63, and 60. Unit 60 became SB slug No. 10. Numbers 58, 64, 65 and 69 went to S&H to become Nos. 68, 65, 64, and 69. RF&P No. 66 sold to Agrico in 12/1967 and renumbered 12.

7 - Numbers 62, 70, and 71 rebuilt by RF&P into slugs: 62 became "A" 11/1967, 70 became "B" asnd 71 became "C" in 12/1967.

8 - Numbers 101, 103, and 104 equipped with steam generators.

9 - Numbers 111-118 renumbered 131-138 in 1969.

10 - Numbers 1001, 1005-1008, and 1010-1015 retired in 2/1972 and sold to Amtrak. Renumbered as Amtrak 213-222. RF&P Nos. 1002-1004 and 1009 retired in 9/1972 and traded in to EMD on GP40-2 Nos. 141-147.

11 - Numbers 1051-1054 traded in to EMD on SW1200 switchers Nos. 81-85. EMD resold 1052-1053 to ACL in 6/1965. Renumbered to ACL 765-766, then became SCL 670B-671B.

12 - Numbers 1102-1104 and 1106-1109 traded to EMD in 11/1966 on GP40s 121-127. Number 1110 traded in to EMD in 11/1966 on SW1500 No. 91. Numbers 1101 and 1105 retired in 11/1965 and sold to Strieger (dealer) in 12/1965, which resold them to Precision Engineering in 6/1966. Then sold to L&N and renumbered,1101 becoming 864 and 1105 becoming 657. Finally traded in to EMD by L&N.

13 - Number 1111 was originally Aberdeen & Rockfish No. 201. Bought by RF&P in 10/1952. Sold to David J. Jospeh in 12/1963 and scrapped.

14 - Numbers 1157 and 1159 retired in 11/1965 and sold to Strieger. Resold to Precision Engineering, the resold to Illinois Terminal and renumbered 1507 and 1508. RF&P Nos. 1151-1156 and 1158 retired in 2/1972 and traded in along with Nos. 1002-1004, 1009 to EMD for GP40-2s Nos. 141-147.

15 - Numbers 1201-1203 retired in 2/1972 and traded in to EMD along with Nos. 1003-1004 and 1009 on GP40-2s Nos. 141-147.

16 - Numbers 101 and 104 retired in 12/1979. Numbers 102 and 103 retired in 3/1983. No. 104 rebuilt by RF&P shop forces in 1986 and renumbered 101. Donated by RF&P to the Old Dominion Chpater, National Railway Historical Society and currently leased to the Buckingham Branch Railroad. Nos. 101, 102 and 103 sold to Naporano Iron & Metal for scrap in 5/1986.

17 - Numbers 132, 135, and 137 retired in 6/1985 and sold to Naporano Iron & Metal for scrap. Remaining GP35s became CSXT Nos. 4426-4429 and were retired in 1993.

18 - Nos. 4, 5, 6, and 7 remanufacturered by Chrome Locomotive in 1985. No. 7 named *Wilbur S. Morris* in honor of retired Potomac Yard Master Mechanic. Nos. 1, 2, 3, and 8 retired and sold to Helm Financial Group in 7/1990. Nos. 4, 5, 6, anmd 7 retired and sold to Bethlehem Subsidiaries in 3/1992.

19. - Slugs S-1 and S-2 retired and sold to Bethlehem Subdsidiaries in 3/1992.

20 - Slugs A and B sold to Alexandria Scrap Corporation in 5/1987. Slug C donated by RF&P to Gold Coast Railroad in 9/1988.

21 - No. 91 became CSXT No. 1315.

22 - Nos. 81-85 becames CSXT Nos. 1300-1304.

23 - Nos. 121-127 became CSXT Nos. 6855-6861.

24 - Nos. 141-147 became CSXT Nos. 6392-6399.

Roster Compiled by William E. Griffin, Jr. and Warren Calloway

(Above) The standard first-generation RF&P passenger locomotive was the E8 from Electro-motive Division of GM. Delivered between 1949 and 1953, RF&P owned 15 A-units numbered 1001-1015 and 5 B-units numbered 1051-1055. Each unit was rated at 2,250 horsepower.

(Right) Virginia Governor William Tuck delivered the keynote address during ceremonies at Broad Street Station to inaugurate the operation of RF&P's first road diesels. E8 No. 1001 made its initial trip on Train No. 2/76 on December 9, 1949. The first service trip by an E8 on the RF&P was made by No. 1003 handling Train No. 14 northbound on December 2, 1949.

(all) William E. Griffin Coll.

Members of the RF&P Engineering Department's Bridge & Building Force pause in their duties to inspect the passage of E8 No. 1005 with a southbound passenger train over Occoquan Creek Bridge at Woodbridge.

An array of RF&P first-generation diesel power is assembled at Bryan Park Terminal in this 1968 photo. From left to right are E8 No. 1002, FP7 No. 1201, and F7 No. 1103.

William E. Griffin

Jim Shaw

A number of E8s were repainted with the simplified scheme shown here on No. 1007, heading up a southbound freight train at Alexandria in 1970. In their final years of service on RF&P, E8s were frequently used in freight service. All of the E8A's were off the roster by 1972. Units 1002, 1003, 1004, and 1009 were traded in to EMD for new GP40 diesels. The rest of the units were sold to Amtrak in February 1972.

William E. Griffin Coll.

The standard first-generation RF&P freight diesel was the F7 model. In fact, throughout its entire history of diesel operations, RF&P never owned other than EMD locomotives. The RF&P owned ten A-units numbered 1101-1110, and ten B-units numbered 1151-1160. This builder photo of a set of A-B-B-A F7s was taken in 1950.

RF&P Engineering Department's Track Force pauses in their work on No. 2 track as F7A No. 1108 and two B-units speed by with a southbound freight.

William E. Griffin Coll.

(Below) In 1950 RF&P purchased three FP7A 1,500 horsepower diesels along with two GP7s, to further replace steam. These diesels were four feet longer than the F7s and were equipped with a steam generator for operation in passenger as well as freight service. Numbered in the 1201-1203 series, they were rated for a maximum speed of 83 mph. No. 1203 is seen here at Ivy City Engine Terminal in Washington on July 3, 1965, in company with another unit.

Howard Ameling Coll.

An A-B-B-B-A set of RF&P F7s, led by No. 1106, powers a southbound freight past Alexandria Union Station in 1963. Note that the company's name was not painted on the sides of the B-units.

RF&P's only F5A diesel was built in 1948 for the Aberdeen & Rockfish Railroad and was purchased from that shortline in 1952. It was repainted and made its first trip with extra 1111-1158 on December 12, 1952. The unit is shown with a northbound freight at Alexandria in 1963. It was retired in December of that year and sold for scrap.

(all) Jim Shaw

FP7 No. 1203 approaches Alexandria Union Station in 1968 with a northbound passenger train.

Repainted FP7 No. 1202 with an alternating variety of first and second generation diesels roll a southbound freight through Milford in 1970. All of the RF&P FP7s were traded in to EMD in 1972 along with four E8s in connection with the purchase of seven new GP40-2s.

The rather plain nose of an RF&P GP7. The GP7s were equipped with 16-cylinder, 567-B engines, had 61,186 pounds of tractive power and were geared for a maximum speed of 71 mph. Nos. 101, 103, and 104 were equipped with steam generators and could be used in passenger service. All of the GP7s had dual controls.

William E. Griffin Coll.

RF&P purchased four of the EMD GP7 1,500 horsepower road switchers for use in through and local freight service. Nos. 101 and 102 were delivered in 1951. Nos. 103 and 104 arrived on the property in 1953. Here No. 101 is seen with the number and road name on its long hood, the RF&P decal under the cab window, and air tanks on the roof.

(both) William E. Griffin Coll.

No. 101 heads up a northbound through freight with an E8 and two GP35s, at Summit, south of Fredericksburg, in 1971.

L. W. Rice, T. W. Dixon Coll.

No. 101 again, this time keeping company with FP7s and some PRR GG-1s at Washington's Ivy City Terminal on June 6, 1951.

William E. Griffin

All of the RF&P GP7s were put in storage at Bryan Park Terminal in 1980-81, and in 1982, consideration was given to converting them into slug units for use in hump service at Potomac Yard. That was rejected, but in 1986, a new "No. 101" was restored by RF&P's mechanical forces using parts taken from the three retired units and a retired GP35. The employees who restored the locomotive pose beside it in recommissioning ceremonies at Acca Yard in 1986. From left to right they are Frank Osborn, Kenny Pierce, George Kinley, Bill Smith, Craig Williams, Bob Bowman, Carl Spiller, Lloyd Wrenn, Garland Hazelwood, Mack Wells, Gerald Ward, Harry Whitfield, Ron Farthing, and Bill Reid. On the locomotive is RF&P's General Manager - Operations J. C. Hobbs and Vice President-Operations S. R. Johnson.

No. 104 is seen here at Potomac Yard on August 18, 1957.

L. W. Rice photo, T. W. Dixon Coll.

RF&P's first diesel, EMD SW1 No. 50, at Boulton Yard. Built in 1939, this locomotive was originally Richmond Terminal No. 1 and was purchased by RF&P and renumbered in 1944. It was sold to the Canton Railroad in 1956 and subsequently passed through three more owners.

(Below) Dieselization of Acca Yard began in 1942 with the delivery of ALCO 1,000 horsepower model 404 S-2 switchers numbered 51 and 52. No. 52 is seen here in a builder photograph.

Paul B. Wright photo, W. E. Griffin Coll.

William E. Griffin Coll.

William E. Griffin

Richmond Terminal ALCO S-2 No. 51 was originally owned by RF&P and went to the terminal company for service at Broad Street Station because SW-1 No. 1 (later RF&P No. 50) was too light to handle the switching work at the station. Behind the S-2 are E8s of SAL, ACL and RF&P.

(Left) Dieselization of Potomac Yard began in 1946 with the delivery of four ALCO S-1 switchers numbered 58-61. Ten additional S-2s were received there in 1948 to complete dieselization of the facility. S-2 No. 68 is shown switching a Southerm Railway caboose at Potomac Yard

J. R. Quinn Coll.

(Below) RF&P acquired eight new EMD SW-1500 switchers numbered 1-8 for service at Potomac Yard in October 1967. This builder photo shows the as-delivered appearances of the new locomotives.

William E. Griffin Coll.

SW-1200 No. 5 with slug unit "C" at Potomac Yard on April 14, 1978. The SW-1500s were used with a slug when performing service as hump engines. Slug "C" was made from S-2 No. 71 in December 1967.

Warren Calloway

In 1986 RF&P retired slugs A, B, and C, that had been rebuilt from ALCO S-2 switchers, when it purchased two new power booster units (S-1 and S-2) that had been designed and constructed for the RF&P by Chrome Locomotive, Inc. specifically for use at Potomac Yard. The new S-2 slug is seen with remanufactured SW-1500 No. 7 in 1987.

(both) William E. Griffin

The ALCO S-2s were replaced from Acca Yard in Richmond with the acquisition in 1965 of five SW-1200 switchers from EMD. No. 84 is seen here at Bryan Park Terminal in 1970.

William E. Griffin Coll.

SW-1500 No. 91 was built by EMD in 1966. The unit was photographed on its delivery date at Bryan Park Terminal.

SW-1500 No. 91 was equipped with dual cab controls and for road freight service. With a gear ratio of 61:16, it could attain a maximum speed of 71 mph, and was used in both local and through freight service. In this photo No. 91 is heading up a through freight near Fredericksburg in 1971.

The RF&P began replacing its F7s in 1965 with the acquisition of eight new 2,500 horsepower GP35 units from EMD. These locomotives were originally numbered 111-118. No. 112 is shown at the builder in 1965.

The new GP35s were equipped with dual control stands that permitted operation with long or short hood forward. No. 118 heads up a southbound freight at Alexandria in 1968 with long hood forward.

The GP35s were renumbered in 1969 to the 131-138 series. No. 132, assisted by two E8s and another GP35, takes northbound TOFC train TT-24 around the curve at Potomac Run (Daffan) in 1969.

(Above) RF&P retired seven F7As in 1967 with the acquisition of seven GP40 3,000-horsepower units from EMD. Nos. 121-125 were delivered in 1966, while Nos. 126-127 arrived in 1967. Here No. 123 is shown at the builder.

(Below) The GP40s were also equipped with dual control stands and, along with the GP35s, handled both through and local freight assignments. Here No. 127 has all the horsepower needed to handle Train No. 227 at Aquia Creek in July 1985.

GP40 No. 123 leads Train No. 275 southbound through Ashland streets in December 1981. Depot building is to the left in the distance.

Front view of GP40 No. 124 at Bryan Park Terminal with the new style RF&P logo applied to the short hood nose of the locomotive.

William E. Griffin

In their final years of service, RF&P locomotives sported a new emblem designed by Mechanical Manager L. F. McGahey. This new design combined the circular emblem of the RF&P's past with the stylized logo used on diesels beginning in 1983. Placement of the new emblem is illustrated by this photo of GP40 No. 127.

William E. Griffin

The RF&P completed replacement of first generation diesel power in 1972 when it retired four E8s and three FP7s and purchased seven new 3,000 horsepower GP40-2s from EMD. The last diesels purchased by the RF&P, they were numbered 141-147. The new GP40-2 No. 143 is seen at Bryan Park Terminal in 1972.

Alex M. Mayes

(Above) Unlike GP35s and GP40s, the GP40-2s were not equipped with dual control stands. Hence, they were always operated low nose forward. No. 147 is about to cross the C&O Railway's Piedmont Subdivision at Doswell with Train No. 227 in January 1982. The neo-classical redbrick station was a joint C&O/RF&P agency, as was the interlocking tower, now boarded up in this era.

RF&P
Linking
NORTH
and
SOUTH

WASHINGTON

RICHMOND

(Left) GP40-2 No. 141 handles Train No. 227 at Hunton on September 26, 1981. TOFC traffic became an important part of RF&P's through business, linking the northeast with the south.

William E. Griffin

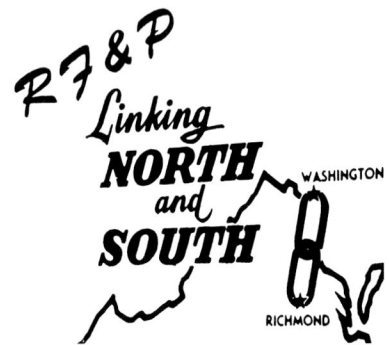

GP40-2 Nos. 145 and 142 and GP35 No. 136 handle southbound Train 191/175 across the old double-track bridge over Quantico Creek on December 12, 1987.

Having just completed a run from Potomac Yard, RF&P F7 diesels wait at the running repair track door of Bryan Park Terminal in August 1962. The mechanical forces will hostle the units into the building for servicing.

William E. Griffin Coll.

David E. George

(Above) In the backshop of RF&P's Bryan Park Terminal in Richmond, diesels of RF&P and Seaboard Coast Line Railroad were serviced. In this photo RF&P and SCL E8s, an SCL switcher and several second-generation RF&P road units are being overhauled.

(Right) GP40 No. 122 on the elevated servicing track at Bryan Park Terminal. The shop forces kept RF&P diesels in first class operating condition.

Painting/lettering diagram for an RF&P E8 - Taken from an official EMD drawing (William E. Griffin Coll.)

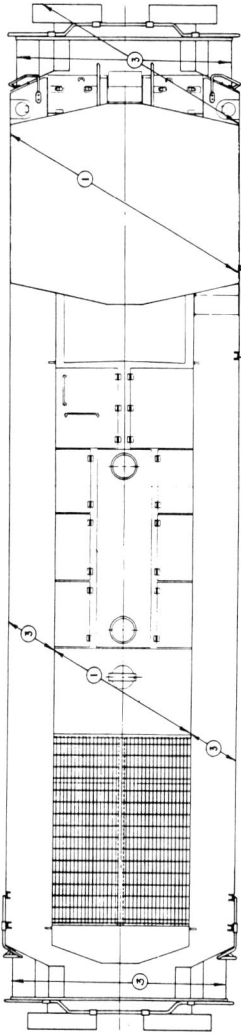

Diagram 135-B goes here, oriented in this direction

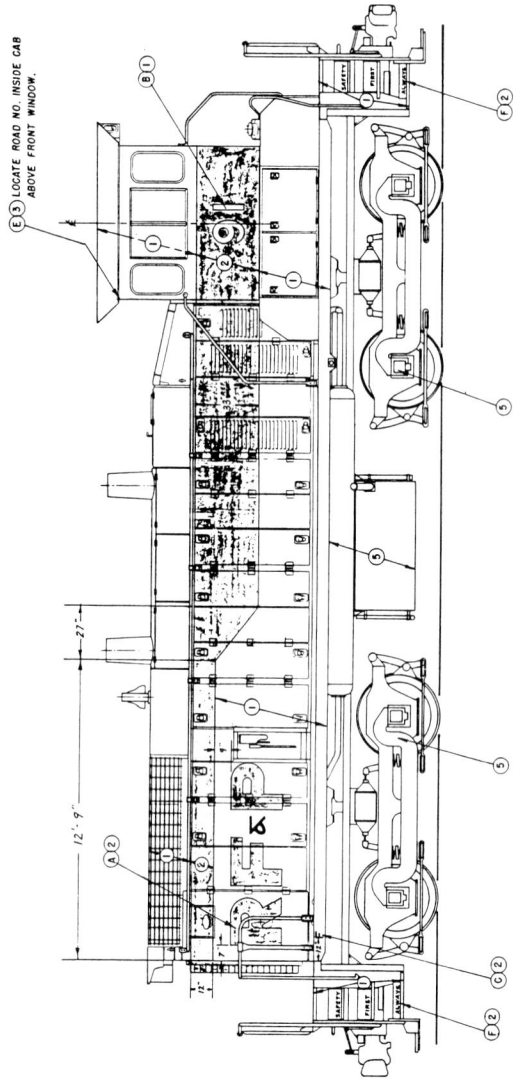

(E)(3) LOCATE ROAD NO. INSIDE CAB
ABOVE FRONT WINDOW.

12' 9"

27"

EMD Painting/lettering diagram for RF&P SW-1500 Switchers *(William E. Griffin Coll.)*

SPECIAL 1" CUT STENCILS:

"ENGINE START SWITCH INSIDE" - ON RIGHTSIDE HOOD DOOR ADJACENT TO ENGINE GOVERNOR.

"FIRE EXTINGUISHER INSIDE" - ON DOORS GIVING ACCESS TO EXTINGUISHERS.

"ENGINE WATER FILL INSIDE" - ON TOP G DOOR GIVING ACCESS TO CONNECTION

"JUMPER CABLE INSIDE" - ON DOOR GIVING ACCESS TO CABLE.

ANTI-GLARE PATTERN - CAREY BLUE TO TOP OF RADIUS AS SHOWN.

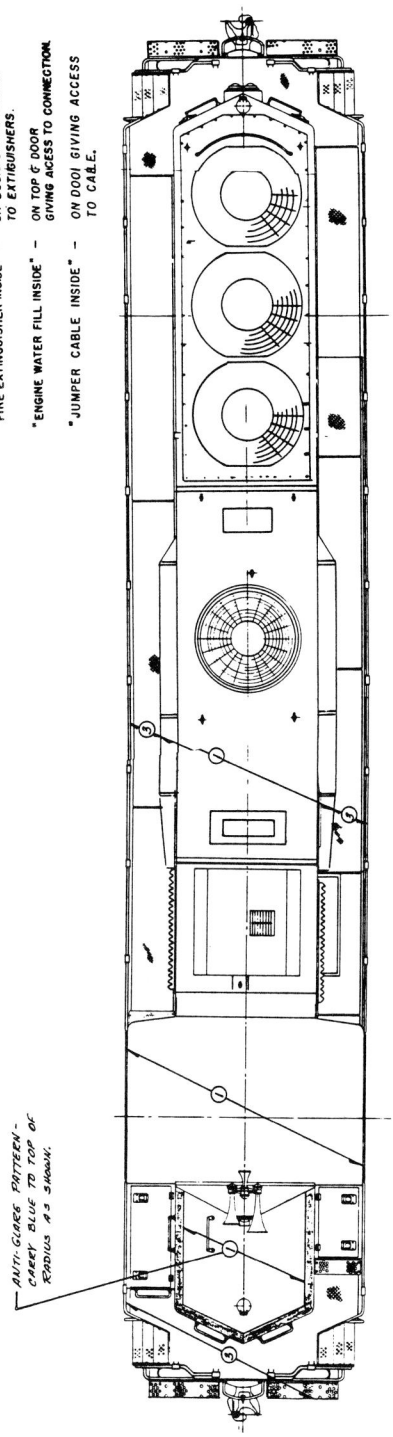

LOCATE ROAD NOS. INSIDE CAB ABOVE FRONT WINDOW ADJACENT TO CAB CARDS IF POSSIBLE

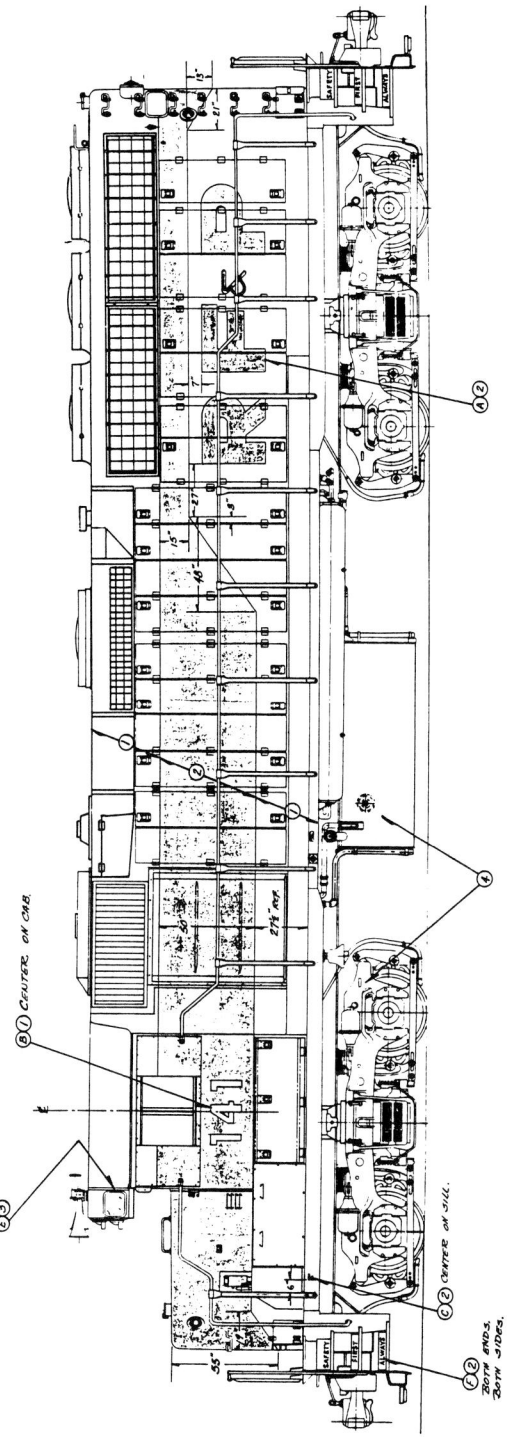

Drawing 135-C goes here, oriented in this direction

CENTER ON CAB

CENTER ON SILL

BOTH ENDS, BOTH SIDES

EMD Painting/lettering diagram for an RF&P GP40 (*William E. Griffin Coll.*)

A light snow covers the platforms at Broad Street Station in Richmond as RF&P E8 No. 1012 departs with Train No. 10, the Seaboard Air Line Railroad's northbound *Palmland*, in January 1964. *(William E. Griffin Coll.)*

Chapter 4
RF&P Passenger Service

For more than one hundred years passenger service was an important source of revenue for the RF&P. In fact, the founders of the Company had looked almost entirely to passenger traffic to sustain the operation. Not until the year 1900 did the revenue from freight trains exceed the passenger train revenue and as late as 1923 the net railway operating income from passenger service represented 64.5 per cent of the total net railway operating income.

As the early rail lines were joined the RF&P became an important link in the transportation of people between North and South. With the construction of the Connection Railroad and the unification of the connecting lines south of Richmond after the Civil War, passengers could travel on through trains, without change, between Weldon, North Carolina and Aquia Creek, Virginia. Through sleeping car service was provided by the Southern Transportation Company as early as 1867. Passenger equipment belonging to the RF&P was also placed in through service, with the Petersburg and the Richmond and Petersburg railroads paying the RF&P the mileage proportions of the cars appraised value.

Passenger travel over the RF&P grew even more dramatically after the all-rail route was established between Richmond and Washington in the 1870's and the Company came under the control of the Atlantic Coast Line System. Of particular significance was the establishment in 1888 of the *New York and Florida Special*, an electric-lighted steam-heated Pullman vestibule train that operated three times a week between New York and Jacksonville, Florida on a schedule of 30 hours and 15 minutes. Later this train's name would be shortened to the *Florida Special* and by 1895 it was operating daily except Sunday. Eventually, its operation was extended to seven days a week during the winter season.

By the turn of the century, the RF&P had opened the new Byrd Street passenger station in Richmond for joint use with the ACL; initiated a connection with the new Seaboard Air Line Railway at Hermitage; and secured a contractual commitment from its connecting lines to route their traffic over the RF&P managed "Richmond-Washington Line". To accommodate the increase in RF&P's traffic, the entire line was double tracked between 1902-1907 and grand new passenger stations were built at Washington (1907), Alexandria (1905), Richmond (1919) and Fredericksburg (1926).

In the handling of through passenger trains over the RF&P, a long standing agreement between the Company and its southern connections (ACL and SAL) provided that all revenues between Richmond and Washington would accrue to the RF&P, the trains being operated with RF&P motive power and crews.

Certain through line train expenses were prorated on mileage between train terminals. In addition, the RF&P supplied its quota of coaches, baggage, mail, express, sleepers and dining cars to equalize mileage as far as practicable.

In the allocation of RF&P passenger train equipment to through-line service, a certain number of coaches, express cars, diners, etc. were designated to be used by the SAL and a certain number were likewise assigned to the ACL. RF&P assigned equipment was allocated such that under normal operating conditions, the cars would run as far north as New York, as far southwest as Birmingham and as far south as Miami. The remaining RF&P passenger equipment was used in local traffic between Richmond and Washington with any excess equipment used as a reserve to protect overflow demands regardless of service.

Through ACL passenger trains were numbered in the 70 and 80 series on both the ACL and RF&P. However, many of the SAL through trains carried low numbers from 1 through 10 on the SAL, which conflicted with the low numbers assigned by the RF&P to its own local passenger trains. Hence, the RF&P added the digits "90" to the actual numbers of the SAL trains. Hence, the SAL Mail and Express Trains 3 and 4 were operated over the RF&P as Trains 93 and 94. Higher

William E. Griffin Coll.

The train bulletin at Broad Street Station reveals that in 1927 RF&P ran passenger trains often and on time.

William E. Griffin Coll.

College students on the way back to school pause for a publicity photo with an RF&P engine crew at Broad Street Station. The year is 1937 and the locomotive is Pacific No. 310. All aboard!

numbers in the 100-series were also used by the RF&P for some of the SAL trains.

Over the tracks of the RF&P the great fleet of ACL and SAL through trains whisked vacation-bound travelers from the East to sunny Florida, and then brought them home. Even their names were magical. On the ACL, there was the *East Coast Champion* and *West Coast Champion*, the *Havana Special*, the *Palmetto Limited*, and the *Everglades*. On the SAL, the trains carried names such as the *Silver Star, Silver Meteor, Cotton States Special, Sun Queen, Palmland* and the *Southern States Special*.

Due to the nature of the RF&P's through passenger business, it participated in the operation of a number of seasonal trains. During the winter months, the SAL's all-Pullman *Orange Blossom Special*, the *Seaboard Florida Limited* and the ACL's *Vacationer, Miamian, Gulf Coast Limited*, and the famous *Florida Special*, all operated over the RF&P.

During the 1930's, five seasonal Florida trains operated over the RF&P during the winter months. With the five in year-around service, the total of Florida trains operated over the RF&P during the winter season was ten each way, or a total of twenty trains per day both ways. No extra fare was charged on the seasonal trains and they operated the finest and most modern equipment obtainable. Club-Library cars with bath and valet service, luxurious Sun Parlor-Lounge cars with soda fountains and every possible convenience offered the traveler the very best in service.

The RF&P also operated an extensive local passenger service. For many years, fast service between Richmond and Washington was provided by Train No. 14. This train departed Broad Street Station at noon making stops at Ashland, Fredericksburg, Quantico and Alexandria. Its southbound counterpart was No. 23, departing from Washington around 5:30 P.M. These trains carried parlor-coach and parlor-dining cars. After 1928, these trains carried the Cafe-Parlor Car *Powhatan*, specially designed and built by the Pullman Company for RF&P service. Other local trains were Nos. 16/15, that likewise provided parlor-coach service on their two and a half hour runs, and through local Nos. 10/29 that made numerous stops between Richmond and Washington.

The RF&P also provided commuter service into both Richmond and Washington. Ashland was the northern turn-around point for the famous Richmond/Ashland Accommodation Train. Fredericksburg was the terminal for other commuter, or accommodation trains, to both Richmond and Washington.

However, the RF&P's local business began to suffer due to automobile competition as early as the 1920's. To reduce the expenses of operating local trains with steam power, the Company purchased an all steel gas-electric train consisting of a motor unit with passenger and baggage compartments and a trailer coach in 1928. It was so successful that a duplicate train was acquired early in 1929. These gas-electrics motor cars were used in RF&P local and commuter service, particularly between Fredericksburg and Washington throughout the 1930's and 1940's.

In an effort to stimulate passenger business during the Great Depression, the RF&P took steps to improve its equipment. In 1931, the Boulton shops began improving the seats on the Company's standard coaches by replacing the antiquated walk-over seats with bucket type deluxe seats. The coaches were also equipped with smooth running roller bearings and the trucks were completely rubberized to prevent shocks and jolts. Since the cars were not air-conditioned, new inside sliding screens were installed to keep out dirt and cinders and linen covers were placed on the seats to protect the passengers clothes. These coaches, which were put in service on Train Nos. 14/23, were also richly carpeted and decorated to harmonize with the Company's dining cars.

In the two year period 1934-1935, the RF&P started a program of air conditioning and deluxing a total of 17 cars, ten of which were assigned to the connecting lines and seven to the local service. The Parlor-Cafe Car "Powhatan" was also air conditioned at this time.

To further improve the through passenger business, the SAL purchased several diesel-electric locomotives in 1938 and began operating this power on the *Orange Blossom Special* winter train. The Seaboard also acquired a diesel powered stainless steel streamlined coach train (the *Silver Meteor*), which was placed in tri-weekly service between New York and

Florida beginning in 1939. The following winter season two similar trains were purchased by the ACL, one by the Florida East Coast Railway, and two additional trains by the SAL. On December 1, 1939, daily service was inaugurated between New York and Miami with the *Silver Meteor* via the SAL route and with *The Champion* via the ACL-FEC route. Under agreements with the SAL, ACL and FEC, the RF&P hired the diesel locomotives of those lines for service between Richmond and Washington in charge of RF&P crews. North of Washington, the trains were operated to and from New York with Pennsylvania Railroad electric locomotives.

During World War II, rationed gas, a halt in automobile production, and the transportation of military personnel pushed the RF&P's passenger traffic to all-time highs. So crowded were passenger trains late in 1942 and thereafter that the Office of Defense Transportation, the Association of American Rail-

RF&P conductor D. C. Olgers (left) and Trainman J. B. Poates are ready for another run from Richmond to Washington.

roads and the individual carriers were forced to appeal frequently to the public to discontinue non-essential travel. The RF&P participated in this publicity program through a liberal series of display advertisements in the newspapers at Richmond, Washington and intermediate points.

While the War Production Board permitted railroads to build a limited number of locomotives and freight cars, no materials were made available for new passenger equipment between 1942-1944, except that the Government arranged for the construction of 1200 troop sleepers and 400 troop kitchen cars which were put into service late in 1943. Additional troop cars were built in 1945 and they were leased to the Pullman Company for operation under a special agreement with the railroads. These troop sleepers provided more sleeping accommodations for long distance troop movements and released some of the railroads' cars for the shorter hauls.

However, due to the pressing need for sleeping cars on long distance troop movements, the seasonal winter train service between New York and Florida was not operated after the 1941-1942 season until resumed for the season 1947-1948. To obtain more sleeping cars for military traffic, the Government in 1945 ordered the discontinuance of all regular Pullman lines having runs of 500 miles or less. This resulted in the elimination of RF&P sleeper service between Richmond and Philadelphia, Richmond and New York, and Norfolk and New York. This service was restored in 1946.

Even with the severe restrictions on travel, passenger business surged to unprecedented levels. In 1943 the travel exceeded 30,000 passengers a day, with the all-time peak reached on April 22, 1943 when 33,324 passengers were carried. During that year the RF&P operated 20,898 passenger trains of which 2,363 were troop trains for an average of 57 passenger trains per day. In 1944 the RF&P operated 21,948 passenger trains including 2,467 troop train. The daily average of freight and passenger trains was 103, the same as in 1943, setting a record of a train each 14 minutes day and night for two full years.

In the midsummer of 1943, the RF&P leased 23 old steel coaches from the Erie, New York Central, and Lackawanna railroads to aid in its ever growing passenger traffic. These cars, the only coaches found available, had open platforms and were of the type used in the New York commuter service. It was contemplated that they would remain in RF&P local service but for lack of better equipment they frequently moved to other lines in through service. These cars were returned to their owners in June 1945.

After the war, government restrictions were removed on the construction of passenger equipment and the railroads placed orders for new, lightweight equipment to replace the heavy-weight, all-steel cars. For its quota of the through passenger service (which was based on route mileage) between New York and the South, the RF&P purchased one dining car and seventeen lightweight coaches. The RF&P's connecting lines also placed orders for a large number of lightweight sleeping cars of the bedroom-roomette type to replace the open section cars theretofore used. As its quota of such equipment the RF&P ordered thirteen of these cars for service between New York, Philadelphia, Richmond and Norfolk, and between New York and the South in connection with the ACL and SAL. The RF&P participated in three different interline Pullman agreements, all involving the Pennsylvania Railroad, which carried the sleepers between Washington and New York. South of Richmond, the interline routes were via the SAL, ACL/FEC and N&W (ACL from Richmond to Petersburg).

The RF&P also purchased a lightweight, streamlined train of four coaches and a cafe-parlor car for operation between Richmond and Washington. After much delay in delivery, the new five car streamline train was received in November of 1947. Named the *Old Dominion*, this steam powered streamlined train made a daily round trip between Richmond and Washington as Train Nos. 11 and 12. Northbound No. 12 made a 7:30 A.M. departure from Broad Street Station with a scheduled arrival of 9:40 A.M. in Washington. The southbound train departed Union Station at 5:00 P.M. for a 7:15 P.M. arrival in Richmond. Regular stops were made at Alexandria, Quantico and Fredericksburg. These trains averaged 50 MPH and sported a tail sign lettered the *Old Dominion Limited.*

As in the case of motive power, the improvement of the RF&P's passenger equipment since the pre-war days was remarkable. In 1940 the Company's passenger carrying equipment included 37 coaches of which only 19 were air conditioned, 2 air conditioned combination passenger-baggage cars and one air conditioned cafe-parlor car. There was no equipment of the modern, lightweight type. At the close of 1947, there were 62 coaches, 2 combination passenger-baggage cars, 2 full parlor cars and 2 cafe-parlor cars. Forty-three of the coaches were air-conditioned and 18 were of the most modern lightweight construction. The combination cars, parlor cars and cafe-parlor cars were also air-conditioned and one of the cafe-parlor cars (the *Virginia Dare*) was of the new lightweight type. During 1948 the RF&P also received 3 additional lightweight coaches for through service; 13 lightweight roomette-bedroom sleepers to run between New York and the South and between Richmond-New York, Richmond-Philadelphia and Norfolk-New York; and one lightweight dining car for through service.

Operation of the *Old Dominion* was inaugurated on November 16, 1947 with much fanfare. Fast luxury service was now available between Richmond and Washington on a train that offered the latest in the art of car building. The RF&P had anticipated that the train would be heavily patronized by the Richmond travelling public. Unfortunately, after only four months of operation it was readily apparent that the train was a dismal failure. The train had cost the Company nearly half a million dollars and from the out of pocket costs of operations, it was losing between $20,000 and $25,000 a month. The financial results were keenly disappointing.

The *Old Dominion* was discontinued on March 21, 1948. The streamline deluxe coaches and the parlor-dining car "Virginia Dare" were reassigned to RF&P Local Trains 16/23 and were later used in other RF&P local passenger operations.

The shocking failure of the public to embrace a train of modern design such as the *Old Dominion* was a harbinger of the desertion of trains by the general public in the post-war era. It was clear that the public preferred other modes of transportation, particularly the airlines for long-haul travel and the automobile for short-haul.

In a last bid for passengers, big railroads

dieselized trains and placed orders for new lightweight equipment to replace the old heavyweight cars. However, the exodus from the passengers trains was dramatic. In 1929 the nation's railroads operated over 20,000 trains and carried 77 per cent of the intercity passenger traffic. By 1950, more than half of the trains had disappeared and the share of traffic had declined to 46 per cent.

To stimulate passenger business, the RF&P developed the "Special Train" concept in the 1950's. These operations will be discussed in detail in Chapter 5 of this book. It also made one last attempt to operate high speed morning service from Richmond to Washington. On September 25, 1955, the RF&P inaugurated *The Blue and Gray Clipper*, Train No. 20, that departed Broad Street Station at 7:45 A. M., and even with stops in Ashland, Fredericksburg, Quantico and Alexandria, it had a scheduled running time of one hour and 59 minutes between Richmond and Washington.

The *Clipper* was pulled by diesel power and assigned refurbished coaches that had been air-conditioned and equipped with comfortable reclining seats. Usually operated with 5 to 7 coaches, a diner was also assigned to the train. Chimes announced breakfast and there were morning mints, comic books and special menus for the youngsters. The RF&P boasted that the "Clipper" was "the hottest thing on the rails."

However, on August 15, 1959, slightly less than four years after it began operation, the *Clipper* would make its last trip.

Even with exemplary service and an extensive advertising campaign, the RF&P couldn't attract the public to the train. The RF&P had attempted to promote the train by offering special tours and parties on the *Clipper*. However, after deducting the Blue and Gray Tour passengers, the train averaged only 46 regular passengers per day. When discontinued, its service was consolidated with that of Train No. 34, an SAL northbound passenger train with a scheduled morning departure from Richmond.

By the 1960's, one famous passenger train after another was being discontinued by the railroads. Railroad passenger traffic had dropped to only 7 per cent of the commercial share and less than 450 passenger trains were being operated nationwide. Passenger train discontinuances were accelerated by the railroads' loss of mail contracts with the Federal Government. In many instances it had been the revenue from the transportation of mail that had made the difference between the railroads breaking even or incurring a loss from the operation of a passenger train.

In 1969, for the first time since the Great Depression, the number of passengers carried by the RF&P dropped below the one million mark. On May 1, 1971 the Company ended its long history in the passenger business. On that date, the National Railroad Passenger Corporation (Amtrak) assumed responsibility for the operation of intercity rail passen-

Always a promoter of its passenger business, RF&P advertised its trains on roadside billboards in the late 1920s, when automobile competition had already begun to sap away local and short-distance travelers from the railroads.

ger service over the RF&P and on most other remaining rail passenger routes throughout the United States. Amtrak purchased nineteen of the RF&P's streamlined passenger cars and eleven of the RF&P E-8 locomotives. The RF&P disposed of its passenger equipment not required by Amtrak. By the end of 1971, the RF&P was operating only four Amtrak trains daily in each direction between Richmond and Washington.

However, Amtrak would prove to be the savior of the passenger train and during the more than two decades of its existence many trains were returned to the RF&P route. Today, daily service is offered by the *Silver Star* and *Silver Meteor* from Boston/New York to Tampa/Miami; the *Palmetto* from New York to Jacksonville; the *Carolinian* from New York to Charlotte, North Carolina; and, the *Colonial* from Boston/New York to Newport News, Virginia. Amtrak's *Cardinal* and *Crescent* also stop at the RF&P's former Alexandria station and, with the daily congestion on the highways in the Northern Virginia area, Amtrak found a market for its *Virginian*, which operates on a high speed schedule between Richmond and Washington.

Even commuter service has returned to the rails of the RF&P, operated between Fredericksburg and Washington. In 1989 the RF&P signed an operating access agreement with the Northern Virginia and the Potomac and Rappahannock Transportation Commissions for the operation of commuter train service between Fredericksburg and Washington by the Virginia Railway Express. Actual operation of the commuter service after the acquisition of the RF&P by CSXT.

The innovative Auto Train service also operates over the RF&P, transporting both passengers and their private automobiles from Lorton, Virginia on the RF&P to Sanford, Florida on the former SCL. This service was inaugurated by the private Auto Train Corporation on December 6, 1971. When that Company went out of business, the service was revived by Amtrak in 1983.

Once again the RF&P route is serving as a important link in the transportation of people between the North and South.

R. F. & P. Local Trains

SOUTH—Read down			Miles	Eastern Standard (War) Time	NORTH—Read up		
31 Ex.Sun.	29 Daily	23 Daily			32 Ex. Sun.	10 Daily	94 Daily
PM	PM	AM			AM	AM	PM
5 40	3 10	7 45	0.0	Lv **Washington** (Un. Sta.) RF&P Ar	8 00	10 25	8 35
5 45	.....	.....	.....	Lv Washington (7th St. Sta.) " Ar	7 55	.....	.....
5 59	3 33	8 09	8.2	Lv **Alexandria** " Lv	7 38	10 03	8 16
f6 01	f3 36	.....	9.6	Lv Seminary " Lv	f7 33	f9 58	f8 11
f6 11	f3 44	.....	14.2	Lv Franconia " Lv	7 25	f9 53	f8 06
f6 17	3 50	8 27	17.8	Lv Accotink " Lv	7 18	9 48	f7 57
f6 25	3 56	8 34	21.0	Lv Lorton " Lv	7 08	9 38	f7 48
f6 30	4 00	8 40	24.1	Lv Occoquan " Lv	7 01	9 32	f7 42
f6 39	4 11	8 50	31.1	Lv Cherry Hill " Lv	6 49	9 18	f7 28
6 45	4 18	8 55	34.7	Lv **Quantico** (Marine Base) " Lv	6 43	9 12	7 22
f6 53	4 27	f9 02	39.1	Lv Wide Water " Lv	6 27	f8 57	f7 14
f7 05	4 40	f9 13	45.4	Lv Brooke " Lv	6 13	f8 46	f7 05
Ar 7 18	4 56	9 30	54.1	Lv **Fredericksburg** " Lv	5 55	8 31	6 51
PM	f5 11	.....	62.0	Lv Summit " Lv	AM	8 15	s6 39
	5 19	f9 49	66.6	Lv Guinea " Lv		8 07	f6 33
	5 24	9 53	69.0	Lv Woodford " Lv		8 00	s6 29
	5 38	10 04	75.7	Lv Milford " Lv		7 44	f6 21
	5 45	f10 11	80.5	Lv Penola " Lv		7 37	f6 15
	5 55	f10 20	86.4	Lv Rutherglen " Lv		7 29	s6 08
	6 02	f10 28	91.7	Lv Doswell " Lv		7 20	6 01
	f6 06	.....	93.8	Lv Taylorsville " Lv		f7 14	s5 56
	6 14	10 40	98.7	Lv Ashland " Lv		7 10	5 51
	6 25	.....	105.4	Lv Glen Allen " Lv		7 00	s5 41
	6 27	.....	106.9	Lv Laurel " Lv		f6 55	s5 36
	6 45	11 05	113.5	Ar **Richmond** (Broad St. Sta.) " Lv		6 45	.....
	.....	.....	116.5	Ar **Richmond** (Main St. Sta.) SAL Ry Lv	.....	.....	5 10
	PM	AM				AM	PM

(Motor Train notation appears in the 31 and 32 columns)

From the December 20, 1943 RF&P timetable.

Effective December 20, 1943

SOUTHWARD—Read Down

Miles	Eastern Standard (War) Time except as shown	191 Daily	75 Daily	89 Daily	45 Daily	23 Daily	375 Daily	93 Daily	15 Daily	9 Daily	11 Daily	107 Daily	29 Daily	91 Daily	43 Daily	77 Daily	331 Daily	1 Daily	7 Daily	21 Daily	95 Daily
0.0	Lv. **Boston** (South Sta.)....NYNH&H	PM 1 00	PM 1 00	PM 6 00	PM 6 00	PM 6 00		†7 00							AM 11 40						AM 8 00
229.1	Ar. New York (Gr. Cen. Term.)....	5 35	5 35	11 00	11 00	11 00	†7 50	†7 50	11 55						12 07						1 00
229.1	Lv. **New York** (42d St.)....B&O.R.R.	5 45	5 45	12 25	12 30	x12 35	x12 35	x12 35	5 40						12 07	12 35	12 35	12 35	12 35	12 35	2 20
229.1	.... Philadelphia (Chestnut St.)....	6 15	6 15			x12 35	x12 35									1 00	1 00	1 00	1 00	1 00	2 52
322.9	.... Wilmington....	8 34	8 34			3 36	3 36	3 36	8 11						2 24	3 50	3 50	3 17	3 17	3 17	5 06
347.9	.... Baltimore (Camden Sta.)....	10 35	10 35		1 25	6 15	6 15	6 15	8 43						4 23	6 13	6 13	5 25	5 25	5 25	5 38
418.8	.... Washington (Union Sta.)....	11 23	11 23			7 05	7 05	7 05	9 47						5 10	6 13	6 13	6 13	6 13	6 13	7 12
455.6	Ar. Washington (Union Sta.)....							AM													
0.0	Lv. **Boston** (South Sta.)....NYNH&H	PM 1 00	PM 3 00	PM 6 00	PM 6 00	PM 6 00	AM	AM	11 55	AM r12 30	AM r12 30	AM r12 30	AM r12 30	AM 8 00	AM 8 00	AM 9 00	AM 9 00	AM 9 00	AM 10 00	AM 11 00
229.1	Ar. New York (Penna. Sta.)....	y5 35	7 45	11 00	11 00	6 00				6 10	6 10	6 10	6 10		y1 00	y1 00	2 12	2 12	2 12	y2 45	y3 50
229.1	Lv. **New York** (Penna. Sta.)....P.R.R.	©7 35	©9 15	12 25	12 30	12 30	3 50		6 30	9 30	9 30	©10 05	9 00	©11 45	©1 45	1 30	©2 35	©43 05	©43 05	3 30	4 30
...	.... New York (Hudson Term. H&M)....	©7 20	©9 20	12 15	12 15	12 15	3 00		6 15			©10 11	9 25	©11 30	©11 30		©2 50	©3 20	©3 20	3 45	4 10
239.2	.... Newark....	©7 49	©9 30	12 48	12 44	a12 44	4 06		6 44	9 42	9 45	©10 45	11 31	©12 01	©2 00	1 45	©2 50	©3 20	©3 20	3 45	4 44
314.9	.... North Philadelphia....	©9 09	©10 51	k2 19	2 10	2 20	5 26		8 02	11 00	11 00	©11 39	12 01	©11 22	©2 00	d3 02	©4 09	©4 39	©4 39	5 13	5 49
320.4	.... Philadelphia (Penn.Sta.,30th St.)....	©9 19	©11 01	3 10	2 57	2 57	5 36		8 11	11 10	11 10	©11 56	12 10	©12 10	©3 29	d3 22	©4 52	©4 49	©4 49	5 43	5 57
347.1	.... Wilmington....	©9 50	©11 39	4 10	4 15	4 15	6 15		8 11	11 39	11 39	©12 27	12 39	©2 10	©4 03	d3 44	©6 06	©6 30	©6 30	6 46	6 24
415.0	.... Baltimore (Penna. Sta.)....	©11 08	©12 50	5 05	5 00	5 05	7 13		9 47	1 25	1 25	©2 02	1 42	©3 26	©4 55	d5 10	©6 45	©6 15	©6 15	7 24	7 24
455.6	Ar. Washington (Union Sta.)....	©11 50	©1 01	5 15	5 05	5 05	8 00		10 30	2 05	2 05	©2 20	2 25	©4 10	©5 55	d5 35	©6 45	©7 15	©7 15	7 30	8 05
	For R. F. & P. local trains, see reverse side																				
455.6	Lv. **Washington** (Union Sta.)....R.F.&P.	AM 12 15	AM 2 40	4 35	AM 6 40	AM 7 45	AM 9 30	AM 10 00	AM 10 40	PM 1 45	PM 1 45	PM 2 45	PM 3 10	PM 4 40	PM 6 10	6 40	PM 7 00	PM 7 30	PM 7 40	7 45	PM 9 00
463.4	.... Alexandria (See Note)....	12 37	3 01	5 57	7 03	8 09			11 00	2 06	2 06	3 06	3 33		7 01	7 01				8 06	9 21
473.4	.... Accotink (See Note)....								&11 18			f3 06	3 50							&8 23	&9 39
490.3	.... Quantico (Marine Base)....	1 15	3 40	6 35	8 15	8 55	10 50		11 40	2 45	2 45	3 42	4 18	6 02	7 38	7 38		8 43	8 43	8 43	10 00
509.7	.... Fredericksburg....	1 40	4 13	7 02		9 30	11 26		12 40	3 10	3 10	f3 42	4 56	6 02	8 05	8 05		9 09	9 09	9 09	10 27
531.3	.... Milford....					10 04			12 58			4 07	5 38								
547.3	.... Doswell....			b7 55		f10 28			1 08	4 04			6 02								
554.3	.... Ashland....			8 15		10 40			1 30				6 14								12 01
569.1	Ar. **Richmond** (Broad St. Sta.)....	3 12	5 45	8 15	10 18	11 05	12 10	12 55		4 45	4 45	5 25	6 45	7 20	9 20	9 20	9 50	10 10	10 10	10 45	12 01
572.1	.... Richmond (Main St. Sta.)....S.A.L.Ry	AM 3 25			10 45			1 10	1 45	PM 4 55	PM 4 55	PM 5 45			PM 9 03		PM 9 50	10 10		AM 11 10	AM 12 20
	Lv. Richmond (Main St. Sta.)....S.A.L.Ry	4 00	6 15	8 35	11 25			1 45	2 40	5 30	5 30	6 27		7 30	p9 30	c10 10	p10 18	10 10		11 45	1 00
	.... Richmond (Broad St. Sta.)....ACLRR	7 35	c7 00	c9 15	3 30	12 20	12 20	5 00	2 40	8 30	8 30	9 15			12 05		1 05		8 45	3 40	4 35
	Ar. Petersburg....	7 35			5 55			f6 46		10 08					4 15	8 45	5 30	z5 20	z5 40	1 30	5 56
	.... Raleigh....			6 30	10 25	10 25	10 25	10 25								9 55		7 15	11 05	1 30	6 35
	.... Southern Pines (See Note u)....	1 10	v3 10	1 45												12 40				11 40	1 30
	.... Wilmington....		6 05	10 40	1 47	v7 45	v7 45	1 47					5 25			8 45		10 45		3 40	11 40
	.... Columbia....	4 50	9 30	2 50	5 00	10 00	10 00			8 00			5 20		6 35	12 40			z5 20	2 50	2 50
	.... Augusta....		7 50	7 35		1 00	1 00								9 05	8 45			z5 40	4 00	6 24
	.... Charleston....	5 45	7 50	5 45								2 05					3 10	10 45	11 05	4 00	7 24
	.... Savannah....	8 25	8 15	6 15						12 00 NOON		4 10					5 10			4 00	8 05
	.... **Jacksonville**....	8 30			10 25			6 30				7 15			4 55					8 25	
	.... Tampa....													3 00							4 55
	.... St. Petersburg....													3 15							
	.... **Miami**....			‖7 20		‖10 00	‖10 00	6 30						6 15							
	.... Atlanta (Eastern Time)....															†6 35		†6 25	†6 40		
	.... **Birmingham** (Central Time)....																				8 55

Via SAL / **Via ACL** / **No coaches** / **Coach seats reserved** markings appear at the feet of the respective columns.

● Southward, stops only to take for south of Washington; northward, stops only to leave from south of Washington.

‡ Stops on signal to receive or discharge revenue passengers.

‖ Through coaches to **Florida**.

§ Via Georgia R. R.

† Via F. E. C. Ry.

● Southward, leaves only from Richmond and beyond; northward, takes only for Richmond and beyond.

O This train held indefinitely for through car connection, when necessary—southward, at Washington; northward, stops only to leave from Richmond.

⊕ Southward, stops only to take for south of Richmond; northward, stops only to leave from south of Richmond.

ᐃ Through coaches to New York (via PRR).

† Except Sunday over this line

a Stops only to receive passengers.

b Stops to discharge through sleeping car passengers only, from Philadelphia or New York.

c Time is for North Petersburg Station.

d Sleeping car passengers use PRR Train No. 149 leaving New York 1:50 p.m., arriving Washington 6:10 p.m. (no coaches, except Washington).

e **The Federal**—Through coach and sleepers from Boston arriving Washington 8:15 a.m.

f Stops on signal.

h Sleeping cars: coach train leaves 12:45 a.m. except Sunday morning leaves 12:30 a.m.

‖ **The Federal** leaves Washington 11:00 p.m., arriving Boston 8:10 a.m. Through coach and sleepers Washington to Boston.

k Sleeper for Richmond leaves Broad Street Station 1:40 a.m. (open 10:00 p.m.).

m Stops on signal to receive revenue passengers.

n No coaches; coach train leaves Washington 9:00 a.m. arrives New York 1:00 p.m.

o Sleeper from Richmond arrives Broad Street Station, Philadelphia, 5:35 a.m. 12:01 may be occupied until 8:00 a.m.

p Southward, stops only to receive; northward, stops only to leave. This stop is conditional Consult ticket agent for details.

q On Sundays, arrives Wilmington, 9:41 p.m., Philadelphia 10:09 p.m., North Philadelphia 10:20 p.m., Newark 11:33 p.m., New York 11:50 p.m.

r Sleeping cars: coach train leaves 12:45 a.m. except Sunday morning leaves 12:30 a.m.

s Through coach service southward from Washington, northward to Washington.

t Sleeping cars only, except coach service Saturday night.

u Also Pinehurst, by bus from and to Southern Pines.

v Time is for North Charleston Station; connecting bus service to and from Union Station.

w Through train Washington to Boston.

x Earlier motor coaches leave 42d Street 10:30 p.m.; Liberty Street, 12:01 a.m. Sleeping cars open Jersey City Terminal 10:00 p.m.

y Time is for Grand Central Terminal.

z Time is for North Charleston Station.

& Stops on signal to discharge revenue passengers.

Note.—Fort Belvoir, Va., is four and one-half miles from Accotink Station, reached by Government railroad operated for military traffic only. Trains handling through cars will stop on signal to discharge revenue passengers occupying such cars from north of Washington or south of Richmond. Bus service for the general public is available between Alexandria and Fort Belvoir.

(This page and next) Through train schedules and through car arrangements from the December 20, 1943 RF&P Timetable. At the peak of its business RF&P was handling this huge volume of passenger traffic as well as being one of the most congested railroads with war-time freight. (William E. Griffin Coll.)

12:01 a.m. to 12:00 noon—Light Face Type
12:01 p.m. to 12:00 midnight—**Bold Face Type**

Miles	Eastern Standard (War) Time except as shown	076 Daily	24 Daily	080 Daily	046 Daily	0376 Daily	094 Daily	16 Daily	14 Daily	0110 Daily	0108 Daily	022 Daily	092 Daily	10 Daily	096 Daily	078 Daily	8 Daily	044 Daily	0332 Daily	02 Daily	0192 Daily
	Lv. Birmingham (Central Time)																				
	.. Atlanta (Eastern Time)																				
	.. **Miami**																				
	.. St. Petersburg																				
	.. Tampa																				
	Jacksonville																				
	.. Savannah																				
	.. Charleston																				
	.. Augusta																				
	.. Columbia																				
	.. Wilmington																				
	.. Southern Pines (See Note **u**)																				
	.. Raleigh																				
	.. Petersburg																				
	Ar. Richmond (Broad St. Sta.) ..ACLRR																				
	For R.F.&P. local trains, see reverse side																				
0.0	Lv. Richmond (Main St. Sta.) ..S.A.L.Ry																				
	Lv. Richmond (Broad St. Sta.) ..R.F.&P.																				
3.0	.. Ashland																				
17.8	.. Doswell																				
24.8	.. Milford																				
40.8	.. Fredericksburg																				
62.4	.. Quantico (Marine Base)																				
81.8	.. Accotink (See Note)																				
98.7	.. Alexandria (See Note)																				
108.5	Ar. Washington (Union Sta.)																				
116.5	Lv. Washington (Union Sta.) ..P.R.R.																				
156.5	Ar. Baltimore (Penna. Sta.)																				
225.0	.. Wilmington																				
251.7	.. Philadelphia (Penn. Sta. 30thSt.)																				
257.2	.. North Philadelphia																				
	.. Newark																				
332.9	.. New York (Hudson Term H&M)																				
	.. New York (Penna. Sta.)																				
343.0	Lv. New York (Gr. Cen. Term.) ..NYNH&H																				
572.1	Ar. Boston (South Sta.)																				

THROUGH CAR SERVICE
(Coaches on all trains unless otherwise shown)

Nos. 1 and 2 (via ACL)—Through reserved seat coaches between New York (via PRR) and Miami. Dining car.

Nos. 7 and 8 (via ACL)—Through sleeping cars and limited reserved seat coach service between New York (via PRR) and Miami. Dining car.

No. 9 (via SAL)—Through sleeping car New York (via PRR) to Birmingham; Washington to Atlanta. Dining car. Parlor and dining cars New York to Washington (via PRR and via B&O).

No. 14—RF&P parlor car and dining car Richmond to Washington. Parlor and dining cars Washington to New York (via PRR and via B&O).

Nos. 15 and 16—RF&P parlor-dining car Washington and Richmond. Parlor and dining cars New York and Washington (via PRR).

Nos. 24—Sleeping cars from Richmond (open 9:30 p.m.) to Philadelphia and New York (via PRR); may be occupied until 8:00 a.m. at Philadelphia, 7:00 a.m. at New York.

Nos. 43 and 44 (via SAL)—Through sleeping cars and reserved seat coaches New York (via PRR) and Miami. Dining and tavern cars.

Nos. 75 and 76 (via ACL)—Through sleeping cars New York (via PRR) and Jacksonville, St. Petersburg, Sarasota and Miami; Washington and Orlando. Dining car. Pullman and dining cars New York to Washington (via B&O).

Nos. 77 and 78 (via ACL)—Through sleeping cars New York (southward on PRR No. 149 leaving 1:50 p.m.) to coach; also coach-lunch service Washington and Hamlet. Sleeping cars New York to Washington on PRR and B&O night trains.

No. 89—Through sleeping cars (via PRR), New York (open 11:00 p.m.) and Philadelphia (open 10:00 p.m. at Broad Street Station) to Richmond. Dining car Washington to Richmond.

Nos. 91 and 92 (via ACL)—Through sleeping cars and reserved seat coaches New York (via PRR) and Tampa, St. Petersburg. Dining car. Pullman and dining cars Washington to New York (via B&O).

Nos. 93 and 94 (via SAL)—Through coach; also coach-lunch service Washington and Hamlet. Sleeping cars New York to Washington on PRR and B&O night trains.

Nos. 95 and 96 (via SAL)—Through sleeping cars Washington and Raleigh; Birmingham; also Washington to Columbia. Dining car. Parlor and dining cars New York (via PRR) and Washington (via B&O).

Nos. 107 and 108 (via SAL)—Through sleeping cars New York (via PRR) and St. Petersburg, Miami; also Sarasota-Venice to New York. Dining car. Parlor and dining cars New York and Washington (via B&O).

No. 110 (via SAL)—Through sleeping car Birmingham to New York (via PRR) and Atlanta to Washington. Dining car. Parlor and dining cars Washington to New York (via B&O).

Nos. 191 and 192 (via SAL)—Through sleeping cars New York (via PRR) and Hamlet, St. Petersburg, South Boca Grande and Miami; Washington and Miami (open 10:00 p.m.). Sleeper Columbia to Washington. Dining car. Pullman and dining cars New York and Washington (via B&O).

Nos. 331 and 332 (via SAL)—Through sleeping cars and reserved seat coaches New York (via PRR) and St. Petersburg; also New York to Sarasota-Venice. Dining car.

Nos. 375 and 376 (via ACL)—Through sleeping cars and reserved seat coaches, Washington and Miami. Dining and tavern cars. Sleeping cars New York to Washington on PRR and B&O night trains. Parlor car Washington to New York (via PRR).

Station force handles express and mail from one train as another waits for its locomotives to couple for a northbound run in this 1950s photo of the east end of Broad Street Station. All mail/express activities were concentrated on this end of the platform since all trains arrived and departed from the station in the same direction by means of a loop track. Note the PRR box express cars on the head-end of one of the trains, undoubtedly through cars from New York.

(both) William E. Griffin Coll.

Mr. H. T. Anthony, the Stationmaster of Broad Street Station. His was a busy job in the heyday of passenger service. Initially RF&P shared this station with ACL, but in 1962 SAL trains moved here from Main Street Station, leaving it to the C&O alone. By that time Southern trains serving Richmond had all been discontinued.

William E. Griffin Coll.

(Above) RF&P's force of passenger train porters poses for a group photo in March 1925.

(Right) RF&P 4-8-4 No. 611, *Governor William Smith*, departs Broad Street Station on April 9, 1950 with No. 94, the SAL's Passenger Main & Express train.

D. Wallace Johnson

William E. Griffin Coll.

E8A No. 1006 and a B-unit are on the ready track at Broad Street Station, awaiting the arrival from the south of the train they will take north to Washington.

This aerial photo illustrates Broad Street Station's unique loop track that allowed RF&P and ACL trains to operate through the station in the same direction. The neo-classical building with its Roman dome stands out in contrast with the commercial and residential housing across from it on Broad Street.

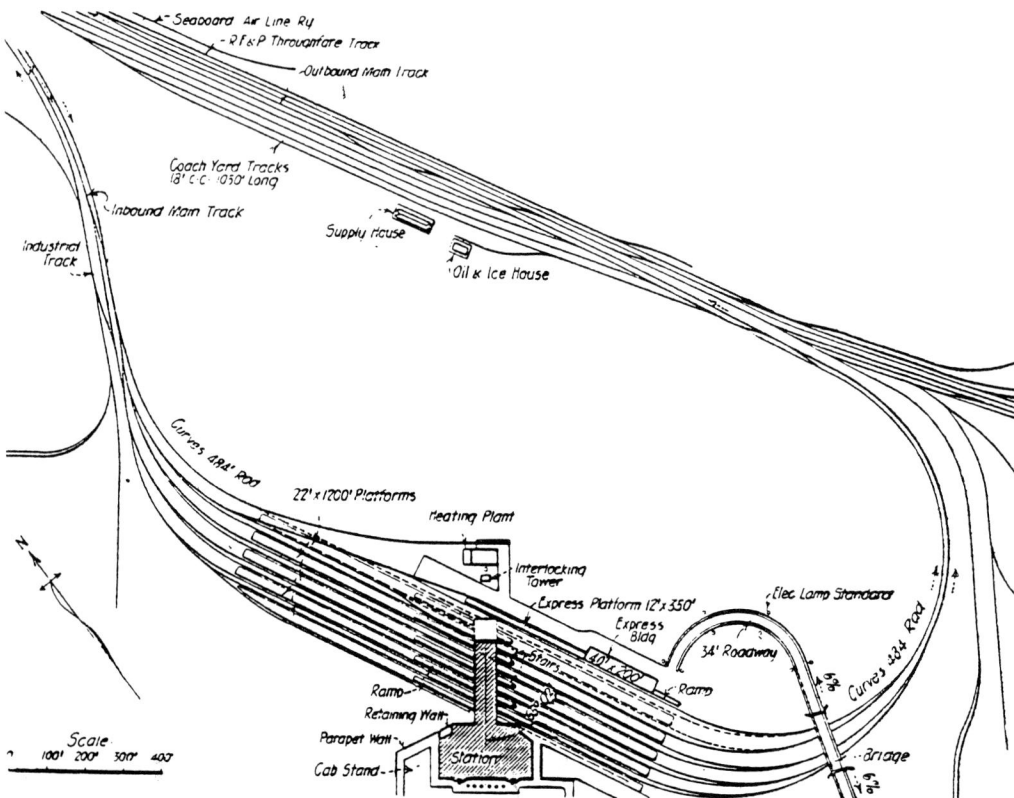

This track layout diagram shows the loop arrangement and location of servicing facilities, coach yard, etc. that served Broad Street Station.

(both) William E. Griffin Coll.

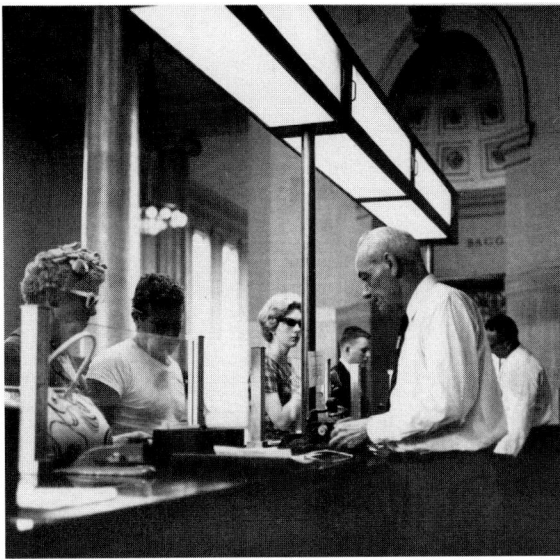

By 1957 modern marble and glass ticket counters had replaced the old-fashioned iron-barred ticket cages in Broad Street's vaulted waiting area. The concourse, above the tracks is to the right background.

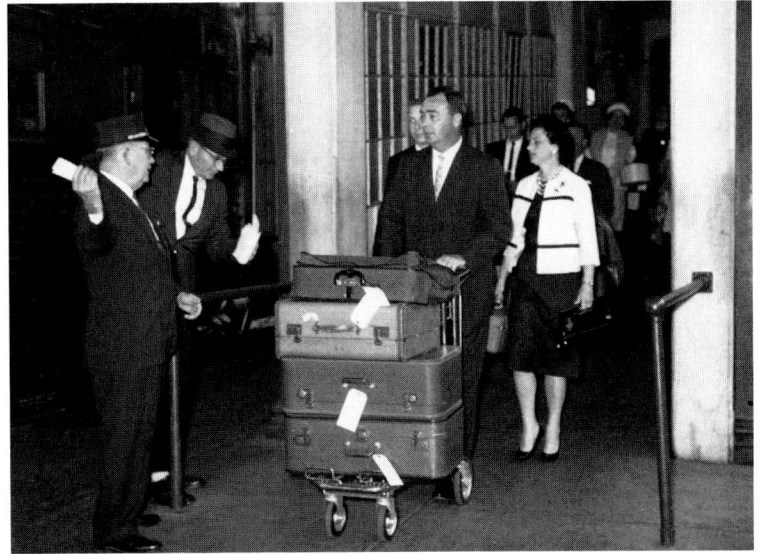

Access to the train platforms at Broad Street Station was gained through enclosed stairways and ramps. Passengers are being directed to their car by a trainman as they arrive from the concourse above.

Pacific No. 328 charges past Franconia station with a 12-car northbound passenger train in July 1945. The first two cars are Army hospital cars with the red-on-white-background red cross marking visible on each end. Wartime traffic continued for some time after the end of hostilities, as military men were taken to camps and bases in the US for discharge and subsequently sent on their way home.

(both) E. L. Thompson photo, H. H. Harwood, Jr. Coll.

The *Governor William Smith*, 4-8-4 No. 611, marches a 14-car Train No. 107, SAL's southbound *Southern States Special*, under the signal bridge near AF Tower south of Alexandria in July 1948.

Pacific No. 312 is making time with a 15-car No. 94, SAL's northbound Passenger, Mail and Express train, at Greendale, in 1945. Mail and express shipments were always very profitable for railroads and passenger trains were often profitable only because of their mail revenues in the latter days. In 1945 almost all mail traveled by train.

H. W. Pontin photo, H. H. Harwood, Jr. Coll.

Snow covers the station platform at Fredericksburg as the "Statesman" 4-8-4 No. 616, *George Mason*, arrives with ACL's southbound Train No. 89 in 1947.

Frank Dementi photo, William E. Griffin Coll.

Joseph A. Rose

The *Governor Patrick Henry*, 4-8-4 No. 601, has a clear stack coasting around the "Eastern View Curve," south of Fredericksburg with a northbound passenger train in July 2, 1946. A full-length Railway Post Office car, followed by an express/baggage car, lead a solid heavyweight consist.

SAL's diesels began operating over RF&P to Washington in 1938. In this classic view at Ivy City Terminal in Washington, SAL E4A No. 3007 is next to RF&P 4-8-4 No. 601, *Governor Patrick Henry*, on June 25, 1942.

Ted Gay photo, H. H. Harwood, Jr. Coll.

E8 No. 1003 glides around the Summit curve (Mile Post 51.5) with Train No. 22, Seaboard Coast Line's *Silver Star*, in July 1969.

(both) William E. Griffin Coll.

Northbound Train No. 22, SCL's *Silver Star*, rounds Potomac Run Curve (Mile Post 65.1) powered by RF&P E8 No. 1013 in the new-style paint scheme, an SCL E7, and another RF&P E8.

Anthony Dementi photo, W. E. Griffin Coll.

Single RF&P FP7 No. 1201 speeds Train No. 34, SAL's northbound *Silver Comet*, over new 140-pound pressure butt-welded rail near Laurel in 1955.

(both) William E. Griffin Coll.

(Above) F7 No. 1109 leads a northbound passenger train in April 1950. This photo was taken by the Union Switch & Signal Company, obviously to illustrate the new signal installation to the right.

(Right) FP7 No. 1203 in company with three other units, rolls Train No. 4, the northbound Passenger, Mail and Express train, across the South Anna River Bridge, 18 miles north of Richmond in 1965.

96

Viewed from the caboose of a northbound freight, E8 No. 1005 arrives at Fredericksburg station with Train No. 34, SAL's northbound Silver Comet in May 1963.

(all) William E. Griffin Coll.

A recollection of bygone days, RF&P's Accommodation train between Richmond and Ashland is parked in front of the Randolph-Macon College in Ashland, with a 4-6-0 and coach No. 61.

(Left) There were many attractive passenger stations located along the main line of the RF&P. This view of the Glen Allen station, located 8 miles north of Richmond, was taken in 1956.

(Below) Passenger shelters were provided at many local stations along the line. This is the Hunton shelter station looking northward up the main line on July 30, 1941.

RF&P Motor Car No. 1 and trailer coach T-11 comprise a southbound local passenger train stopping at the Potomac Yard station in June 1939. The yard is out of the photo to the right. The highway to the left is US Route 1. In the 1920s and 1930s, as local passenger traffic declined steeply, many railroads adopted the motor train concept for their remaining branch and local services, thus saving on the expense of a steam locomotive. RF&P received No. 1 and T-11 in 1928 and was so pleased that a duplicate set was ordered in 1929.

L. W. Rice photo, H. H. Harwood, Jr. Coll.

Traveling under catenary on the Pennsylvania Railroad, RF&P motor car M-2 and trailer coach T-12 comprise a southbound local train passing 14th Street in Washington in 1946.

L. W. Rice photo, T. W. Dixon Coll.

E. P. Wallis photo, H. H. Harwood, Jr. Coll.

Another excellent view of M-1 and T-11 at the north end of Washington Union Station in 1948.

Pacific No. 311 leads southbound local passenger Train No. 23 across the Little River Bridge at Taylorsville in 1948. Note the three 840-series streamlined coaches originally purchased for use on the Old Dominion that have been reassigned to the consist of No. 23.

J. I. Kelly photo, E. D. Siler Coll.

E. L. Thompson photo, H. H. Harwood, Jr. Coll.

Its run from Washington to Richmond almost complete, Pacific No. 309 charges past SAL's Hermitage Yard, south of AY Tower, en route to Broad Street Station with 5-car local No. 23 in November 1947.

D. Wallace Johnson

4-8-4 No. 606, *Governor John Tyler*, leads northbound local passenger Train No. 14 across South Anna River Bridge on November 13, 1949. No. 14 provided fast service between Richmond and Washington, with stops at Ashland, Fredericksburg, Quantico, and Alexandria.

99

Passengers in RF&P's dining car *Fredericksburg* were treated to a delicious cup of coffee—"an early morning eye opener on the house"—followed by a breakfast menu that offered country ham with eggs, grits with ham gravy, corn muffins, or Virginia fried apples with bacon.

R. F. & P.
Country Ham Breakfast

Choice of
Fruit, Fruit Juice or Cereal

COUNTRY HAM
with Eggs (Any Style)
Grits with Ham Gravy

Orange Marmalade

Toast			Corn Muffins
Coffee	Tea	Milk	Cocoa

1.85

RF&P's tiny breakfast menu!

The 1931 improvements to RF&P coaches for local passenger Train No. 14 included rotating deluxe lounge seats in 2-and-1 arrangement (pioneered by C&O a year before), inside sliding screens to keep out dirt and cinders, and linen covers on the seats to protect the passengers' clothes. The cars were also equipped with smooth running roller bearings and the trucks were completely rubberized to prevent shocks and jolts.

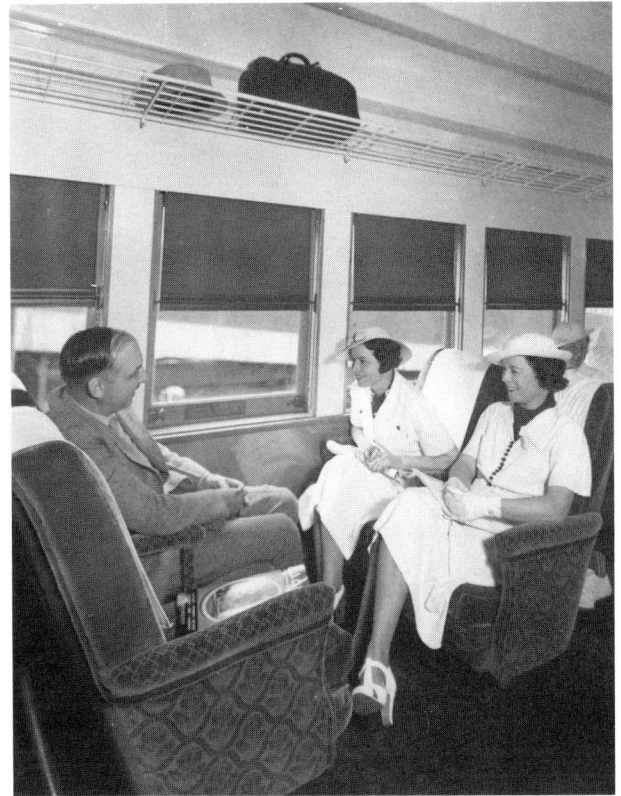

(both) William E. Griffin Coll.

(Above left) A lady attired in typical 1931 fashions enjoys the bucket-type rotating seat that replaced the old straight walk-over type on RF&P coaches. *(Above, right)* In 1934 RF&P started air-conditioning and deluxing its coaches. In this publicity photo, the ladies are dressed in white to emphasize that passengers cound travel without the discomfort and annoyance of the steam locomotive's smoke and cinders.

J. I. Kelly photo, E. D. Siler Coll.

The *Governor Thomas Jefferson*, No. 602, crosses over passing SAL's Hermitage Yard after having moved through RF&P's Acca Yard en route to Broad Street Station with southbound Passenger, Mail and Express Train No. 93 in 1946.

The Old Dominion

Anthony Dementi photo, W. E. Griffin Coll.

The complete *Old Dominion* poses with its five-car consist on the Rappahannock River Bridge at Fredericksburg in November 1947.

Like so many railroads in the immediate post-World War II-era, after restrictions on building new cars were lifted, RF&P ordered a modern streamlined train for use on its own short route. After much delay the equipment finally arrived in November 1947. So many railroads were ordering new cars that the builders were unable to work out of the backlog until 1950. The train consisted of a cafe-parlor car named *Virginia Dare* and four coaches. As Nos. 11 and 12 the consist made a daily round trip over the line but was discontinued only four months later because of losses.

"A railroad man's railroad"*
is now proud to present

Between Washington, the Capital of the Nation

The OLD DOMINION

...and Richmond, the Capital of the Old Dominion

THIS new train provides old-fashioned comfort in an ultra-modern setting . . . not a Hollywood version with multitudes of flashy, photogenic gadgets . . . but a truly modern, utterly practical train which combines beauty with utility, solid comfort with de luxe service.

Two hours and fifteen minutes between Washington, D. C., and Richmond, Va. A round trip each day with hotel comfort all the way.

"The OLD DOMINION" comfortably seats more than 300 passengers in modern, beautifully decorated coaches and a luxurious parlor-cafe car. High tensile steel construction throughout. Tight-lock couplers, roller bearings, and shock absorbers insuring a smooth ride from start to stop.

The interiors, in every detail . . . from floor to ceiling . . . are a supreme delight. Completely air conditioned; modern, restful lighting; stainless steel kitchen (Southern cooking, you know!) colorful murals of historic interest; *plus* !

Yes, "The OLD DOMINION" provides 117 miles of de luxe service so typical of Virginia, the Old Dominion.

RICHMOND, FREDERICKSBURG AND POTOMAC RAILROAD

W. M. TAYLOR, *Traffic Manager*

(Above) This ad appeared in the November 15, 1947 issue of *Railway Age*, advertising RF&P's new train.

Anthony Dementi photo, W. E. Griffin Coll.

(Above) William M. Tuck, Governor of Virginia, addresses the crowd during christening ceremonies for the Old Dominion at Broad Street Station on November 7, 1947. Governor Tuck's remarks were also broadcast to the people of Richmond over WRVA. The governor's wife was the official christener of the new train, with water taken from the James (Richmond) and Potomac (Washington) Rivers.

(Right) One of the many first-class touches added to the *Old Dominion* was this drumhead mounted on the rear of the train.

The *Old Dominion's* Parlor-Cafe car was numbered 844 and named *Virginia Dare*. It featured a parlor section, a lounge, and a dining room seating twenty people, and served to supply both the first class accommodations for the short trip between Washington and Richmond, and the train's food service. It and the coaches for this train were built by American Car and Foundry in St. Charles, Missouri.

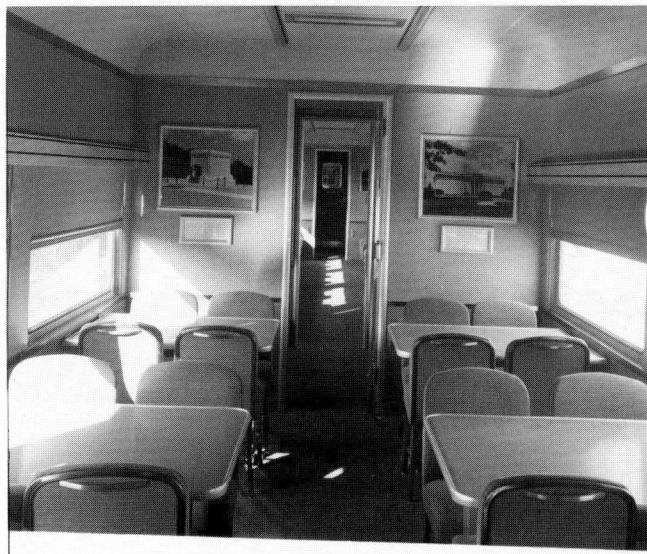

(Above, left) The *Virginia Dare's* spacious lounge, where passengers could relax in chairs upholstered in red. Blue curtains and green carpets were used throughout the car. *(Above, right)* The dining room seated 20 people in chairs upholstered in gray needlepoint. The interiors of each car on the *Old Dominion* featured large pictures of Virginia historical sites.

(Left) The well equipped kitchen and pantry assured a complete variety of meal service for passengers. The long tank in the ceiling contains the water supply for the kitchen, which had three large sinks on the left, and ranges and other cooking appliances on the right.

(Above) The lightweight streamline coaches of the *Old Dominion* were numbered 840-843. The entire train was built of special high-strength steel by American Car and Foundry and featured roller bearings, tight-lock couplers, and shock absorbers to ensure smooth rides and stops. The exteriors were painted gray with blue and gold stripes.

(Left) The interior of the *Old Dominion's* coaches was tastefully decorated, with ivory ceiling and aluminum and tan walls. Green and gold window shades contrasted with the blue upholstered individual seats. The floors were covered with asphant tile of blue and gray agate. As shown in the photo, the coaches were divided by a glass partition into smoking and non-smoking compartments.

(all) William E. Griffin Coll.

Seating capacity of the *Old Dominion* was 302 passengers, which included the 22 parlor seats. The train was, of course, all air-conditioned. In this publicity photo, passengers are boarding the *Virginia Dare.* This photo gives a good view of the wide diaphragms between the cars which gave the train a smooth outside appearance. Also obvious are the wide blue stripes and narrow gold fine-lining.

William E. Griffin Coll.

RF&P made one last bid for fast morning service from Richmond to Washington with the inauguration in 1955 of Train No. 20, the *Blue and Gray Clipper*. RF&P established a special same-day round trip fare of $4.95 and ran a contest offering a $100 savings bond to the person submitting the name most fitting the new train. The billboard on the lawn of Broad Street Station advertising the new train was photographed on September 19, 1955.

Anthony Dementi, W. E. Griffin Coll.

(Above) Mr. Irvin W. Guthman of Stafford County submitted the name *Blue and Gray Clipper*, which *was chosen from over 4,500 entries, as the win*ner of RF&P's $100 bond contest to name Train No. 20. In this photo RF&P President W. Thomas Rice (left) presents Mr. Guthman with his prize for naming the train.

Richmond *News-Leader*

(*Left*) The *Blue and Gray Clipper* was advertised as "the hottest thing on rails." E8 No. 1012 departs Broad Street Station with the morning "Clipper" that will cover 110 miles between Richmond and Washington in less than two hours. This cut 15 minmutes off the previous schedule of even the fastest through train.

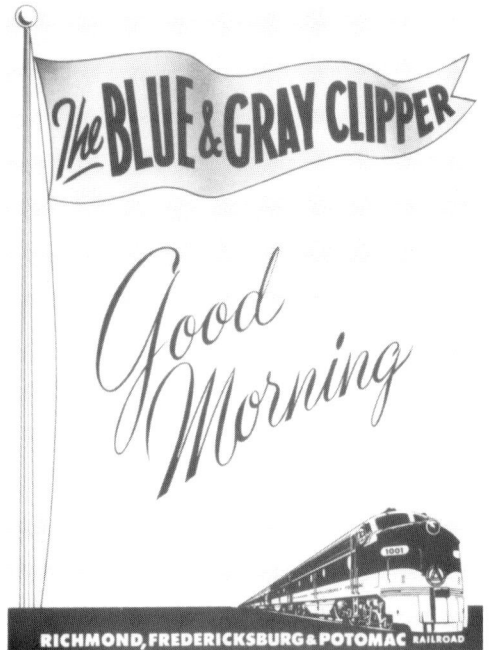

The *Blue and Gray Clipper* made its last trip on August 15, 1959, just four years after its inauguration, but in the meanwhile it offered the fastest schedule ever over the RF&P, with chimes to announce breakfast, morning mints, comic books for the children, and menus like this one.

Welcome... Your Breakfast is Ready

Let Us Give Thanks!

JEWISH

BLESSING BEFORE MEALS

Eternal God and Father, we are grateful for thy loving care and providence. Humbly we ask Thee to bless our food, that we, who partake of it, may gain strength to carry on Thy work.

We recite our traditional blessing of Thanksgiving: Praised art Thou, O Lord, our God, King of the universe who bringeth forth bread from the earth. Amen.

SUGGESTED BY RABBI ARIEL L. GOLDBURG, D.D.
CONGREGATION BETH AHABAH, RICHMOND, VA.

CATHOLIC

BLESSING BEFORE MEALS

Bless us, O Lord, and these thy gifts which we are about to receive from Thy bounty—Through Christ our Lord, Amen.

BLESSING AFTER MEALS

We thank Thee, Oh Lord, for these and all thy gifts which we have received, through the merits of Christ our Lord, Amen.

These traditional prayers recommended by
RT. REV. PETER L. IRETON BISHOP OF RICHMOND
in behalf of Catholics in Richmond and this Diocese

PROTESTANT

BLESSING BEFORE MEALS

Our Father—I thank Thee for all thy goodness and mercy. Grant that I may be strengthened in body, mind and spirit as I have need. Bless those I love and all who need Thee, and bless this food to my use and me in Thy service through Jesus Christ, our Lord. Amen.

SUGGESTED BY REV. THEODORE F. ADAMS, D.D.
PASTOR, FIRST BAPTIST CHURCH, RICHMOND, VA.

CLUB BREAKFAST

PLEASE WRITE ON CHECK "CLUB BREAKFAST" AND EACH ITEM DESIRED

CHOICE OF
Fruit, Fruit Juice or Cereal

VIRGINIA FRIED APPLES with Link (3) Sausage 1.65
VIRGINIA FRIED APPLES with sliced (3) Bacon 1.65
VIRGINIA FRIED APPLES with Sugar Cured Ham 1.85
SUGAR CURED HAM with Eggs (any style) 1.85
KIPPERED HERRING with Scrambled Eggs 1.65
EGGS (ANY STYLE) with Bacon Strips (3) or Sausage Links (3) 1.65
GOLDEN OMELETTE with Guava Jelly 1.55
SELECTED FRESH COUNTRY EGGS, Boiled, Fried or Scrambled 1.35
GRIDDLE CAKES with Sausage (3) or Fried Eggs 1.65
BROWNED CORNED BEEF HASH with Poached Egg 1.55
FRENCH TOAST with Syrup 1.15

Florida Orange Marmalade

Toast   Corn Muffins

Coffee   Tea   Milk   Cocoa

A LA CARTE

Hot or Dry Cereals with Cream .45, with Sliced Banana .60

Fruit or Vegetable Juice .25   Florida Orange Juice .25   Double Juice .40
Grapefruit .30   Lemon Juice with Water .20   Sliced Florida Orange .25
Stewed Prunes .40   Sliced Banana .45   Individual Strained Honey .30
Broiled Ham with Eggs 1.35   Broiled Ham 1.30: Half Portion .75
Broiled Bacon (6 strips) 1.25: Half Portion (3 strips) .70 Browned Corned Beef Hash with Poached Egg 1.25
Bacon (3 strips) with Eggs 1.20   Kippered Herring with Scrambled Eggs 1.20
Eggs—Boiled, Fried, Scrambled, Shirred (1) .40; (2) .70   Eggs Poached (1) .45; (2) .75
Toast or Muffins .25   Hominy Grits .30   Omelette with Guava Jelly .95   Plain Omelette .85
Griddle Cakes or French Toast, Syrup or Honey .75: with Bacon Strips (3) 1.25
Coffee, Cocoa, Sanka, Postum, Tea .30   Milk, Buttermilk .25
PARENTS MAY SHARE THEIR PORTIONS WITH CHILDREN WITHOUT EXTRA CHARGE

Please Write Your Order—Waiters Are Not Allowed to Accept Verbal Orders

YOU ARE ALWAYS "WELCOME ABOARD"
THE RICHMOND, FREDERICKSBURG AND POTOMAC RAILROAD

The BLUE & GRAY CLIPPER

Good Morning

RICHMOND, FREDERICKSBURG & POTOMAC RAILROAD

William E. Griffin Coll.

Amtrak assumed the operation of passenger service over RF&P on May 1, 1971. Here Amtrak's Train No. 82, the northbound *Silver Star*, passes RF&P's AY Tower behind SDP-40 Nos. 611 and 639 after departing Broad Street Station en route to Washington in July 1974. At this writing Amtrak operates 12 trains between Richmond and Washington over RF&P daily, making it one of the most heavily trafficked corridor on the system. Broad Street Station long ago became a museum and the tracks were taken up, with Amtrak trains now using a suburban location just north of Richmond.

(both) William E. Griffin

Auto-Train Corporation's northbound train rounds the Potomac Run Curve behind U-36B Nos. 4003 and 4002 en route to its terminal at Lorton, in January 1972. Pursuant to an August 1, 1970 operating agreement among Auto-Train, RF&P and SCL, the two railroads operated the Auto-Trains over their respective lines between Lorton, Virginia and Sanford, Florida. Auto-Train supplied the trains and terminal facilities and the railroads furnished the crews. Later Auto-Train was liquidated and Amtrak assumed the Auto-Train function and as of this writing it is one of the national system's best operations.

107

RF&P sponsored special trains to boost aware-
ness of its passenger business. One of the
most successful was the *Santa Claus Special*
starting in 1956 and ending in 1971.

Chapter 5

Special Trains

Football, baseball, plays, flower shows, little folks, and even Santa Claus. Do these things sound out of place as part of railroad operations? Perhaps so, but not on the RF&P where these items were lumped under one heading - Special Trains.

These trains were conceived by the RF&P's genial Manager/Passenger Sales, Mr. Eugene B. "Gene" Luck, who joined the RF&P's Traffic Department in August, 1955 at age 51 after a thirty-one year career as a salesman in the paper industry. Working on the principle that people enjoyed riding trains, particularly when the trip included planned events, Luck and his assistant, William A. "Billy" Griffin (no relation to the author), began week end and holiday trips to New York and Washington. Next came tours of Washington, specially designed for school children.

This led to Washington Redskin football trips, Washington Senator and Baltimore Orioles baseball trips, flower show trains and embassy tours in Washington, race track trips to Maryland and Delaware, and even theater trains to Washington and New York. Theater trains were operated out of Richmond in the late afternoon to Washington, serving dinner enroute, and returning to Richmond the same evening. New York theater trains provided five nights in New York and Broadway productions each evening. For at least 10 years, the RF&P was the Redskins biggest season ticket holder. Until 1971, the railroad controlled a block of 600 tickets, which it sold to passengers who rode excursion trains to the home games.

Mr. Luck's "Special Trains" were designed to stimulate passenger business and win friends for the RF&P. The concept was so successful that it soon developed into a lucrative sideline extending outside the Company's regularly scheduled Richmond to Washington runs. In 1962, the RF&P operated 175 such trains with over 43,000 passengers. In 1966, over 56,000 people rode the Special Trains, with over 30,000 of those passengers being the children and their escorts that rode the Santa Claus and Little Folks Trains.

In 1956, a Caboose Car Train was operated for fathers and sons from Richmond to the Quantico Marine Base, consisting of fourteen cabooses and two passenger coaches. The Marine Corps provided the sons and their dads with a tour of the military reservation and allowed the group to eat in the mess hall prior to the return trip to Richmond.

Beginning in l956, the most memorable of all the Special Trains began operation. Santa Claus trains came on the scene.

The first "Santa Claus Specials" came to the town of Ashland, Virginia with Santa brought into town on an RF&P passenger train. Santa detrained and then visited with the children and their parents at Cox's Department Store.

These early specials, operated in 1955 and 1956, evolved into a trip - courtesy the RF&P and Cox's Department Store - that ran from Ashland to Richmond and back again. The first such trip was operated from Ashland on Friday, December 6, 1957. The public response was tremendous and during the year, the RF&P operated three Santa Claus trains with 6,600 passengers between Richmond and Ashland.

The trains left Richmond's Broad Street Station with a fairy princess in each car, several clowns and wandering minstrels. The clowns, fairy princesses and Santa's helpers were located throughout the train and led the children in Christmas songs and music on the trip from Richmond to Ashland. As the train approached Ashland the tempo of excitement increased and when the princess in each car announced that Santa could be seen just ahead, the children rushed to their windows for a view of the jolly old elf sitting on his red sleigh.

Santa and his beautiful Snow Queen boarded the train in Ashland and visited with the children throughout the train all the way back to Richmond, gathering their wish lists for Christmas morning. Upon arrival at Broad Street Station, Santa lit the RF&P's mammoth Christmas tree and started the organ music program for the Yuletide Season.

Gene B. Luck, RF&P's genial Manager of Passenger Sales and creator of the company's special trains.

By 1958 the Santa Claus Specials had become an unqualified success and were operated from Richmond to Doswell with ticket sales taking place from a caboose parked at Broad Street Station. Six special Santa Claus trains were operated to the delight of over 8,000 enthusiastic children and parents. During 1958 the Miller and Rhoads Department Store in Richmond took over control of ticket sales for the Richmond area and trains were also run from Alexandria under the sponsorship of the J. C. Penney Department Store.

By the 1960's, more than 18,000 children and adults were riding twelve Santa Claus Specials each year - six from Richmond, five from Alexandria and one from Fredericksburg. A train of 21 coaches traditionally operated round trips between Richmond and Doswell, picking up Santa at Ashland; and, between Alexandria and Possum Point (Quantico), picking up Santa at Newington.

From the Santa Claus trains, Luck hit on the idea of a "Little Folks Train" - one designed to familiarize kindergarten and first and second grade children with train operations. Equipment included 12 coaches and three Pullman cars, with RF&P people on board to explain the operations. The first Little Folks Trains were run in 1961 and attracted over 6,000 children for the one and 1/2 hour trip from Richmond to Doswell and return.

The RF&P continued to operate these popular trains until the Company ceased its operation of passenger service with the take-over of intercity passenger trains by the National Railroad Passenger Corporation (Amtrak) in 1971.

Over 200 parents and children rode RF&P's Santa Claus trains. Among them was columnist and humorist Charles McDowell, Jr., whose "hasty journal of a weary father" from the December 8, 1957 edition of the Richmond Times-Disptach is reprinted below:

Accompanied by daughter 3, traveled to Ashland by automobile Friday evening to rendezvous with Santa Claus Special and high adventure. Daughter had never been on a train or seen Santa Claus; was anxious to make acquaintance of both. Accomplishment of dual objective made possible through ingenunity of Cox's department store in Ashland and RF&P Railroad.

Twenty-two car train carrying Santa Claus would pull into Ashland from north (from North Pole actually), pick up children and adults, carry them nonstop to Richmond and back while everyone met Santa Claus. Advance ticket sale: 2,200. Approximate population of Ashland 2,700. Appalling.

Arrived Ashland after dark, parked car on outer fringe of classic traffic jam, walked with daughter to railroad station to find what looked like 3,000 people waiting along tracks that run down principal street of town. Daughter kept jumping up and down. Children everywhere in murk kept yipping and whooping. Loudspeakers kept saying, "Stay back from tracks, please"....Turned to pleasant lady beside me and said ' You know, only a fool would drive all the way from Richmond to get into this.' She smiled, replied, "We drove from Petersburg."

Loudspeakers announced regular train to Florida would now come through-Santa Claus Special to follow-so please keep back from tracks. Ashland children fearless; grew up with trains running down main street. Daugher, a Richmonder completely, retreated 60 feet. Regular train came through at crawl, amazed faces of Florida-bound passengers making quite a show in windows.

Considerably later, Santa Claus train announced—"direct from the North Pole." Cheers. High school band began to play suitable number. Santa Claus waved from cab of engine. Very impressive.

Boarded train with daughter, gave her seat next to window, realized she was sitting stiffly, staring straight ahead. "This train isn't going to go," she said suddenly with strange inflection. Analysis of inflection indicated daughter meant she didn't want the train to go anywhere; she didn't much like train. Took three minutes to make reassuring, pro-train speech to daughter. "But this train doesn't have a driver," she said finally, pointing to absence of driver in front left seat of coach.

Train started at this point, fairy princess appeared in front of car, waved wand, said "Hello children," and everything was all right. People began to stream through train from front looking for seats. Took in three little girls with daughter, stood in aisle.

Led by fairy princess, children sang Christmas songs. Daughter sang lustily although she was not familiar with words except "Jingle Bells." When in doubt about others, she sang "Jingle Bells." Parents began to circulate, get acquainted. Found one brave, unruffled man with five of his own children, two of neighbor's; he said he had been carrying too many little cups of water, that he hadn't had time to worry about responsibilities, nerves, anything. Found ruffled-looking man with one child sitting on his shoulder singing and kicking. "My wife and I flipped a coin," he said. "I lost."

Clowns came through coach entertaining small fry, explaining to parents Santa Claus was working his way through...talking with each child, three minutes each.

Fairy princess stopped to chat with parents across aisle, mentioned that little girl in next coach had become somewhat sick. "I got away just in time," said fairy princess, smoothing her wings.

Train wheeled in great circle near Broad Street Station...Great roar in vestibule announced appearance of Santa Claus. Excellent Santa Claus. Daughter whimpered uneasily....warmed up as great man approached, suddenly extended her hand...

Progress back to Ashland rather slow. Everything considered, though, all hands behaved acceptably. Daughter discueed Tiny Tears doll in almost proprietary way...with small girl in seat with her.

When train reached Ashland, carried daughter on shoulders toward car. Fell into step beside man carrying daughter same way. Daughters glowed at each other sleepily.

(Above) Santa Claus gets ready to board his special train as it arrives at Newington from Alexandria in 1968.

(Right) Clowns rode the trains to entertain the children as they waited for Santa to board.

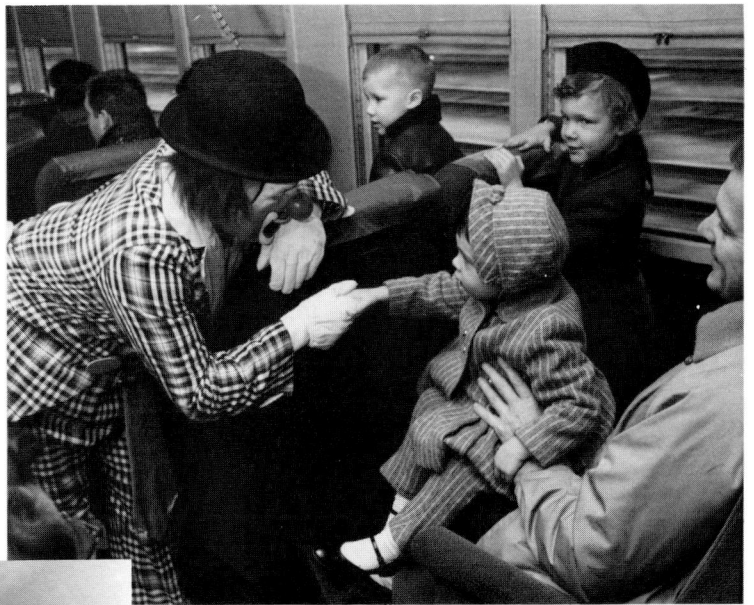

(all) William E. Griffin Coll.

(Left) Santa greets children on his way through one of the 1963 specials that operated between Richmond and Doswell.

111

E8A No. 1005 and its huge 21-car Santa Claus Special ready to depart Doswell in 1967 returning to Broad Street Station

Santa and the Snow Queen wave to children as the Santa Claus Special arrives at Ashland in 1962. RF&P gathered inestimable good-will among the public by operating these trains, and certainly achieved another goal of attracting young people to passenger trains and introducing them to this means of travel.

Car ONE Football Specials

When the RF&P operation of special trains ended in 1971 with the assumption by Amtrak of the operation of intercity passenger train service, the company relinquished its block of almost 600 season tickets to the Washington Redskins football games. The RF&P did retain 12 season tickets and for a number of years, the company operated Football Specials to entertain clients and to take company guests to Washington for the Redskins home football games. The clients and guests included the railroad's shippers, State and local legislators and officials, the company's Board of Directors, officers and officials.

Transportation was provided in the railroad's Business Car, known on the RF&P simply as Car *ONE*. This car was built in 1919 by the American Car and Foundry Company and was originally known as *Berwick.* It was acquired by RF&P from AC&F for $13,023.75 in 1936. Renamed "ONE," it was placed in service on RF&P on October 23, 1936.

The car was of all-steel construction, weighed 190,200 pounds and measured 82 feet, 4.5 inches in length. It contained an observation room, four bedrooms, a kitchen and a dining room. Originally the car had an ice-activated air-conditioning system which was replaced in 1947 with an electric one. Car *ONE* was extensively renovated over a two-year period beginning in 1981.

Even so, it had received few modifications to its original construction and decor over the years and was a fine example of a vintage railroad private car. Although not as opulent as some of the business cars used on much larger railroads, the *ONE* was well-appointed and it was lovingly maintained by the RF&P.

Football trips were run as special trains and, after 1982, Car *ONE* was accompanied by a kitchen car that had been converted from an old RF&P coach. The locomotive assigned to power the Special was always spotlessly clean.

In addition to the football trips, Car *ONE* could also be seen coupled to the rear of Amtrak passenger trains that operated over the RF&P between Richmond and Washington. On such occasions, the car was being utilized by the RF&P's President or other company officials to make inspection and/or business trips over the railroad.

RF&P's Business Car *ONE* on the private car track at Broad Street Station. The *ONE* was built in 1919 by American Car & Foundry Company and purchased by RF&P in 1936.

(both) William E. Griffin Coll.

These football fans are leaving Broad Street Station to board one of the RF&P's specials to travel to Washington for a Redskins home game in 1962.

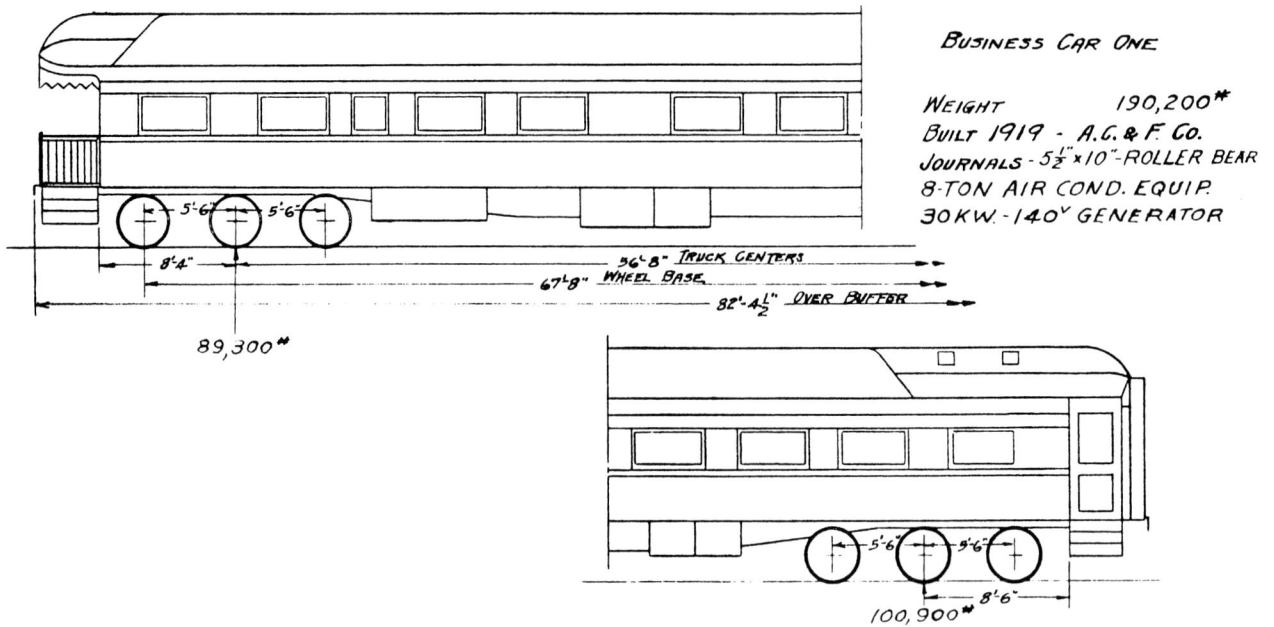

BUSINESS CAR ONE

WEIGHT   190,200#
BUILT 1919 - A.C.& F. CO.
JOURNALS - 5½" x 10" - ROLLER BEAR
8-TON AIR COND. EQUIP.
30KW. - 140V GENERATOR

56'-8" TRUCK CENTERS
67'-8" WHEEL BASE
82'-4½" OVER BUFFER

89,300#

5'-6"   5'-6"
8'-4"

5'-6"   5'-6"
8'-6"
100,900#

RF&P official mechanical diagram showing the elevations of Business Car *ONE*. This car was typical of railroad business cars, but unusual in that it was the only one on the roster. Many larger lines had cars built to their specifications, but just as often purchased them second hand as did RF&P in this case.

RF&P's Football Special discharges its passengers at Alexandria on the December 6, 1981 trip. The Chessie System diesel was required because it was equipped with a steam generator to operate the car's heating equipment.

GP40-2 No. 141 heads north through Fredericksburg with an RF&P Football Special. The locomotive will have no trouble handling its tiny two-car train, which consists of a power car equipped with steam and electric generating equipment and Business Car *ONE*.

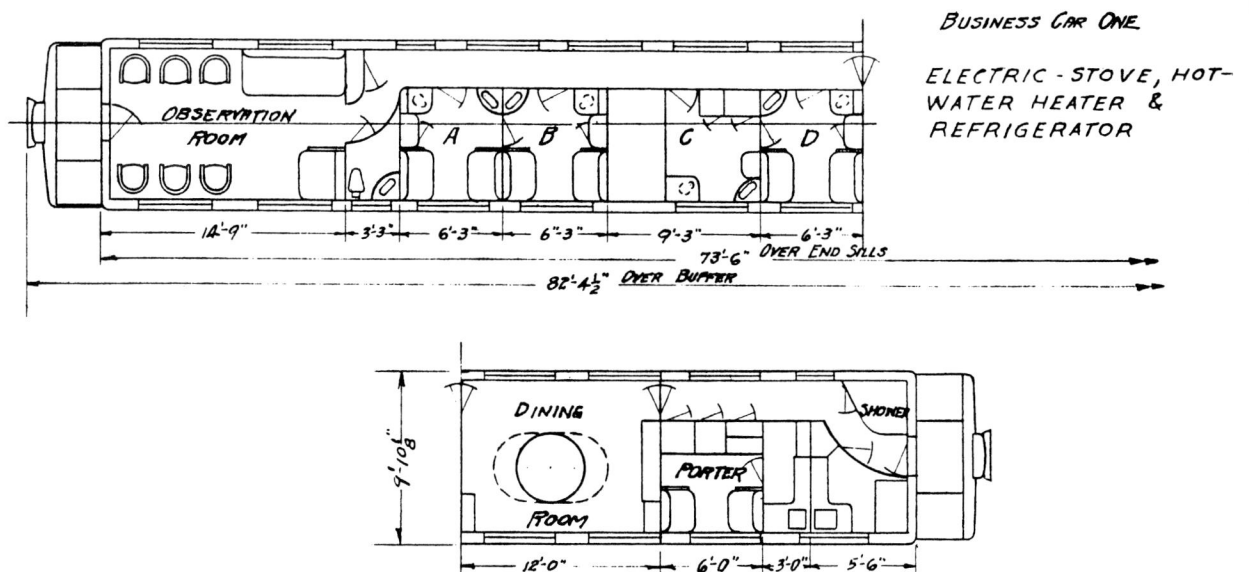

The other part of the official mechanical diagram of *ONE* shows its floorplan, including a spacious observation area, four bedrooms, dining room and galley with steward's quarters.

40 FAST FREIGHTS DAILY between Potomac Yard and Richmond!

CARRYING on its urgent wartime assignment, in close cooperation with connections North and South, and with much appreciated aid from shippers, the R. F. & P. is handling *more* freight *faster* than ever before through Potomac Yard and Richmond.

The expenditure of $4,000,000 for new road locomotives, new diesel-electric switching engines and additional yard trackage has facilitated the task of moving expeditiously over this vital connecting link wartime tonnage just three times the volume of pre-war 1940 traffic. Fast and frequent service between terminals keeps the yards clear and the freight moving.

JOHN B. MORDECAI, Traffic Manager
RICHMOND, VIRGINIA

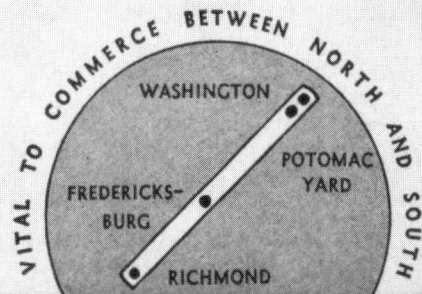

VITAL TO COMMERCE BETWEEN NORTH AND SOUTH

WASHINGTON
FREDERICKS-BURG
POTOMAC YARD
RICHMOND

RICHMOND, FREDERICKSBURG AND POTOMAC RAILROAD

The July 24, 1943 issue of *Traffic World* magazine carried this RF&P ad, proclaiming the road's ability to cope with recordbreaking war-time traffic.

Chapter 6

Freight Service

During the early years of the RF&P's corporate existence, the Company derived very little of its gross revenues from the transportation of goods and commodities. Freight shipments moved to river landings on wagons drawn by teams of oxen, horses or mules and were routed via water between the various coastal ports on the Atlantic Seaboard. The RF&P's freight revenues were secured primarily from the handling of local service.

This situation changed in the years following the Civil War as the little ante bellum railroads were tied together in a national system. Strategically located on the principal route over which commerce between North and South would flow, the RF&P's share of through freight traffic increased dramatically.

In 1870, when the RF&P was still operating to the steam boat landing at Aquia Creek, the Company transported only 8,999 tons of through freight producing revenues of $8,398. In 1880, only eight years after the all-rail route was established at Quantico, through freight revenues exceeded local freight revenues for the first time in the Company's history. By the year 1886, the RF&P was transporting 186,398 tons of through freight producing revenues of $130,537.

In 1888, the RF&P became an important link in a new through freight service—the "Atlantic Coast Dispatch"—which was established by William T. Walters' Atlantic Coast Line Railroad to provide fast rail movement of fresh fruits and vegetables from the South to the Northern markets. It was the beginning of what would become a major source of through freight tonnage for the RF&P.

Strawberries, melons and vegetables from the Carolinas and vegetables and citrus fruits from the winter gardens of Florida moved over both the SAL and ACL to the Eastern markets via the RF&P during the months of winter and early spring. Special ventilated and insulated box cars were built for the service. Later, refrigerated cars were introduced and whole train loads of perishables were handled in high speed service. During the steam era, the speed limit of RF&P freight trains was 45 miles per hour (raised to 50 miles per hour after World War II) and a four hour schedule was advertised between Acca Yard and Potomac Yard.

The RF&P's first separate record of northbound perishable shipments was reported in June, 1892 with 6,717 cars handled during the previous 12-month period. Soon the demand for perishable cars was so great that the railroads handling this business organized the Fruit Growers Express Company in 1920 to supply refrigerated and ventilated cars for the service. These cars were leased to the western railroads during the summer and fall seasons. The peak of the RF&P's perishable business was reached in 1931 when it handled 85,964 car loads of fruits and vegetables.

In the 1890's, each year brought a new record for freight traffic handled and in 1900 revenue from freight trains exceeded that derived from passenger trains for the first time in the RF&P's history. During this period the Company's physical plant was constantly upgraded to accommodate the ever increasing business. The entire railroad was double tracked between the years 1902 and 1907. In 1906 the new Potomac Yard became the northern freight terminal for the newly established Richmond-Washington Line.

Potomac Yard included tracks for the receipt and dispatch of northbound and southbound trains, northbound and southbound classification facilities operated by gravity (humps), an engine terminal, facilities for making running repairs to locomotives and freight cars, pens for feeding and resting live stock in transit, icing facilities for perishable freight and tracks upon which fruits and vegetables could be held

A 400-series 4-6-2 rolls a northbound perishable train north of Ashland in the 1930s. Traffic in perishable agricultural products bound from the South to the Northeastern US has always accounted for considerable traffic over the RF&P. This appears to be a solid train of wooden icecooled refrigerator cars, typical of the era.

William E. Griffin Coll.

for reconsignment to markets.

Often perishable traffic was billed from the South to Potomac Yard with the privilege of reconsignment to a point beyond for the purpose of controlling or meeting the various produce markets. In fact, for many years Potomac Yard was claimed by perishable produce dealers as the most important distribution point in the eastern section of the country.

Until 1934, Potomac Yard also contained extensive facilities for transferring less than carload freight (LCL) from car to car in the interchange of such traffic among the several tenant lines. Until 1926, it also provided shop tracks to the Fruit Growers Express.

At Potomac Yard, commerce primarily from the north and south was sorted, made up into trains, and sent on to its final destination. From the north, the Pennsylvania and B&O sent their trains. From the south, came the trains of the RF&P (handling the traffic of the SAL and ACL), the C&O and the Southern. Daily, thousands of freight cars were shoved atop the north and southbound humps and then were propelled by their weight, a gently descending grade, and the force of gravity into the proper tracks for assembly into outbound trains.

For many years the most efficient method for slowing a car as it descended the hump was to have a rider put his back to the car's brake wheel. Car riders were used on the northbound hump until the late 1930's and on the southbound until November of 1945. As the yard modernized, the humps were equipped with automatic route selectors which routed the cars' movement to the desired track and automatic and semi-automatic car retarders controlled the speed of the cars during their transit from the apex of the hump into the classification tracks.

Throughout its history, the RF&P was fortunate to have a highly diversified freight traffic that safeguarded its revenues from the abnormal conditions affecting any particular commodity or industry.

The Company's business was reduced alarmingly during the years of the Great Depression, but it not only remained solvent - it was also able to pay its guaranteed dividend obligations to its stockholders each year.

While the Company's freight traffic was depressed during the 1930's, tonnage surged to record levels during the decade of the 1940's as the RF&P helped the nation go to war. Beginning late in 1941, the withdrawal of all Atlantic coastal steamship service account the threat of German submarines, gave the railroads - and particularly the RF&P - much of the freight that had moved by water. In addition, the great military camps of World War I had to be rebuilt or enlarged, and many new centers were established to accommodate the highly mechanized nature of the modern warfare. This gigantic construction program, which began in late 1941 and continued throughout the war, produced substantial new freight traffic for the railroads. Due to its unique location, the volume of wartime freight and passenger traffic on the RF&P increased over normal figures to a much greater extent than on any other Class I American railroad.

In 1942, the tons of revenue freight handled by the RF&P increased 78% over that handled in 1941. The Company operated 15,683 freight trains during the year.

The year 1943 shattered all previous records. The RF&P handled 14 million tons of revenue freight in 16,616 freight trains. That exceeded the entire tonnage handled in the depression years of 1933 and 1934 combined. The Company operated an average of 103 trains per day, or one every 14 minutes, with the freight peaking on November 1 when 1,281,240 tons were hauled in 47,759 freight cars.

At Potomac Yard, the loaded and empty cars cleared through the yard in 1943 increased 96% over that handled in pre-war 1940. The peak day in the history of Potomac Yard occurred in 1944 when 2,724 northbound cars were classified on a single day in January. On this day a total of 1,107 cars were classified over the northbound hump during a single 8-hour shift. To relieve congestion at Washington Terminal, troop trains were also routed through Potomac Yard from the Spring of 1943 until April 1, 1947.

In the post-war era the railroad's freight business suffered as barges, trucks and pipelines reclaimed much of the profitable traffic. The railroads' share of intercity freight traffic declined from 68% to 44% between 1944 and 1960. To stem the decline in their freight business, railroads inaugurated new services in the form of "Piggyback"—trailer-on-flat car (TOFC) service, operation of unit trains, and the con-

D. Wallace Johnson

4-8-4 No. 553, *General J. E. B. Stuart*, passes GN Tower (Greendale) arriving Richmond on July 7, 1950, with a southbound freight train that seems to be mainly hopper cars.

struction of larger freight cars built to shipper specifications. The RF&P was in the forefront of the innovative new services.

The RF&P inaugurated its first TOFC service by participating in through "piggyback" movements between Jacksonville, Florida and Potomac Yard. The first "piggyback" cars handled through Acca Yard arrived on the head end of ACL Train No. 112 on the morning of June 3, 1959. The RF&P handled 272 such loads during that first year of through TOFC service.

Another milestone in the RF&P's "Piggyback" service was reached on the afternoon of January 8, 1961 when the first solid TOFC train was handled over the line. This solid "piggyback" train, consisting of 39 TTX flat cars loaded with 76 new aluminum trailers filled with perishables, was delivered to Acca Yard by the ACL at 12:58 p.m. and thirteen minutes later it was on its way to Potomac Yard with an RF&P caboose and three RF&P F-7 diesels. The first solid "piggyback" train from the SAL was received by the RF&P at Acca Yard on January 25, 1961.

"Piggyback" service quickly became one of the brightest aspects of the RF&P's freight business. In the early 1960's, most of the TOFC traffic was handled in regular through freight service, but special solid TOFC trains were also operated with an average consist of 34 cars each. These trains were expedited

through Acca Yard in from eleven to about twenty minutes and made the run to Potomac Yard in less than two hours.

Thereafter, TOFC service was substantially expanded in cooperation with the RF&P's northern and southern connections. "Piggyback" loading and unloading facilities were constructed at Potomac Yard in 1959 and at Acca Yard the following year. At that time, the loading and unloading was done "circus style" - attaching the truck trailer and using a ramp to either back the trailer on the flat car or pull it off. In 1970 the Potomac Yard facility was expanded to include two open-ended tracks of increased capacity.

The Company also purchased its first "Piggy Packers", powerful rubber-tired, off-rail vehicles that operated like forklifts to load and unload trailers from the flat cars.

By the 1980's, TOFC represented thirty-six percent of the RF&P's total revenue carloads and solid "piggyback" trains with a maximum authorized speed of 60 miles per hour were operated in conjunction with the connecting lines.

In 1964 the RF&P acquired the Dahlgren Railroad line that had been put up for sale as surplus property by the Federal Government. This line, built during World War II as a means of transporting guns manufactured at the Naval Weapons Plant in Washington, D.C. to the Dahlgren Naval Weapons Testing Station, connected with the RF&P main line just north of Fredericksburg at Dahlgren Junction in Stafford County. The RF&P purchased the entire 28-mile line with the intention of promoting industrial development on the branch.

The first industry, the Republic Lumber Company, located on the line late in 1964 and, four years later, the RF&P rehabilitated and reopened eleven miles of the line to serve Solite Corporation, a sand and gravel industry that opened a plant on the branch at Sealston, on the Rappahannock River. The formal inauguration of commercial service on the eleven miles of rehabilitated track was marked with the placement on April 24, 1969, of 21 hopper cars for loading at the Solite plant. In 1973, the RF&P established a road switcher, known as the "Sealston Switcher", to handle the sand and gravel business between Sealston and Waterloo, at the north end of Potomac Yard.

The RF&P's freight business was forever changed in 1967 when its two competing southern connections - the SAL and ACL - merged to form the Seaboard Coast Line Railroad. For many years, the ACL had conducted its freight interchange with the RF&P at Acca Yard.

Hermitage Yard was the northernmost termi-

Local freight at Doswell on June 22, 1947 with Pacific No. 308 for power. Doswell was an interchange point with the C&O's Piedmont Subdivision which ran from Charlottesville to Richmond.

C. A. Brown

nal of the SAL and freight shipments arriving in Richmond from the SAL for movement beyond over the RF&P had to go to Hermitage Yard and then be switched to the RF&P at Acca.

Pursuant to an agreement reached with the SCL, effective January 1, 1970, the SCL closed Hermitage Yard and moved the operations formerly performed there to the RF&P's Acca Yard. To accommodate the additional work to be performed at Acca Yard, the facilities at the yard and at the RF&P's Bryan Park Terminal were expanded and upgraded.

One of the expected benefits of this consolidated operation was the faster scheduling of through trains. This benefit was quickly realized on June 9, 1970 with the inauguration of the Tropicana unit "Juice Trains". Tropicana Products, a citrus fruit company of Bradenton, Florida had purchased 150 snow-white painted new refrigerated boxcars (later repainted orange) equipped with shock-absorbing devices from the Fruit Growers Express Company and built a distribution center at Kearny, New Jersey. Tropicana required the operation of a 60-car unit train of its refrigerated boxcars to move its products from Florida to market in the northeast at least once every eight days. The SCL, RF&P and Penn Central (later Conrail) shared about $2 to $4 million in annual revenue from the unit juice train that ran from Bradenton to Kearny in 36 hours with stops only for locomotive and crew changes. Empties were returned daily to Bradenton for reloading at the headend of a merchandise freight train.

In 1977 the RF&P sold approximately 500 acres of its subsidiary Richmond Land Company's Bear Island property in Hanover County, some twenty miles north of Richmond, to the Bear Island Paper Company. To enable the RF&P to serve this Company's new $100 million newsprint mill, the RF&P worked out a trackage rights arrangement with the C&O Railway granting to the RF&P the right to use the C&O's main line track between Doswell and the Bear Island tract, a distance of 4.8 miles. Thereafter, traffic was handled to and from the paper company by the RF&P's south

end local freight.

Also during the late-1970's, the Bi-Modal Corporation was attempted to develop the "RoadRailer", a highway/rail trailer equipped with a dual set of wheels, one with rubber tires and the other steel-flanged, to permit operation on railroad tracks without the conventional loading on a railroad flat car. Commencing late in 1979, RoadRailer units began test runs in commercial service on the RF&P and SCL between Potomac Yard and Jacksonville, Florida. This test phase of solid RoadRailer trains, starting with 15 trailers and increasing to 50 units, ran through early 1981. While the RoadRailers were subsequently operated by both Norfolk Southern and CSX Transportation, they were unable to replace the conventional piggybacking service on the RF&P/SCL route.

Beginning in 1982, the RF&P participated with the Chessie and Seaboard units of CSX Transportation in a joint effort to recapture from trucks a share of the Florida fresh fruit and vegetable traffic moving to the East. In November of that year, a new all-perishable piggyback train, which had been named the "Orange Blossom Special", commenced operation between Orlando, Florida and Wilmington, Delaware transporting gleaming new forty-five foot refrigerated highway trailers on flat cars. At Wilmington the trailers were transferred to the highway and moved via Chessie Motor Express to consumer markets in the Northeast.

In the final years of its corporate existence, the RF&P's Potomac Yard was downsized and eventually closed as Norfolk Southern and Conrail diverted the interchange of their north/south traffic to Hagerstown and CSX Transportation implemented new run-through train service, thus decreasing the traffic moving through Potomac Yard and eliminating the requirement for car-by-car classification. However, to the end, the RF&P continued to provide superior service to its customers with a direct, high-capacity, high-speed freight service over a superbly maintained physical plant of double-track railroad equipped with an automatic block signal system and a total CTC (Centralized

Traffic Control) system.

During this period the RF&P operated six pairs of through freight trains daily, northbound unit Tropicana "Juice Trains" once every five or six days, and extra unit coal trains as required to Virginia Power's Possum Point power station located just north of Quantico. It operated a south end local freight/road switcher assignment five days per week making a daylight roundtrip between Acca Yard and Fredericksburg, or some other intermediate point. It also operated a north end local freight/road switcher making an overnight roundtrip between "RO"

(Potomac Yard) and Fredericksburg. The Sealston Switcher sand and gravel train operated three days a week, or on an as needed basis. The assignment went on duty at Potomac Yard in the late afternoon and made an overnight run between Waterloo and Sealston and return, often pushing the Hours of Service Law on its return trip to Potomac Yard.

The maximum authorized speed of solid piggyback trains over the RF&P was 60 miles per hour, mixed freight trains 55 miles per hour, and trains handling 30 or more cars in a block of coal, phosphate rock and sand and gravel were restricted to 45 miles per hour.

Arriving Richmond on the inside track is a TOFC train led by two of RF&P's new GP35s, Nos. 113 and 114, while another trailer train moves north. RF&P was an early leader in TOFC traffic, again because of its bridge-line status that put it in the middle of major merchandise routes.

(both) William E. Griffin Coll.

The auto carriers loaded on the TOFC flats in this photo, each carrying four new Ford Falcons, look hopelessly archaic. ALCO S-2 switcher No. 65 shoves the 12 loads at Potomac Yard in October 1960.

121

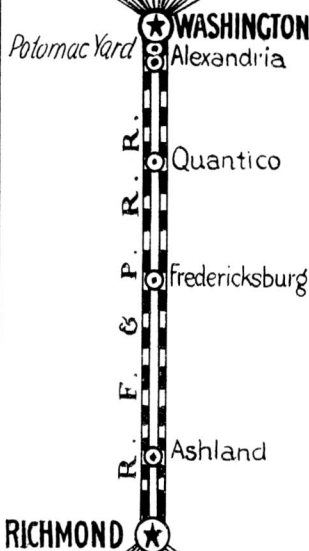

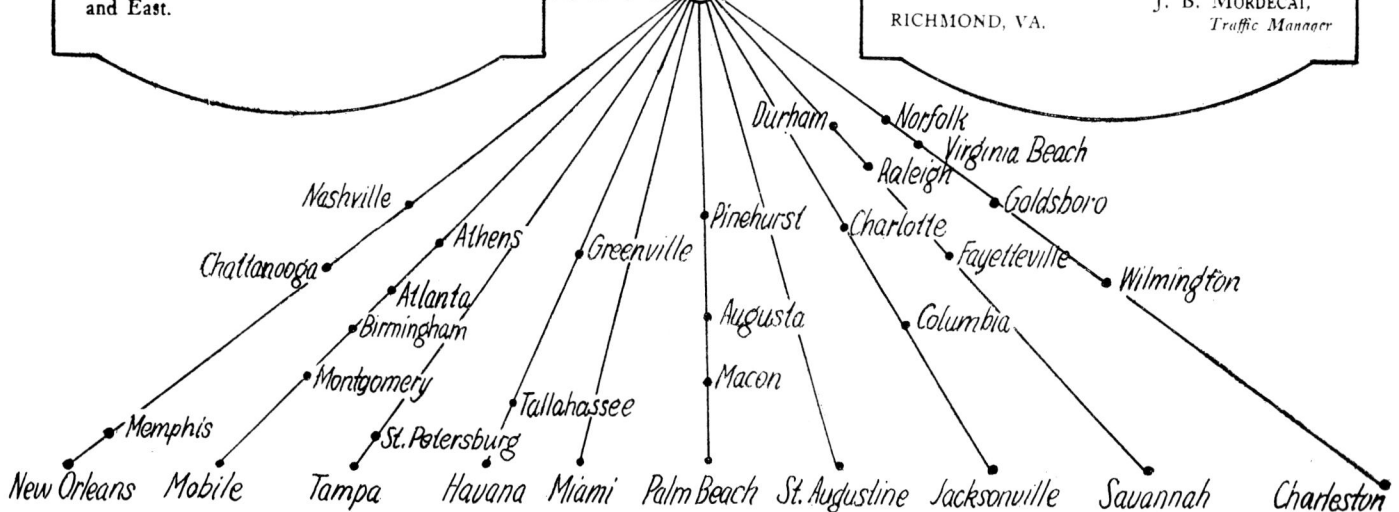

Northern terminal of the RF&P was Potomac Yard, which included an area of 520 acres. It was six miles long, 2,000 feet wide, and contained 136 miles of track. This aerial view was taken in 1963. Here RF&P connected and interchanged traffic with B&O, C&O, Southern, and Pennsylvania. The yard is situated in Alexandria, just across the Potomac from Washington, and since its virtual abandonment in recent years, has become the target for various commercial development projects on this obviously very valuable land.

123

Looking south at Potomac Yard with the northbound receiving yard to the left and southbound classification yard to the right. In the distance the tracks of the Washington & Old Dominion Railroad cross the yard. A set of three C&O GP7s are seen in the left foreground.

(both) William E. Griffin Coll.

Looking north over the shoulder of the car retarder operator gives a view of the northbound classification yard and the Crystal City complex in the distance. Potomac Yard, like a funnel, routed traffic coming to and from the great cities of the Northeast and the South. Because it was so busy during World War II, the N&W's inland route up the Shenandoah Valley into Hagerstown and thence via PRR to the eastern cities was greatly developed.

(Right) Looking across the northbound classification yard toward the coaling station and southbound hump in this steam-era view of Potomac Yard. The yard is populated with a wide variety of wooden and steel box cars of the standard 40-foot variety, as well as a few scattered tank cars and gondolas in this era before the specialty railroad vehicle.

(Below) Potomac Yard car riders await their turn on the northbound hump to ride a cut of cars from the apex of the hump into one of the class tracks in an early view. In later days automatic car-retarders controlled the speed of cars crossing the hump and eliminated this job.

(both) William E. Griffin Coll.

Two tracks in the northbound receiving yard could accommodate 32 cars for re-icing. The Potomac Yard ice house had a capacity of 130 tons per day with a storage capacity of 12,000 tons. Potomac Yard was discontinued as a regular re-icing station in August 1967, the use of its facility having diminished with the virtual disappearance of ice bunker type refrigerator cars by that date. In this photo workers are placing block ice in the bunkers of refrigerator cars undoubtedly on their way from the farms of the South to the cities of the Northeast.

William E. Griffin Coll.

(Right) SW-1500 switcher No. 8 and slug "C" in hump service at Potomac Yard in the 1960s.

(Below) Pacific No. 326 brings a train of refrigerator cars into Alexandria in 1943, during the height of war-time traffic.

William E. Griffin

Homer R. Hill

This aerial view shows RF&P's Acca Yard and Bryan Park Terminal in Richmond on July 22, 1965. The modern shop building is in the upper left. This building is now used as a system maintenance-of-way equipment repair shop by CSX Transportation since its use as a diesel shop was eliminated when CSXT absorbed RF&P.

The *General Robert E. Lee*, No. 551, departs with its train from the southbound classification yard at Potomac Yard in 1947 en route to Richmond with a merchandise train.

H. H. Harwood, Jr.

SW-1500 No. 91 performs switching duties with a cut of RF&P boxcars at Richmond with the Acca Transportation Center in the background.

Pacific No. 403 at Franconia with a perishable train in 1947. Note the auxiliary tender and the ventilated box car ahead of the train of refrigerated cars. By this date a few old wooden ventilator cars could still be seen, but they had become scarce. They had vents in the ends and sides that allowed air to flow through the car and naturally cool the contents.

Pacific No. 405 storms through Ashland with a merchandise freight on March 3, 1946.

With Atlantic coast steamship service suspended because of the threat of German submarines, RF&P Berkshire No. 575 is handling a cut of tank cars southbound past Laurel en route to Acca Yard in a wartime photograph. Much of the oil from the Southwestern U. S. had to be sent to the East and North via rail rather than through the Gulf of Mexico and up the coast on ships, so during the war big tank car trains were often seen, After the war pipelines were soon completed or enlarged and took over much of the traffic as well as the return to coastal shipping.

Anthony Dementi photo, W. E. Griffin Coll.

William E. Griffin Coll.

F7A No. 1105 and two B-units speed a merchandise train north of Ashland. Note the well-kept roadway, ballast in line, ditch and bank free of brush.

A matched set of A-B-A F7s, led by No. 1104, speed a perishable train over RF&P's well-maintained right of way just north of Richmond.

RF&P issued this time-freight schedule in 1957 for the convenience of its customers. The map, similar to one that the road had used in advertising for many years, showed graphically the bridge-line nature of RF&P, with its wide range of connections north and south.

IF YOUR CARLOAD SHIPMENT LEAVES:			IT WILL ARRIVE POTOMAC YARD AT:	See Connection From Potomac Yard
Greenville, N. J. (From NYNH&H & L. I. RR)	via PRR	10:30AM—Tue.	8:15PM—Tue.	#3—#4
Greenville, N. J.: (From NYNH&H RR)	via PRR	6:30PM—Tue.	3:30AM—Wed.	#3—#4
Cumberland, Md.: (From Points West)	via B&O	1:30AM—Tue.	3:30PM—Tue.	#1—#2
		12:01PM—Tue.	10:30PM—Tue.	#3—#4
Harrisburg, Pa.: (From Points West)	via PRR	3:45AM—Tue.	12:15PM—Tue.	#1—#2
		9:30AM—Tue.	5:15PM—Tue.	#3—#4
		5:15PM—Tue.	12:01AM—Wed.	#3—#4
		9:00PM—Tue.	4:30AM—Wed.	#4—#5
New York & Jersey City:	via PRR	9:30PM—Tue.	4:50AM—Wed.	#3—#4
	via B&O	9:00AM—Tue.	9:45PM—Tue.	#3—#4
		8:30PM—Tue.	5:45AM—Wed.	#3—#4
Trenton, N. J.:	via PRR	3:30AM—Tue.	11:00PM—Tue.	#3—#4
Camden, N. J.: (& From PRSL Conn.)	via PRR	6:00AM—Tue.	11:00PM—Tue.	#3—#4
Phillipsburg, N. J.: (& From LV Conn.)	via PRR	6:30AM—Tue.	11:00PM—Tue.	#3—#4
Philadelphia, Pa.:	via PRR	5:00AM—Tue.	1:00PM—Tue.	#1—#2
		7:15AM—Tue.	11:00PM—Tue.	#3—#4
		1:15PM—Tue.	9:00PM—Tue.	#3—#4
		10:00PM—Tue.	3:30AM—Wed.	#3—#4
	via B&O	1:30AM—Wed.	5:45AM—Wed.	#3—#4
		8:15AM—Tue.	4:30PM—Tue.	#3—#4
		2:45PM—Tue.	9:45PM—Tue.	#3—#4
Baltimore, Md.:	via PRR	7:45PM—Tue.	10:40PM—Tue.	#3—#4
	via B&O	7:00PM—Tue.	9:45PM—Tue.	#3—#4

LEAVE POTOMAC YARD VIA RF&P:	#1	#2	#3	#4	#5
ARRIVE RICHMOND, VA.:	8:00PM—Tue.	8:00PM—Tue.	8:00AM—Wed.	10:00AM—Wed.	8:00PM—Wed.
	11:00PM—Tue.	11:00PM—Tue.	11:00AM—Wed.	1:00PM—Wed.	11:00PM—Wed.
	SAL & Conn.	ACL & Conn.	SAL & Conn.	ACL & Conn.	SAL & Conn.
LEAVE RICHMOND, VA.: ARRIVING:	9:15AM—Wed.	2:00AM—Wed.	11:45AM—Wed.	2:30PM—Wed.	9:15AM—Thu.
Hamlet, N. C.	5:00PM—Wed.		6:00PM—Wed.		5:00PM—Thu.
So. Rocky Mount, N. C.		5:00AM—Wed.		5:00PM—Wed.	
Florence, S. C.		11:00AM—Wed.		8:30PM—Wed.	
Charlotte, N. C.	4:00AM—Thu.		4:00AM—Thu.		4:00AM—Fri.
Wilmington, N. C.	1:00AM—Fri.	1:15AM—Thu.	1:00AM—Fri.	1:15AM—Thu.	1:00AM—Sat.
Charleston, S. C.	8:00AM—Thu.	1:30AM—Thu.	8:00AM—Thu.	1:30AM—Thu.	8:00AM—Fri.
Columbia, S. C.	6:00AM—Thu.	12:40AM—Thu.	6:00AM—Thu.	12:40AM—Thu.	6:00AM—Fri.
Augusta, Ga.		1:30AM—Thu.		1:30AM—Thu.	
Savannah, Ga.	2:40AM—Thu.	5:00PM—Wed.	2:40AM—Thu.	1:30AM—Thu.	2:40AM—Fri.
Waycross, Ga.		1:30AM—Thu.		5:45AM—Thu.	
Jacksonville, Fla.	6:00AM—Thu.	12:30AM—Thu.	6:00AM—Thu.	5:45AM—Thu.	6:00AM—Fri.
Tampa, Fla.	9:00PM—Thu.	5:00PM—Thu.	9:00PM—Thu.	5:00PM—Thu.	9:00PM—Fri.
Orlando, Fla.	10:30AM—Fri.	2:10PM—Thu.	10:30AM—Fri.	2:10PM—Thu.	10:30AM—Sat.
W. Palm Beach, Fla.	9:30PM—Fri.	9:15PM—Thu.	9:30PM—Fri.	9:15PM—Thu.	9:30PM—Fri.
Atlanta, Ga.	3:30AM—Thu.	10:40PM—Thu.	3:30AM—Thu.	10:40PM—Thu.	3:30AM—Fri.
" (Via GA)		9:00AM—Thu.		9:00AM—Thu.	
Miami, Fla.	1:30AM—Fri.		1:30AM—Fri.		1:30AM—Sat.
" (Via FEC)		11:30PM—Thu.		11:30PM—Thu.	
Birmingham, Ala.	8:00AM—Thu.	2:20AM—Fri.	8:00AM—Thu.	2:20AM—Fri.	8:00AM—Fri.
Montgomery, Ala.	8:00PM—Fri.	8:30PM—Thu.	8:00PM—Fri.	8:30PM—Thu.	8:00PM—Sat.
" (Via WOFA)		6:50PM—Thu.		6:50PM—Thu.	

Schedules herein contained, including those of connecting railroads, indicate the service that may be expected but not guaranteed. This Company reserves the privileges to alter or vary therefrom without notice to the public. The time of arrival or departure represents standard time.

This southbound time freight schedule is from the inside of the timetable shown on the previous page. It shows five regularly scheduled freights leaving Potomac Yard for Richmond, beginning at 8:00 a.m. and finishing at 8:00 p.m. Since much of the business came from the Northeast, the approximate transit times are given from various cities on the PRR, B&O, New Haven and Lehigh Valley lines. The destination cities in the South also cover RF&P's major connections. A car leaving New York at 9:30 a.m. on Tuesday would usually arrive Potomac Yard 4:50 a. m. Wednesday, and leave on No. 3 or 4, getting to Jacksonville, for example, at 6:00 a.m. on Thursday. This was good, fast service.

The first "piggyback" shipment of new auto-mobiles (Ford Falcons) moves over the RF&P on July 2, 1960. The autos are loaded on highway trailers, 4 each, for immediate off-loading and transportation to dealerships.

Two TOFC trains arrive in Richmond in this 1967 view taken from the Dumbarton Road overpass. On the far track GP7 No. 101 splices F7 1109 and another F7, while two GP35s had charge of the train in the left distance.

All three of RF&P's FP7s, led by No. 1203, plus GP7 No. 102, arrive at Potomac Yard with a northbound freight in July 1965. The George Washington National Masonic Memorial, built in the shape of the ancient lighthouse of Pharos at Alexandria Egypt, looms in the mist in the background, a sure landmark of railroading in Alexandria.

Snow covers the ground as southbound Atlanta TOFC Train No. 227 with GP35 No. 131 and GP40-2 No. 144 passes through the neat RF&P layout at Doswell. The railroad in the bottom of the photo is the C&O. This scene is so reminiscent of a model railroad that one has to look at it twice to be sure that it's an actual aerial photo!

(both) William E. Griffin Coll.

GP7 No. 104 leads three GP40s and a northbound merchandise freight train around the curve at Summit.

William E. Griffin

GP40 No. 127 splits the signals at Elmont with southbound Train No. 109 in this July 1980 photo.

Train No. 109 southbound across the Neabsco Creek Bridge in September of 1981 is powered by GP40 No. 127, GP35 Nos. 134 and 132.

Certainly one of the more famous modern operations on the RF&P is the Tropicana "Orange Juice Train", seen here getting under way from Richmond on its northbound run. The train carries Florida orange Juice to the Northeast on regularly scheduled trips, the white cars making an attractive sight.

The southbound "Orange Blossom Special," the all-perishable TOFC train passes the Jefferson Memorial in Washington in February 1985, while on Conrail tracks headed south to the RF&P. GP40-2 No. 145 is in the lead because of the cab signal/train control operation of RF&P.

GP40-2 No. 145 departs the Potomac Yard TOFC facility with a Bi-Modal "RoadRailer" test run over the RF&P in 1980. The Roadrailers are highway trailers with retractable railroad wheels that can be carried by train without having to be set on flat cars.

(Left) RF&P motive power assembled in the Relay Yard at Potomac Yard in 1990. All wear the new RF&P logo on the long and short hoods.

(Below) The southbound "Orange Blossom Special" with RF&P GP35 No. 133 and a consist of Chessie System and Seaboard System diesels passes the northbound Tropicana "Juice Train" just north of Fredericksburg.

Doug Koontz

Conrail/RF&P run-through Train No. R410 crosses the Rappahannock River Bridge at Fredericksburg in January 1992.

Alex M. Mayes

The RF&P south end local freight is shown on C&O tracks crossing the RF&P main line at Doswell in January 1982, en route to the Bear Island Paper Company. Motive power is provided by GP40 No. 126.

(Right) GP40-2 No. 147 rounds the curve and will have no trouble climbing Franconia Hill with a southbound test run of RoadRailers over RF&P in 1980.

Linking NORTH and SOUTH
WASHINGTON
RICHMOND
Richmond Fredericksburg and Potomac Railroad Co.

(Below) GP40 No. 127 is shown at Sealston, shoving a cut of RF&P hoppers for loading at the Solite sand and gravel plant on the Dahlgren Branch in 1969. Although most of RF&P's business has always been through traffic, it has generated some of its own as well.

(both) William E. Griffin Coll.

Gravel is dumped into an RF&P 8000-series hopper at Doswell for outbound shipment. Doswell was always an important station on the RF&P, both from the point of view of its connection with the C&O, and also for incoming and outgoing shipments of merchandise, farm implements, agricultural, forest, and mineral products.

William E. Griffin

Fifty new woodrack cars, the first to be owned by RF&P, were purchased in 1965. Five of the cars are shown while being loaded at the North Doswell pulpwood yard.

(both) William E. Griffin Coll.

A bevy of classic automobiles witness the southbound passage through Ashland of GP7 No. 103 with the RF&P's south end local freight in May 1962.

The RF&P's "RO" Local Freight sets off a string of coal loads at the Possum Point Power Plant in July 1962 as a southbound passenger train heads for Quantico on No. 3 track. The remainder of the local freight, consisting of a hopper, two box cars and a gondola and caboose, sits on No. 2 track.

GP40 No. 121 leads a southbound merchandise train through Woodbridge in 1985, each locomotive in the consist wearing the last RF&P paint scheme with the stylized logo.

RF&P Brakeman C. E. Karns signals to his engineer to bring F7 No. 1103 to a coupling with their train in November 1963.

Brakeman A. S. Bankert (left) and Conductor E. H. Meredith (right) depart the caboose and head for the yard office at Acca Yard after completing their tour of duty on RF&P's south end local freight on May 1, 1962. Their day began with the 10:00 a.m. departure from Acca and ended with return at 6:00 p.m. Northbound their local switched Ashland, Doswell, Ruther Glen, and Milford. Doswell, Ellett and Laurel were switched on the return trip.

This advertisement strikes the familiar tones of RF&P's publicity, the North-South Link, and the vital connection.

Interior of Lightweight cafe-parlor car *Virginia Dare*, built for RF&P's ill-fated *Old Dominion* in 1947. The ceiling was ivory, with tan walls and rose wainscoting. The chairs were upholstered in gray, cardinal red or blue-green. *(William E. Griffin Coll.)*

Chapter 7

RF&P Passenger Train Equipment

Illustrated in this chapter are many of the cars used by RF&P in its passenger service in the heavyweight and lightweight steel car eras from the 1920s through the end of passenger service. RF&P not only had to supply cars for its local service and its own Richmond-Washington trains, but had pool arrangements whereby it supplied a portion of the cars used on the Florida trains operated through over the Pennsylvania Railroad, RF&P, Atlantic Coast Line, Seaboard Air Line, and Florida East Coast Railroads. The line had no lightweight streamlined cars until later World War II, although SAL and ACL's pre-war streamliners operated through over its line. The two rosters below show the RF&P passenger car fleet in 1943 and again in 1954 and are taken from the *Official Railway Equipment Register*.

PASSENGER EQUIPMENT.

A.A.R. Mech. Desig.	KIND.	SERIES OF NUMBERS.	SEATING CAP'CTY	LENGTH OF CAR.	No. of Cars.	A.A.R. Mech. Desig.	KIND.	SERIES OF NUMBERS.	SEATING CAP'CTY	LENGTH OF CAR.	No. of Cars.
MA(e)..	Postal...........	101	....	60 ft. & under 70 ft.	1	PB(e). BX	Coaches........ Box Express. Steel Frame & Underframe	550 to 562	....	70 ft. & over	18
MA(e)..	"	102 to 105		70 ft. & over	4			280 to 288			9
BE(e)..	Baggage & Express....	161 to 178		70 ft. & over	18	PC(e)..	Parlor, Chair, Air Conditioned......	Dolly Madison		70 ft. & over	1
BE(e)..	" "	180 to 191		70 ft. & over	12	DP(e)..	Cafe-Parlor, Air Conditioned.......	Powhatan			1
BE(e)..	" "	153, 160		60 ft.& under 70 ft.	2	DA(e)..	Dining, Air Conditioned.	James			1
BE(e)..	" "	141 to 148		60 ft.& under 70 ft.	6	DA(e)..	" "	Pocahontas			1
CA(e)..	De Luxe Pass. & Bagg., Air Conditioned.....	311, 312		70 ft. & over	2	DA(e)..	" "	Potomac			1
PB(e)..	Coaches..........	431		Under 70 ft.	1	DA(e)..	" "	Quantico			1
PB(e)...	"	441 to 449		70 ft. & over	7	DA(e)..	" "	Rappahannock			1
PB(e)...	" DeLuxe Air Conditioned.	501, 502		70 ft. & over	2	DA(e)..	" "	Fredericksburg			1
PB(e)...	" Air Conditioned	517, 519, 524 530, 532		70 ft. & over	5	DA(e)..	" "	Alexandria			1
PB(e)...	DeLuxe Coaches, Air Conditioned..........	511 to 516 518,520 to 523 525, 526, 528 529, 531, 533 534, 535		70 ft. & over	19	PB(e)..	Motor Rail Trailer....	T11	82	Over 70 ft.	1
						PB(e)..	" " "	T12	100	Over 70 ft.	1
						PV(e)..	Business..........	100			1
						"	"	ONE			1
							Total.........				114

Official Railway Equipment Register, April 1943

PASSENGER EQUIPMENT.

A.A.R. Mech. Desig.	KIND.	SERIES OF NUMBERS.	SEATING CAP'CTY	LENGTH OF CAR.	No. of Cars.	A.A.R. Mech. Desig.	KIND.	SERIES OF NUMBERS.	SEATING CAP'CTY	LENGTH OF CAR.	No. of Cars.
MA(e)..	Postal...........	101	....	60 ft. & under 70 ft.	1	PS(e)...	Sleeping Cars, Lightweight Steel, Air Conditioned.......	Byrd Island	21	85 feet	1
MA(e)..	"	102 to 105		70 ft. & over	8	PS (e)..	" "	Fairfax River	20	85 feet	1
BE(e)..	Baggage & Express....	161 to 178		70 ft. & over	17	PS (e)..	Sleeping Cars, Steel, Air Conditioned....	Clover Bed Clover City Clover Woods	26		3
BE(e)..	" "	180 to 190		70 ft. & over	11	PS (e)..	Sleeping Cars, Steel, Air Conditioned....	Belnord McCutchenville Meadenham	27		3
CSB(e).	Baggage-Dormitory, Air Conditioned....	301		85 feet	1	PS (e)..	Sleeping Cars, Steel, Air Conditioned....	Simoda Lake Mary Lake Oliver	24		3
CA(e)..	De Luxe Pass. & Bagg., Air Conditioned....	311		70 ft. & over	1	DP(e)..	Cafe-Parlor, Air Conditioned..	Powhatan			1
PB(e)..	Coaches, DeLuxe, Air Conditioned.	501, 502		70 ft. & over	2	DA(e)..	Dining, Air Conditioned.	James			1
PB(e)..	DeLuxe Coaches, Air Conditioned..	511 to 527		70 ft. & over	17	DA(e)..	" "	Pocahontas			1
PB(e)..	" "	528 to 535		70 ft. & over	8	DA(e)..	" "	Potomac			1
PB(e)...	Coaches..........	550 to 562		70 ft. & over	11	DA(e)..	" "	Quantico			1
PB(e)...	" DeLuxe, Air Conditioned	801 to 806		70 ft. & over	6	DA(e)..	" "	Rappahannock			1
PB(e)..	" " "	810 to 812		70 ft. & over	3	DA(e)..	" "	Fredericksburg			1
PB(e)..	" " "	840 to 843		70 ft. & over	4	DA(e)..	" "	Alexandria			1
PB(e)..	" " "	850 to 857		70 ft. & over	8	DA(e)..	" Lightweight Steel	Henrico			1
BX.....	Box Express, Stl. Frame & Underframe.	280 to 288			9	PV(e)..	Business, Air Conditioned	100			1
PDS (e)	Sleeping-Bar-Lounge Car, Lightweight Stl.	Colonial Beach	36	85 feet	1	"	" "	ONE			1
PS(e).	Sleeping Cars, Lightweight Steel, Air Conditioned....	King William King George King & Queen	22	85 feet	3		Total.........				135
PS(e)...	" "	Caroline County Chesterfield Essex Hanover County Lancaster Spotsylvania County Stratford County	22	85 feet	7						

Official Railway Equipment Register, April 1954

(Above) RF&P owned five Railway Post Office cars, Nos. 101-105. No. 101, shown here in January 1951, was built by American Car & Foundry in 1912 and was retired December 28, 1967. Some of the first steel cars were RPOs, required by government regulations beginning about 1910. The last RPOs were removed by the Post Office Department in the late 1960s, causing many marginal passenger trains to be discontinued.

(Left) Interior of RPO No. 101 looking from the letter-case end toward the general newspaper and parcel sorting area. The letter cases were where letter-size first-class mail was sorted. The bundles were then thrown onto the center table, where clerks "pitched" them into the proper bags, hung on the metal racks seen to the right.

(Right) Looking to opposite direction gives a better view of the general sorting area where the bags were hung. The overhead bins were used primarily for newspapers. The Railway Mail Service personnel were the highest paid and best trained postal employees. They had to learn complicated "schemes" of dispatch so that they could sort letters for connecting trains and to towns along the way, sometimes at locations where the train didn't stop. The intricate system of RPOs, which reached its height about 1925, provided probably the best overall postal service in history—before or since. These cars also were an important revenue source for the railroads, as the Post Office paid well for carrying them.

(all) William E. Griffin Coll.

POSTAL CAR 105
(All Steel)

Weight 141,400
Electric Lights
Length Inside 70'-8⅜"
Width Inside 9'-0½"
Commonwealth Steel Trucks
Journals 5"x9" Wheels 36" Dia.
Built 1925 by Bethlehem Shipbldg Corp
Lot Nº VT 5004

ELECTRIC REFRIGERATOR—
HOT PLATE

5'-6" 5'-6"
Truck Centers 53'-5¾"
13'-7 9/32"
11'-5 25/32"
9'-10 7/8"
9'-9⅛"
71'-5¾" over end Sheets
19 13/16"
74'-9⅜" over Buffers

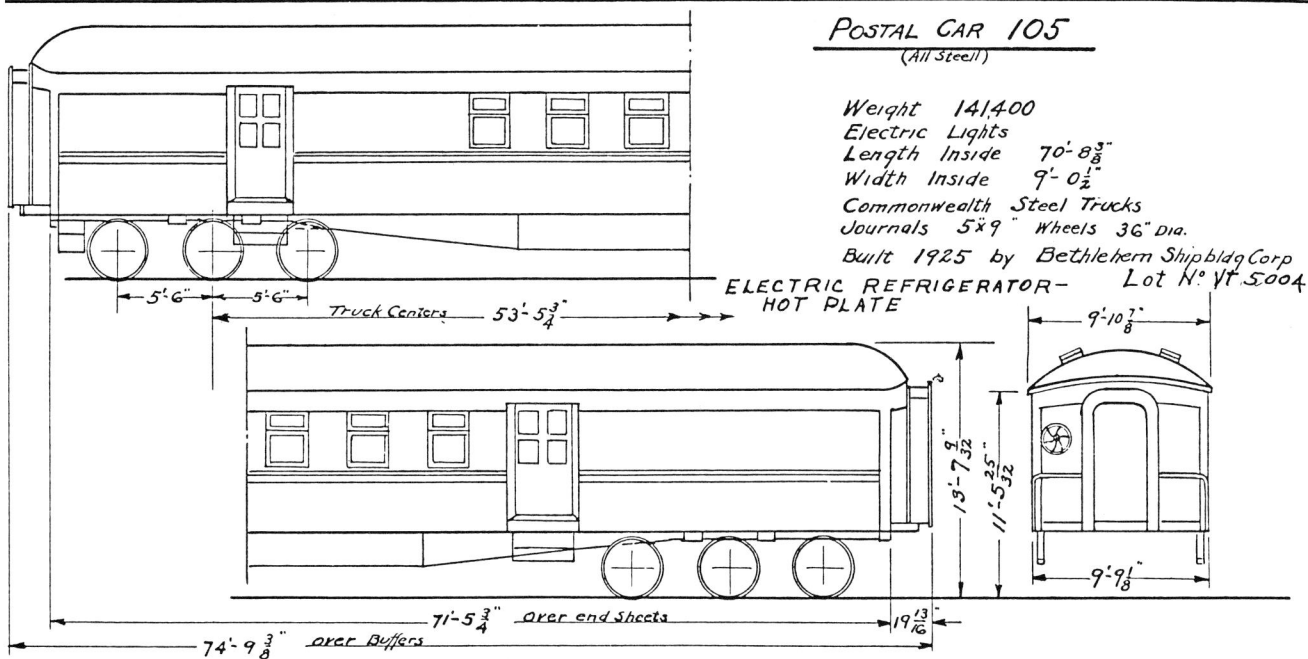

RPO No. 105 was built by Bethlehem Shipbuilding Co. in Wilmington, Delaware in 1925. Like all RPOs it had a catcher arm located at one of the doors so a clerk could extend it at the right moment and catch a bag of mail suspended from a special crane at towns where the train didn't stop. He would, at the same time, kick off a sack destined for the town. Quite a feat of coordination and concentration.

(all) William E. Griffin Coll.

Of course express was an equally important revenue-producer for any railroad. Here RF&P Express car No. 184 is shown new at the American Car & Foundry Co. plant in July 1937. Railway Express Agency contracted, like the Post Office, for the railroads to carry its packages as well as its own "messenger" in the cars to transact business at each station.

Express Car No. 188, built by ACF in May 1940. It is interesting to note that this car was still lettered for the "Richmond-Washington Line" in 1940. It was retired in 1971. Express-type cars were also used for carrying baggage on certain trains when large capacity was needed.

(all) William E. Griffin Coll.

Interior of No. 184 (see page 145) is typical of these cars. The metal poles that are stored in the ceiling were lowered to the floor when needed to provide bracing to stabilize boxes, crates, mail sacks, and luggage that might be carried in the car. The steam heating radiator is behind the screen in the center.

End view of No. 188 with the brake wheel and a grab-iron for the brakeman to hold onto and a stirrup for him to stand on.

Express car No. 160 in service at Dunn, North Carolina, June 2, 1969. As shown in the diagram below this car was built in 1912 as a baggage/mail car, and was converted to full express in 1927. The windows shown in the diagram were subsequently removed as well.

EXPRESS CAR 160
(ALL STEEL)

Capacity 60,000 lbs.

WEIGHT 119140 POUNDS.
ELECTRIC LIGHTS
LENGTH OF CAR INSIDE   60'-1"
WIDTH OF CAR INSIDE   9'-1"
BAGGAGE MAIL CAR 7 ALTD JAN 1927 AS ABOVE
BUILT 1912 BY AMER. CAR & FDY. CO.

COMMONWEALTH STEEL
TRUCKS, 5"x 9" JOURNALS

41'-10" TRUCK CENTERS
60'-10" OVER END SILLS
64'-3¾" OVER BUFFERS

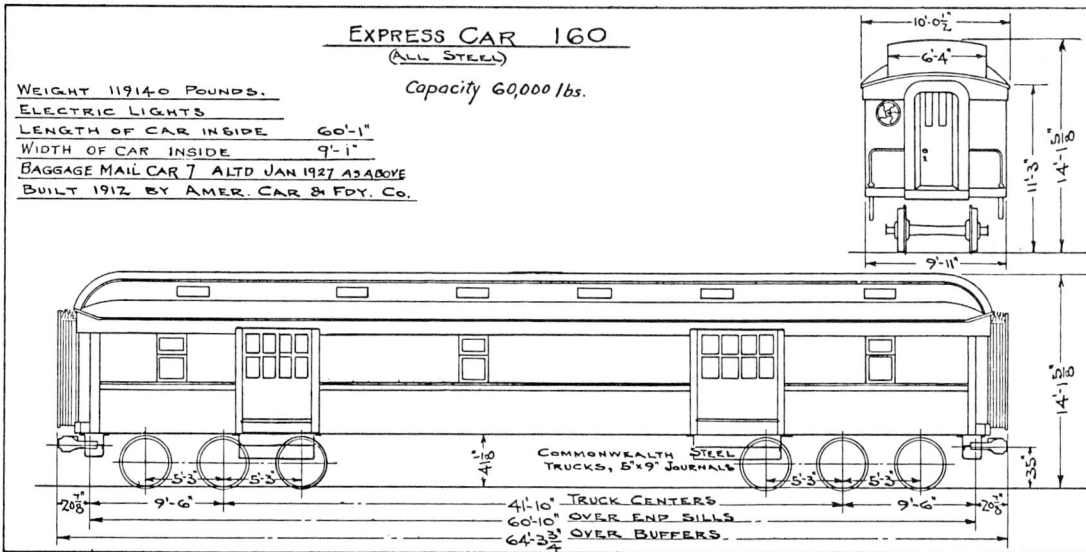

Cafe-parlor car *Powhatan,* built by Pullman in 1928, is under the PRR catenary at Washington Terminal in 1937. It made daily round trips Richmond-Washington assigned to local passenger trains Nos. 14 and 23. It was unusual in that at the time of its construction it was the longest car ever built by Pullman (86 feet, over the couplers).

Heavyweight coach No. 81 was built by Bethlehem Shipbuilding Corporation in 1923. It was one of four all-steel cars (Nos. 81-84) with a seating capacity of 88 passengers. These cars were later renumbered in the series 520-523 and were air-conditioned and modernized in 1941. No. 81, renumbered to 520, was later converted to Office-Sleeper car No. 21. It weighed 147,900 pounds, and rode on 6-wheel Commonwealth trucks.

(both) William E. Griffin Coll.

Steel underframe coach No. 449 was one of four coaches in the series 68-71, purchased by RF&P in 1912. They were later renumbered 447-450 and remained in service until the late 1940s. This car was built during the transition from wooden to steel cars. During that period many cars were built with steel underframes and end posts, but the remainder of the superstructure was wooden. Many of these cars that survived late were also given steel sheeting over their wood sides, but the giveaway is the truss-rods beneath the car.

No. 526 was one of the first coaches air-conditioned for service on the RF&P in the 1930s. In a press release of that era the company noted that the air-conditioned car "...insures the passenger against any cinders, dust, or dirt and places him at his journey's end clean, refreshed, and in a happy state of mind."

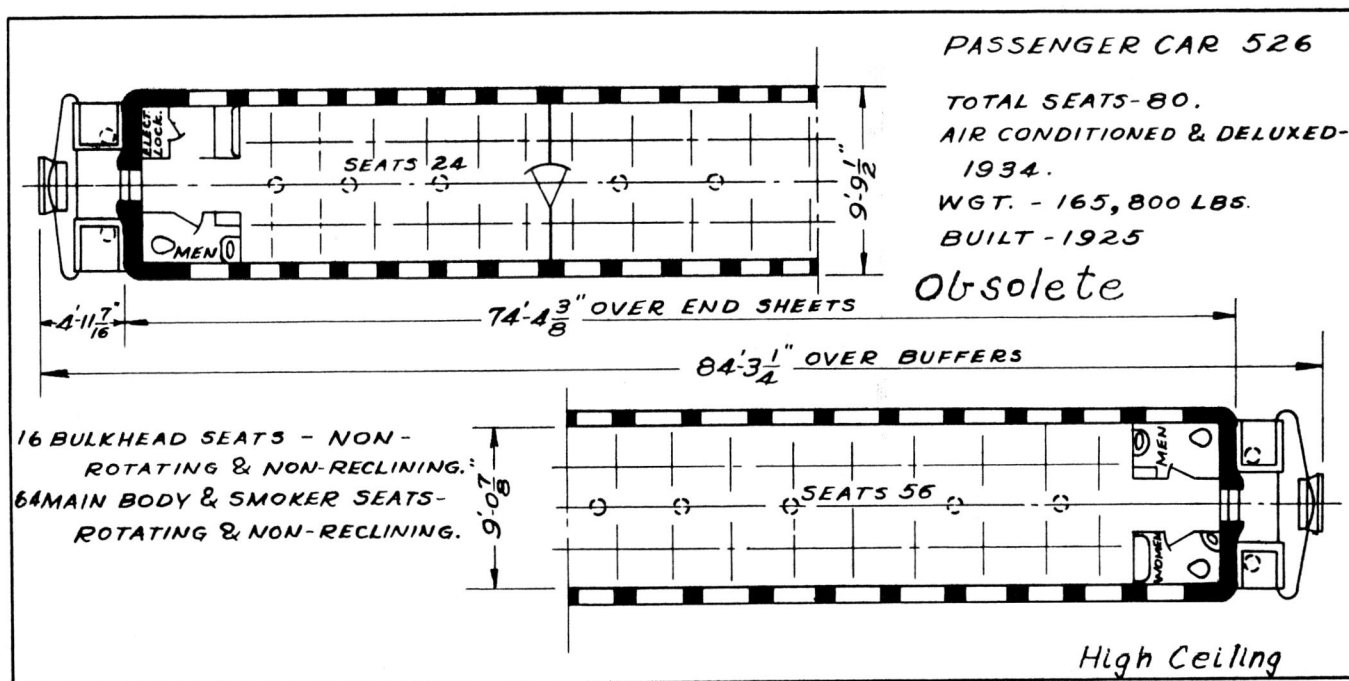

PASSENGER CAR 526

TOTAL SEATS - 80.
AIR CONDITIONED & DELUXED - 1934.
WGT. - 165,800 LBS.
BUILT - 1925
Obsolete

SEATS 24

MEN

9'-9½"

←4'-11⁷⁄₁₆"→

74'-4³⁄₈" OVER END SHEETS

84'-3¼" OVER BUFFERS

16 BULKHEAD SEATS - NON-
   ROTATING & NON-RECLINING.
64 MAIN BODY & SMOKER SEATS-
   ROTATING & NON-RECLINING.

9'-0⁷⁄₈"

SEATS 56

MEN

WOMEN

High Ceiling

(both) William E. Griffin Coll.

As the diagram of No. 526 tells us, the car was originally built in 1925, and of course in the photo above, it is shown before air-conditioning equipment was added to the underbody. The 16 seats that the diagram mentioned as "bulkhead" were ahead of the dividing bulkhead or partition and were for "Colored" passengers. The diagram is at variance with its legend as well as it shows 24 ahead of the Bulkhead and 56 behind it.

In 1941 the RF&P purchased second-hand all-steel re-conditioned coaches 552-559 from Pullman-Standard. These cars were not air-conditioned, and they seated 86 passengers. They were, of course, much needed during the great glut of passengers in the next five years.

The view at right shows the vestibule on one of the 502-559 series cars. An interesting, but prominent detail is the rain gutter atop the door, which diverted most of the run-off from in front of the doorway.

(all) William E. Griffin Coll.

Combination baggage/dormitory car No. 301 was converted from the Cafe-Parlor Car *Virginia Dare* (see pages 103 and 142), originally built for the short-lived *Old Dominion* in 1947. The car was re-built in August 1953 to accommodate 31-feet of baggage space, and sleeping for 24 dining car waiters and one steward (who had a private compartment). A shower and locker space was also provided.

Combination passenger/baggage car No. 311, (shown above and in the two diagrams below) was built by ACF in 1921 and purchased by RF&P from the Pittsburgh & Shawmut Railroad in May 1926. It seated 42 in reclining, rotating chairs and allowed 29-feet of baggage storage space

Air Conditioned

Old Nos 203, 204

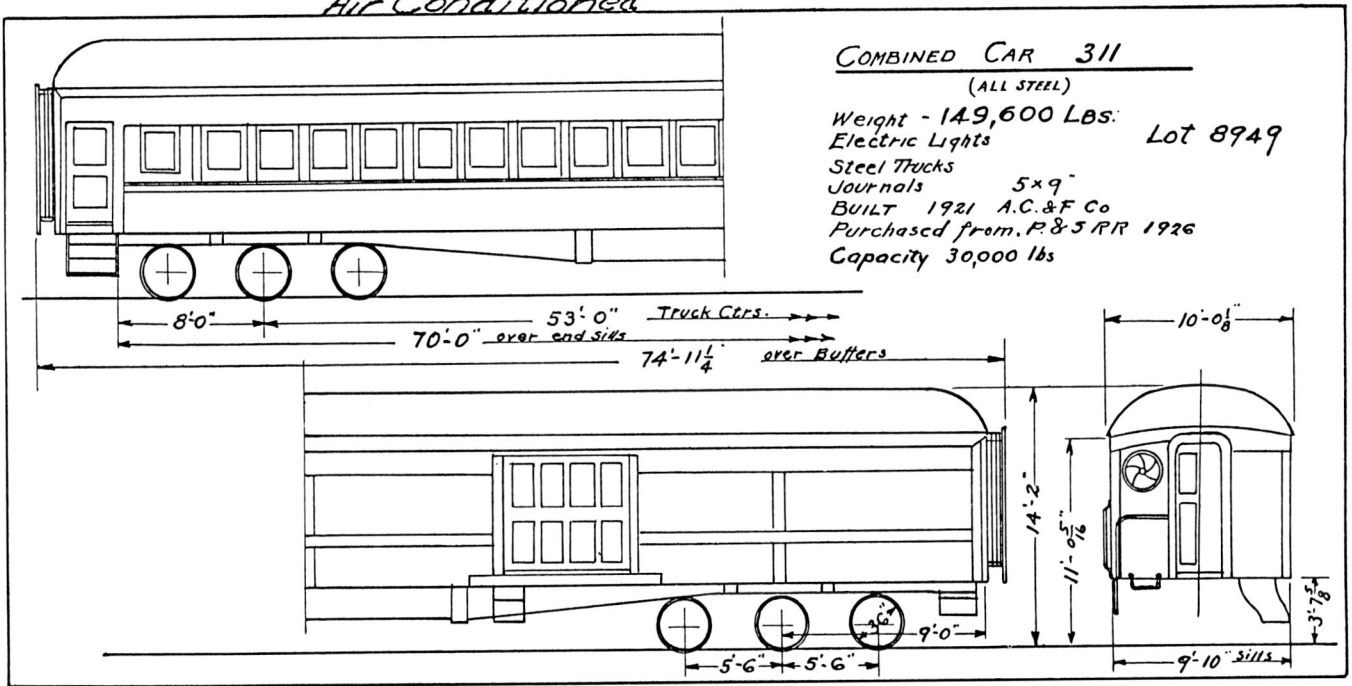

COMBINED CAR 311
(ALL STEEL)

Weight - 149,600 LBS.
Electric Lights   Lot 8949
Steel Trucks
Journals   5×9"
BUILT 1921 A.C.&F Co
Purchased from. P.& S RR 1926
Capacity 30,000 lbs

8'-0"
53'-0" Truck Ctrs.
70'-0" over end sills
74'-11¼" over Buffers

10'-0⅛"

14'-2"

11'-0⁵⁄₁₆"

3'-7⅝"

9'-0"
5'-6" 5'-6"

9'-10" sills

Combined Car 311

4'-8¼"
29'-11¼"

8'-11³⁄₁₆" 9'-0"

ELECT. LOCKER
WC

32 Rotating Reclining Seats With Adjustable Foot Rests

70'-0" Over Sills
74'-11¼" Over Buffers
69'-3" inside

29'-1½" inside

BAGGAGE

5'6"

LUGGAGE

£ of Car

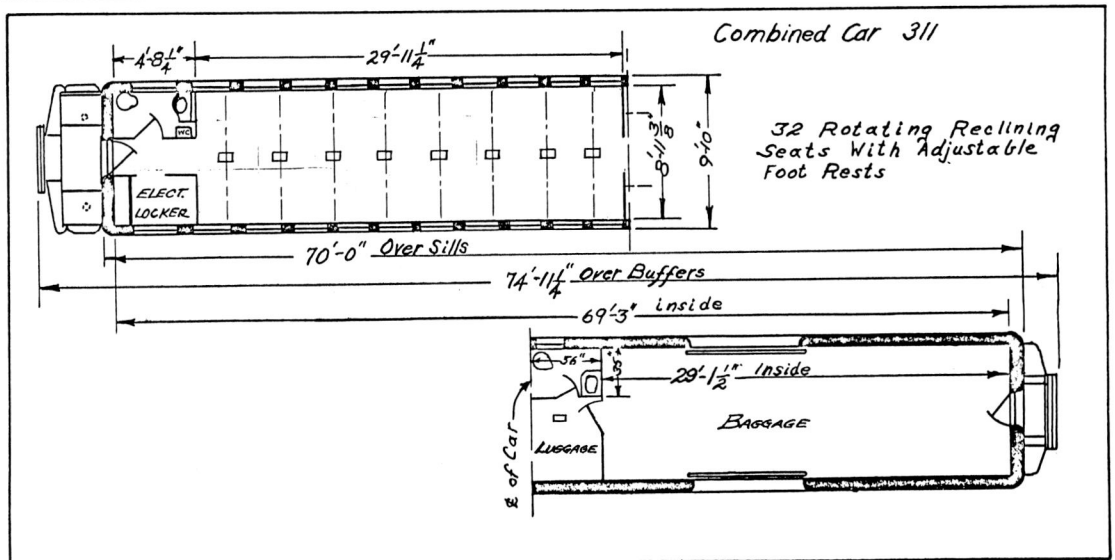

151

Beginning in 1954, RF&P modernized six of its air-conditioned 500-series coaches, upgrading them to better match the latest type of streamlined equipment. Cars 515, 511, 534, 533, 530, 532, and 526 were renumbered respectively 701-707. They were used extensively in RF&P local passenger service. The exterior of the cars was streamlined and new features included vestibule folding steps, trap doors, tightlock couplers, rubber draft gear, and electro-pneumatic end doors that opened at the touch of the finger and then closed automatically. The high roofline which covered the old clerestory was tapered at the ends to conform with the lightweight car roofs.

The pleasant interior (left) was as nice-looking to passengers as any lightweight streamlined car.

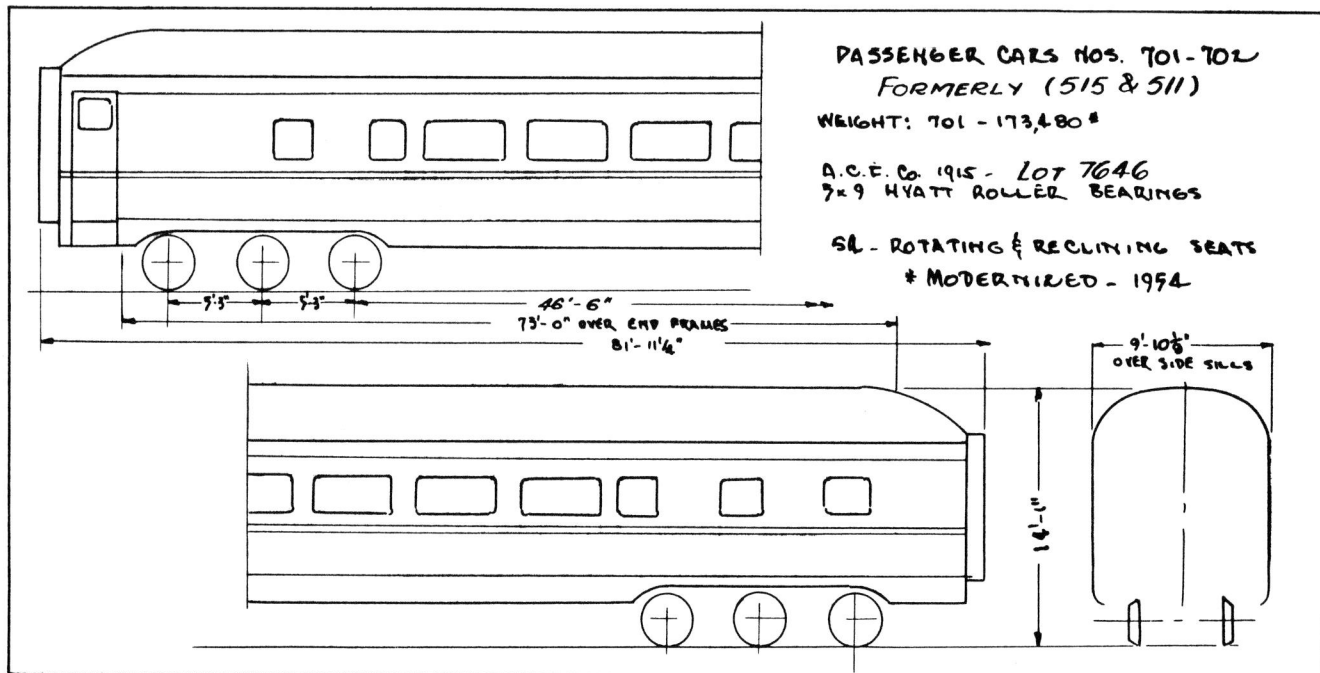

PASSENGER CARS NOS. 701-702
FORMERLY (515 & 511)
WEIGHT: 701 - 173,480#

A.C.F. Co. 1915 - LOT 7646
7×9 HYATT ROLLER BEARINGS

SR - ROTATING & RECLINING SEATS
MODERNIZED - 1954

5'-5" 5'-3" 46'-6"
73'-0" OVER END FRAMES
81'-11¼"

9'-10⅝"
OVER SIDE SILLS

14'-1"

152

(all) William E. Griffin Coll.

No. 703 was built by Bethlehem in 1926 as No. 95. It was air-conditioned in 1937 and renumbered 534, then modernized in 1955 and changed to 705. It was retired in 1971 and sold privately. This photo is at Atlanta in 1968.

Originally No. 75, built by ACF in 1915, it was air-conditioned and modernized in 1941 and renumbered 514, and was retired in 1967. It became maintenance-of-way car No. 205 in 1968, was renumbered 203 in 1971 and finally retired in 1981—a long eventful life!

Modernized heavyweight No. 704 is seen here at Florence, South Carolina, running through on ACL Train No. 75, *The Havana Special*, on February 21, 1956.

153

INVENTORY OF PASSENGER TRAIN EQUIPMENT

CLASSIFICATION	NUMBERS – NAMES	
POSTAL CARS - steel	101, 102, 103, 105	(4 Cars)
EXPRESS CARS - steel	161, 162, 163, 164, 165, 167, 168, 169, 170, 171, 172, 173, 174, 175, 176, 177, 178	(17 Cars)
EXPRESS CARS - steel	180, 181, 182, 183, 184, 185, 186, 187, 188, 189, 190	(11 Cars)
BOX EXPRESS CARS - steel underframe, steel superstructure frame	280, 281, 282, 283, 284, 285, 286, 287, 288	(9 Cars)
DORMITORY-BAGGAGE CAR – LAHT steel, air conditioned	301	(1 Car)
COMBINATION PASSENGER AND BAGGAGE CAR steel, air conditioned - deluxe	311	(1 Car)
COACHES - steel, air conditioned - deluxe	501, 502, 512, 513, 514, 516, 517, 518, 519, 520, 521, 522, 523, 524, 525, 527, 528, 529, 531, 535	(20 Cars)
COACHES - steel	550, 551, 552, 553, 554, 556, 557, 558, 559, 560, 562	(11 Cars)
COACHES - steel - air conditioned streamlined, wide windows, deluxe	701, 702, 703, 704, 705, 706, 707	(7 Cars)
COACHES - stainless steel, air conditioned - deluxe	801, 802, 803, 804, 805, 806	(6 Cars)
COACHES – LAHT and stainless steel, air conditioned - deluxe	810, 811, 812	(3 Cars)
COACHES – LAHT steel, air conditioned - deluxe	840, 841, 842, 843	(4 Cars)
COACHES - stainless steel, air conditioned - deluxe	850, 851, 852, 853, 854, 855, 856, 857	(8 Cars)
COACHES – LAHT and stainless steel, air conditioned - deluxe	861, 862	(2 Cars)
DINING CARS - steel - air conditioned	ALEXANDRIA, FREDERICKSBURG, JAMES, POCAHONTAS, POTOMAC, QUANTICO	
DINING CAR – LAHT and stainless steel, air conditioned	HENRICO	
21-ROOMETTE – LAHT and stainless steel, air conditioned	BYRD ISLAND	
6-DOUBLE BEDROOM, BAR-LOUNGE – LAHT and stainless steel, air conditioned	COLONIAL BEACH	
2-DRAWING ROOM, 14-ROOMETTE – LAHT and stainless steel air conditioned	FAIRFAX RIVER	
6-DOUBLE BEDROOM, 10-ROOMETTE – LAHT steel, air conditioned	KING GEORGE – KING WILLIAM – KING & QUEEN	
6-DOUBLE BEDROOM, 10-ROOMETTE – LAHT and stainless steel, air conditioned	CAROLINE COUNTY – HANOVER COUNTY SPOTSYLVANIA COUNTY – STRATFORD COUNTY CHESTERFIELD – ESSEX – LANCASTER	
5-DOUBLE BEDROOM, 8-SECTION - steel - air conditioned	CLOVER BED – CLOVER CITY – CLOVER WOOD	
1-DRAWING ROOM, 2-COMPARTMENT, 10 SECTION - steel - air conditioned	LAKE MARY – LAKE OLIVER	
1-DRAWING ROOM, 12-SECTION - steel - air conditioned Used in Coach Service	571	
1-DRAWING ROOM, 2-COMPARTMENT 10-SECTION - steel - air conditioned – Used in Coach Service	572	
1-DRAWING ROOM, 12-SECTION - steel - air conditioned Used in Coach Service	573, 574	

This official RF&P passenger car roster from 1958 details equipment then in service, by number or name.

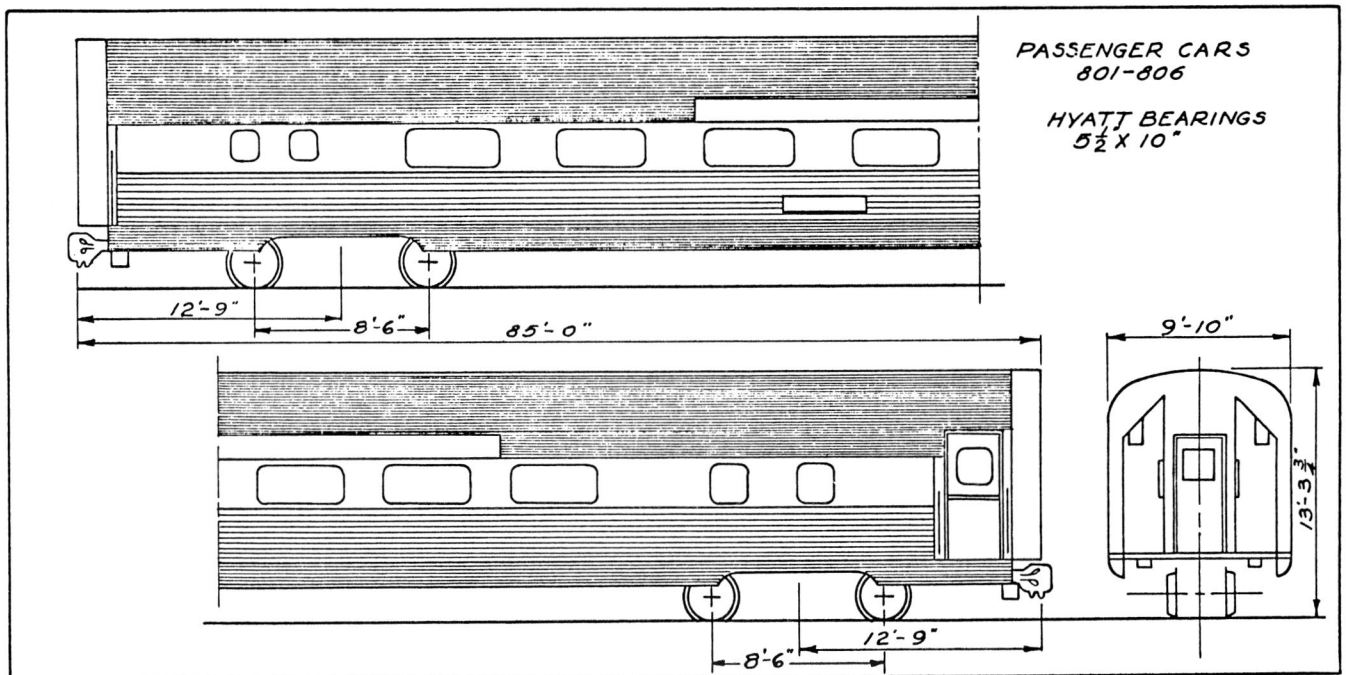

RF&P lightweight stainless-steel coach No. 802 was built by the Budd Company in 1946 as part of a six-car order to help the railroad fulfill its pool arrangements with PRR, ACL, SAL, and FEC for the through train service. Typical of Budd-built cars, there were corrigations on both the sides and roof.

RF&P Passenger Car Painting

Heavyweight Cars:
Bodies were Pullman Green with gold leaf lettering. Under-body appliances, boxes, and trucks were black.

Modernized Heavywight Cars (500 & 700-series):
These cars had two schemes. The early scheme consisted of bodies blue with a gray stripe over the windows and along the base of the car. The blue and gray shades of paint matched those used on diesel locomotives. Later the gray stripe along the base of the car was dropped and cars had blue bodies with just the gray stripe over the windows. The lettering and numbers were in gold leaf. Under-body appliances, boxes and trucks were black.

Lightweight Cars:
Coaches, sleepers, and diners were stainless steel with blue letterboards and gold leaf lettering and numbers, with two exceptions: the sleeper *Fairfax River* had ACL purple letterboards, and sleepers in the PRR/RF&P/N&W pool were painted Tuscan Red with gold leaf lettering.[see page 104 for special paint scheme used on the *Old Dominion* cars.]

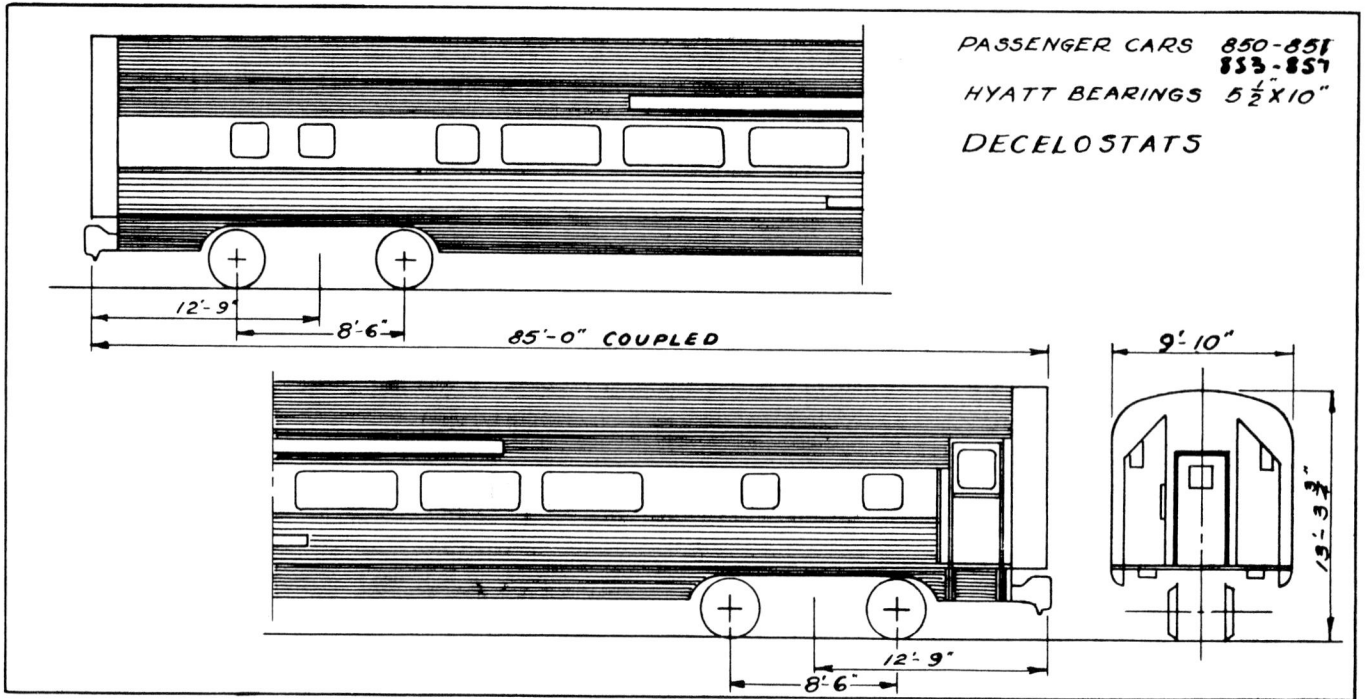

PASSENGER CARS 850-851
853-857
HYATT BEARINGS 5½"X10"
DECELOSTATS

12'-9"

8'-6"

85'-0" COUPLED

9'-10"

15'-3¾"

12'-9"

8'-6"

C. L. Goolsby

William E. Griffin Coll.

Coaches in the 850-857 series were built by Budd in 1947 as part of the post-war upgrade of through New York-Florida passenger service. The cars originally cost $90,072.53 and weighed 124,250 pounds. They were in very good condition at the end of railroad-operated passenger service and were sold to Amtrak. The photo above shows No. 850 at Raleigh, North Carolina, June 2, 1969. The diagram shows major dimensions, side elevation and end of the car.

No. 855, one of the eight cars shown new here at the Budd plant in Philadelphia. The cars were used in New York-Birmingham service as well as on the Florida trains over PRR/RF&P/SAL. No. 855 went to Amtrak in 1971. Note the brightly painted trucks; they soon enough turned dull from road grime and dirt in operation.

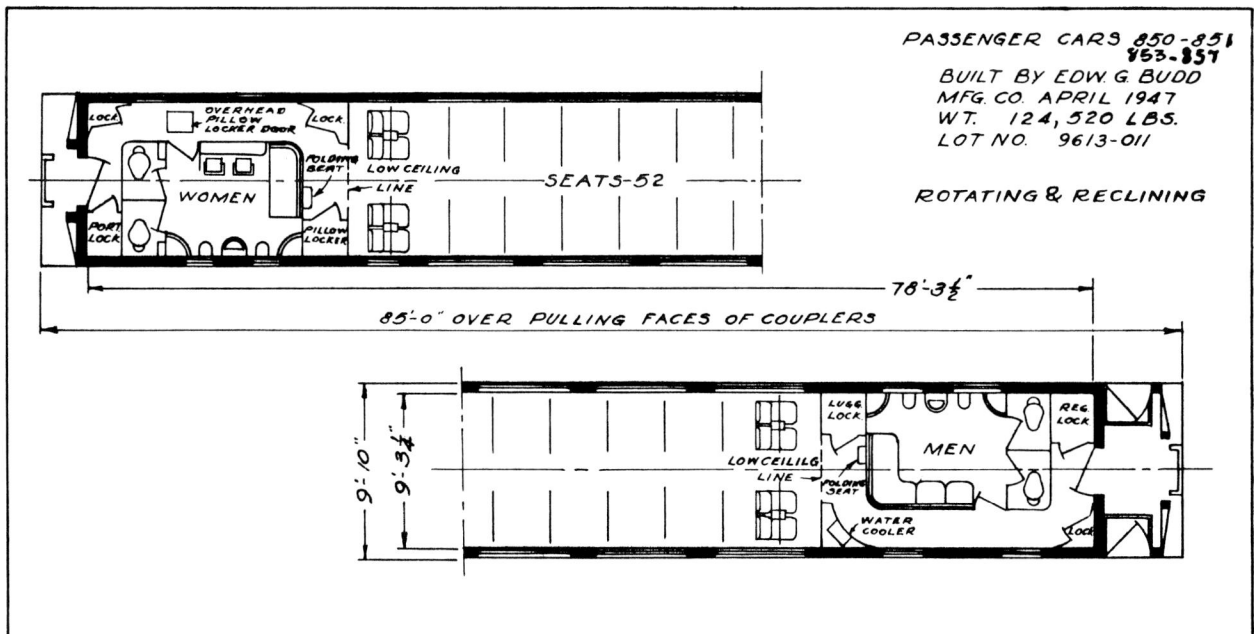

These were indeed deluxe long-distance coaches, with seating for only 52 people, thus providing plenty of leg room between seats. The large lounge areas for both men and women in each end of the cars next to the toilets were also much larger than on ordinary coaches, even of the post-war period.

In December 1955 RF&P purchased two stainless steel streamlined lightweight Coach-lounge cars, Nos. 861-862, from Pullman-Standard Car Manufacturing Co. High-speed 4-wheel trucks, large coil springs, shock absorbers, and roller bearings provided excellent riding qualities for these cars. The interior design comprised of two coach compartments, seating 22 and 30 passengers respectively, separated by a spacious center lounge section accommodating 10 passengers. The lounge/smoking area was separated from the two coach compartments by half-bulkheads, one on each side of the car at each end of the lounge, so in effect the whole long "bowling-alley" effect of the coach was broken up into much smaller, cozier compartments. The cars were placed in the pool service between New York and Florida and were eventually sold to Amtrak in October 1971.

(both) William E. Griffin Coll.

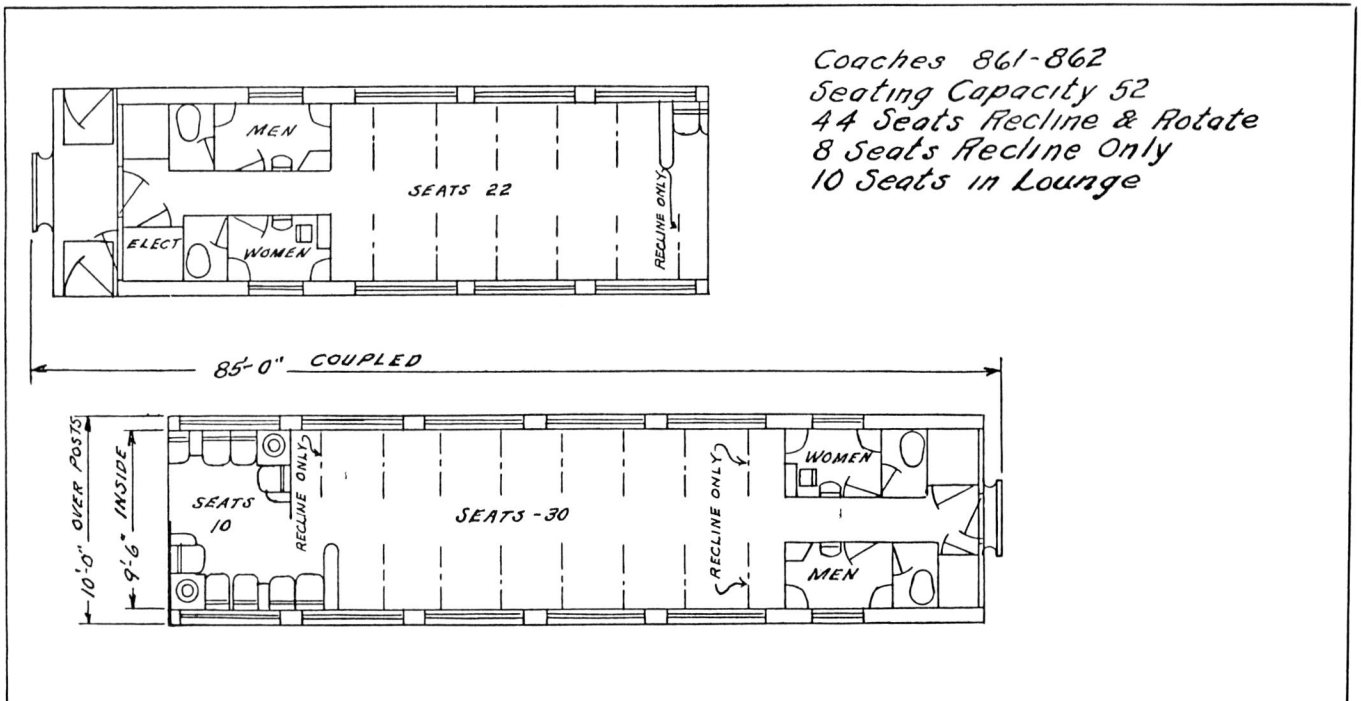

Coaches 861-862
Seating Capacity 52
44 Seats Recline & Rotate
8 Seats Recline Only
10 Seats in Lounge

This diagram shows the lounge in detail, with its seats backed against each wall and bulkhead. The cars had the first trucks specifically designed to accommodate disc brakes and were equipped with the Decelostat anti-wheel slip system. The cars were initially pooled with 7 SAL cars for use on the *Silver Meteor*.

"FAIRFAX RIVER"
2-DRAWING RM.-14 ROOMETTE

85'-0" COUPLED

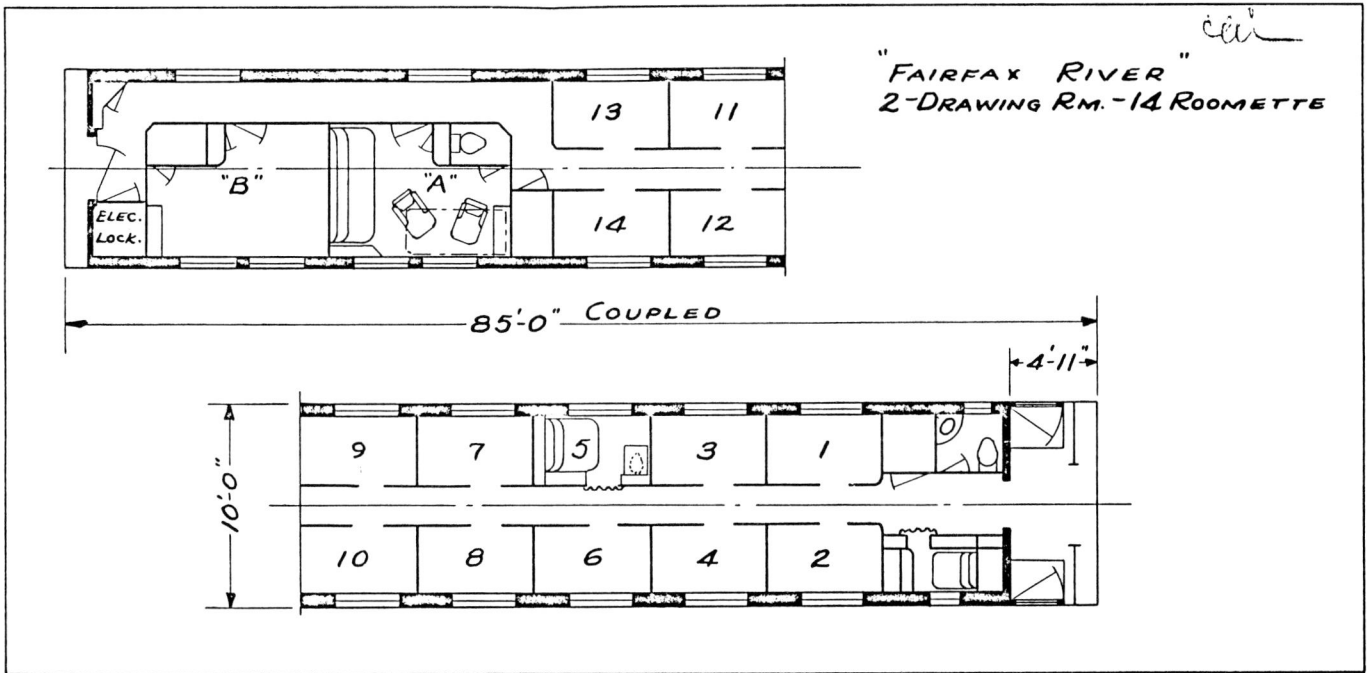

William E. Griffin Coll.

Lightweight stainless steel sleeping car *Fairfax River* was built by American Car & Foundry for use in the PRR/ RF&P/ACL/FEC pool. The car had distinctive purple letterboards and the unusual 14-roomette, 2-drawing room floor plan. This arrangement was popular for only a short time after the war when many railroads believed that they would be able to retain much of the traditional overnight business travel, if good accommodations were provided, thus the many single rooms. But airlines and automobiles soon depleted this market and the single-person accommodations didn't sell very well with the vacationing families that became the main-stay of post-war Pullman business, especially in service like the Florida trains. This car was converted to Kitchen-Diner-Sleeper No. 204 in 1968 for use by the RF&P's Maintenance-of-Way forces, and was finally retired from service in 1980. On the floorplan, the small compartment to the right of Roomette No. 2 was the porter's rest area.

(Left) Bedroom in an RF&P sleeper set up for day use. Not unlike any accommodation on any other railroad of the post-war era. About the only differences among railroads was the color of upholstery and wall paint and sometimes the style of chair.

(Below) A double bedroom made down for sleeping. In Pullman parlance a bedroom, compartment, or berth was "made down" to prepare it for sleeping and "made up" for daytime use. Most of the berth ladders as seen here (which were stored in the closet during the day) had the car name stamped in them and are highly prized collector-items today.

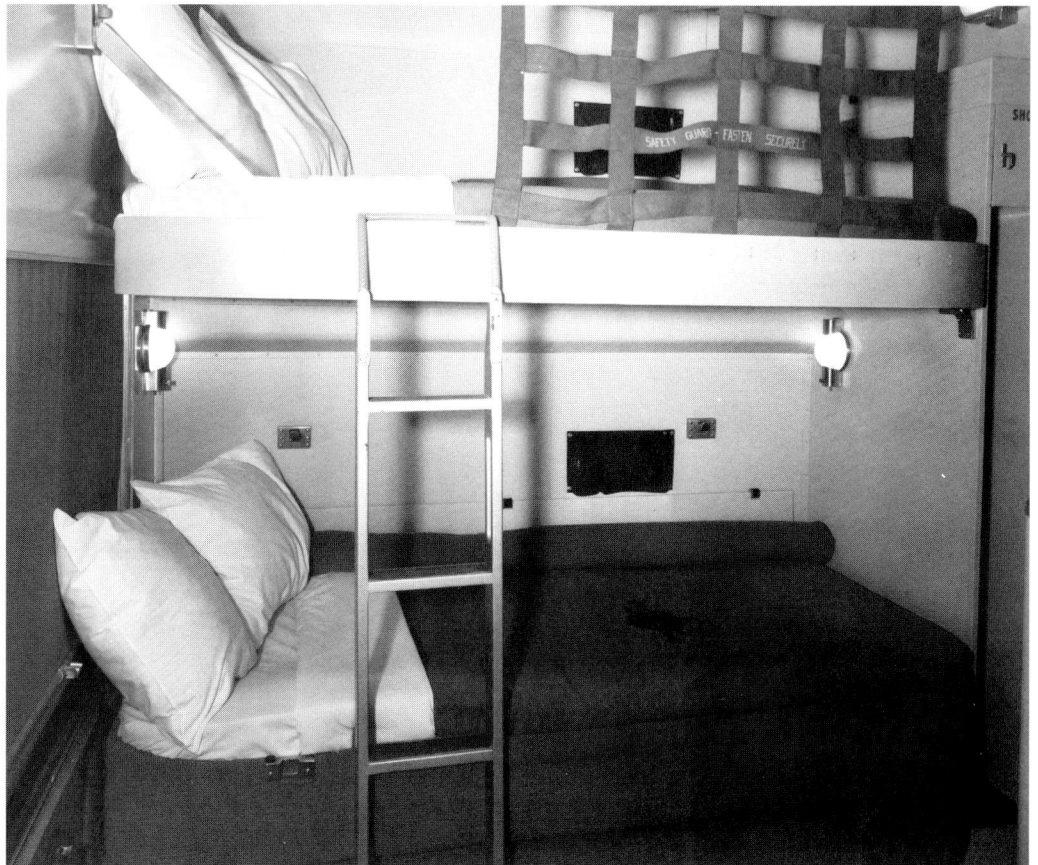

(both) William E. Griffin Coll.

160

Sleeper-lounge car *Colonial Beach* was purchased from American Car & Foundry in 1949 for use in the Florida pool service. This car had six double bedrooms and a bar-lounge. It was sold to Amtrak in 1972, and in 1974 Amtrak renamed it *William A. Griffin, Jr.* in honor of RF&P's late passenger traffic official (no relation to the author).

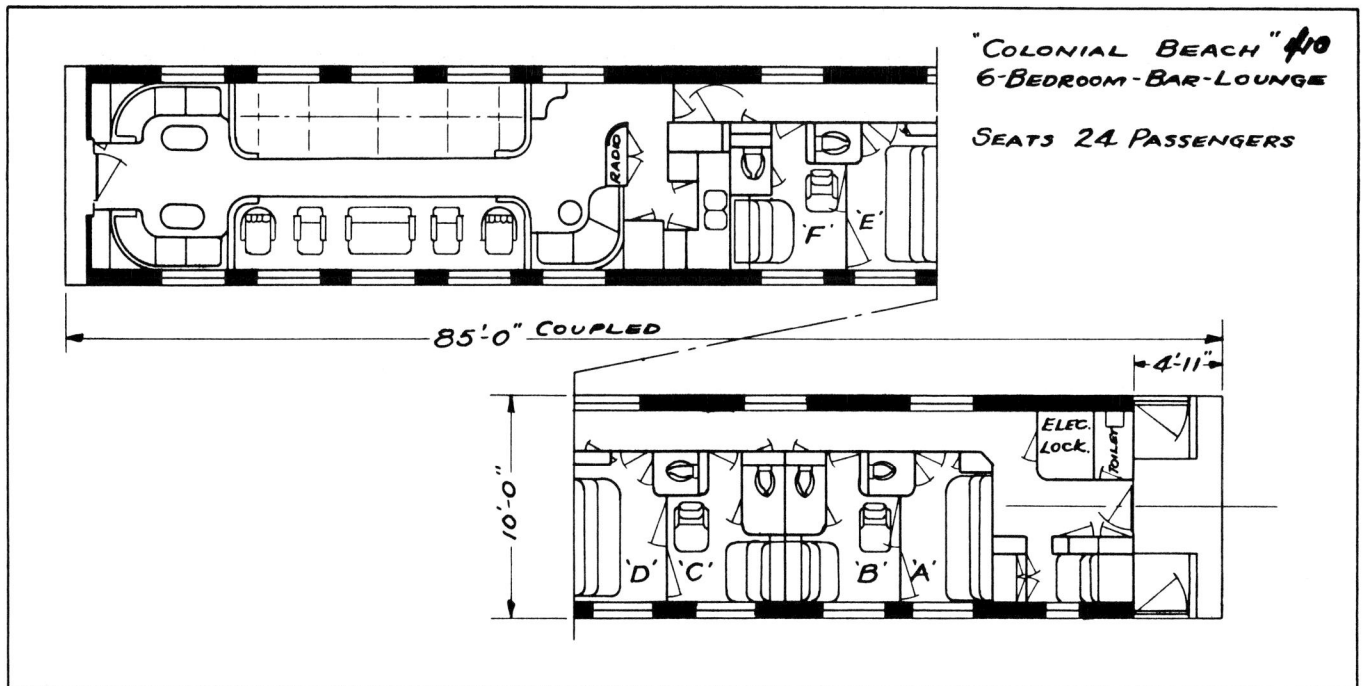

"COLONIAL BEACH" #10
6-BEDROOM-BAR-LOUNGE

SEATS 24 PASSENGERS

85'-0" COUPLED

10'-0"

4'-11"

ELEC. LOCK.

TOILET

RADIO

F' E' D' C' B' A'

(both) William E. Griffin Coll.

The diagram illustrates in detail the lounge-bar arrangement with curved sofas and individual seats, in the approved style of the era. Each of the bedrooms could be opened en suite to accommodate parties of up to four traveling together (often used for families).

Lightweight dining car *Henrico* was built by Pullman-Standard and placed in service in May 1950. It was sold to the Mexican National Railways in 1971. In 1946 RF&P, ACL, and FEC agreed to purchase cars to re-equip the *Florida Special* and *Champion* train-sets. Thirteen diners were ordered from Pullman-Standard (10 for ACL, 2 for FEC and 1 for RF&P), but were not delivered until 1950. As can be seen in the diagram below the seating arrangement in the car was unusual in that booths with triangular tables were used on one side for 2-person seating and the 4-person tables were placed at an angle on the other side. In each case the people nearer the window were seated on built-in sofas. The car still seated 36, as many as a diner arranged in the usual way.

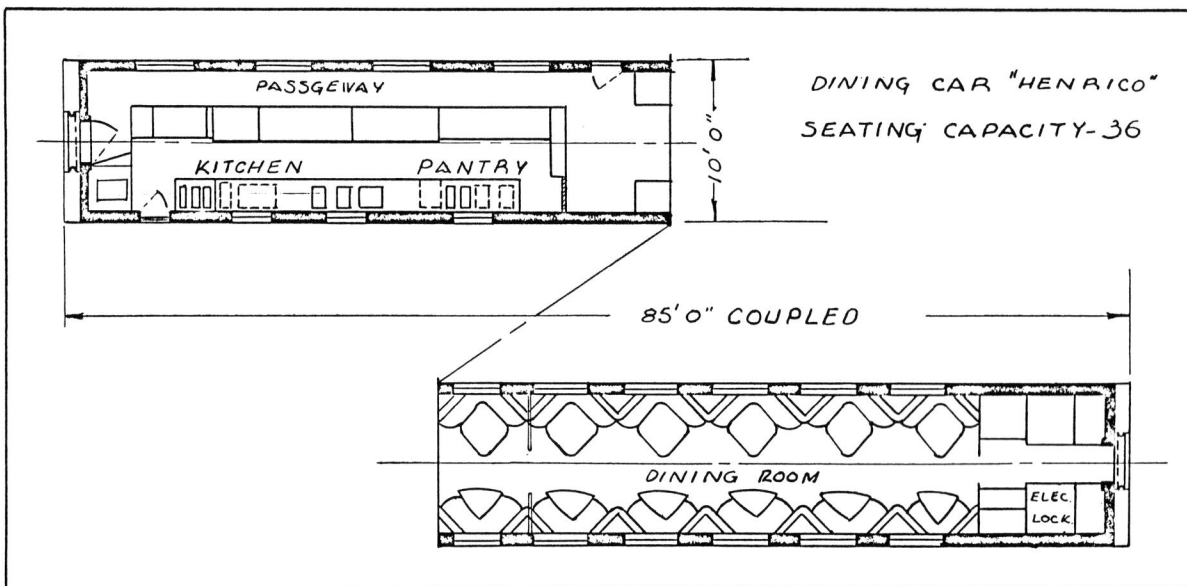

DINING CAR "HENRICO"
SEATING CAPACITY-36

85'0" COUPLED

(all) William E. Griffin Coll.

King George was one of three 10-roomette/6-double bedroom lightweight sleepers purchased from Pullman-Standard in 1949. These cars were in the PRR/RF&P/N&W pool, hence were painted Tuscan red and had smooth sides. It was sold to the NdeM in February 1972.

Lightweight 10-roomette/6-double bedroom sleeper *Lancaster* was built by Pullman-Standard in 1949 for the PRR/RF&P/SAL pool, and was ultimately sold to Mexico in February 1972. It was part of an order for 16 (3 for RF&P and 13 for SAL) cars for the *Silver Meteor* and *Silver Comet* pool placed in March of 1946. *Chesterfield* and *Essex* were the other two cars in the series. They were similar enough to the line's other 10/6 sleepers that the mechanical department made up a single diagram to cover three different orders.

Vestibule end of *Lancaster.*

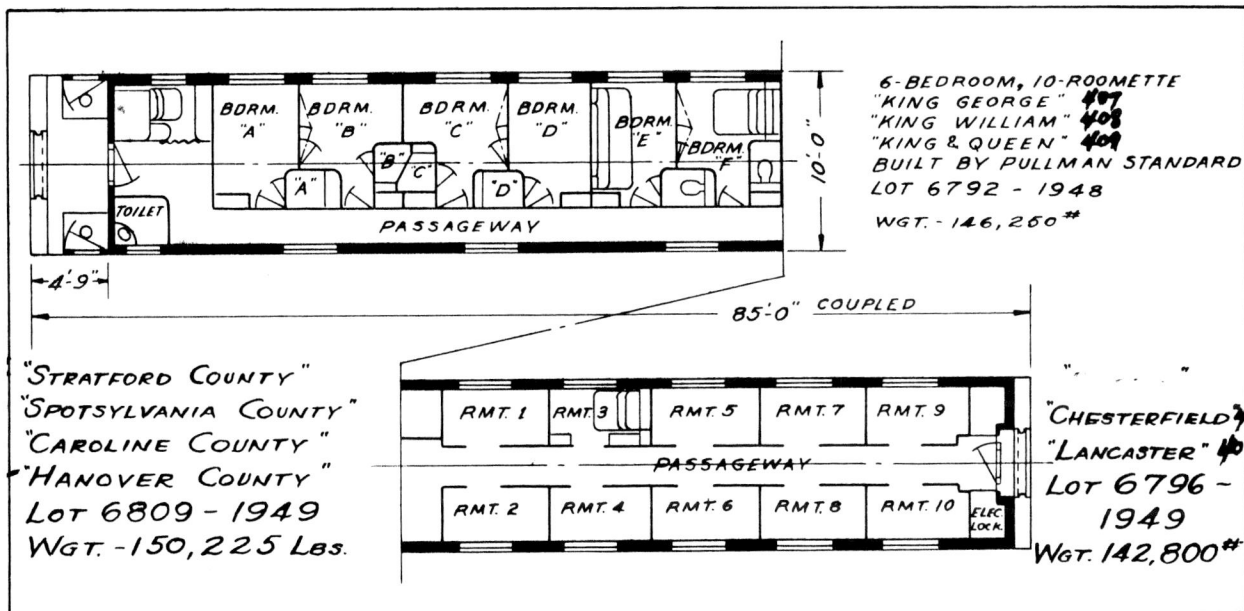

6-BEDROOM, 10-ROOMETTE
"KING GEORGE" 407
"KING WILLIAM" 408
"KING & QUEEN" 409
BUILT BY PULLMAN STANDARD
LOT 6792 - 1948
WGT. - 146,260 #

"STRATFORD COUNTY"
"SPOTSYLVANIA COUNTY"
"CAROLINE COUNTY"
"HANOVER COUNTY"
LOT 6809 - 1949
WGT. - 150,225 LBS.

"CHESTERFIELD"
"LANCASTER" 40
LOT 6796 -
1949
WGT. 142,800 #

Motor Car M-1 poses for builder photo at the J. G. Brill Co. in Philadelphia in May 1928. No. M-1 was divided into engine, baggage, and passenger compartments, and was acquired to help reduce costs of local passenger service.

A Trailer Coach, No. T-11, was purchased at the same time to accompany the M-1. It resembled a standard passenger coach of the period but was a good deal lighter. This two unit motor train was so successful that RF&P ordered a second set in 1929.

The eningeer of the M-1 operated from a seat in front of the No. 1 engine. This photo shows the interior of M-1's engine and control compartment at its front. The units was powered by two 300-horsepower 6-cylinder Hall-Scott engines, which gave it sufficient power to propel itself and one trailer coach at passenger-train speeds.

(all) William E. Griffin Coll.

Head-on view of M-2, the second of RF&P's motor cars. It can easily be seen why engineers on many railroads disliked the placement of the engineer in a dangerous position in a collision.

This builder photo shows the baggage compartment of the M-1 unit, which separated the engine/control compartment from the passengers.

The 73-foot, T-11 trailer-coach was divided into a 24-seat smoking section and a 58-seat passenger compartment. The accommodations were very plain. The motor cars and trailers weren't air-conditioned, but ceiling fans were installed later. In effect the trailer was an interurban electric design which made it lightweight enough to be pulled easily by the motor car.

RF&P shop workman M. C. Ladd completes stenciling of box car in August 1963. *(William E. Griffin Coll.)*

Chapter 8

RF&P Freight Equipment

RF&P was mainly a box-car railroad, with more boxes than any other type freight car. There were a few gondolas, hoppers, and covered hoppers, and in later days some specialty cars, but for the most part RF&P, given its short bridge-line status, relied on other railroads for the cars it hauled. The box cars it did have were primarily for transporting the usual local freight and for what goods did originate on the line, mainly at Richmond. The accompanying photos depict many of the classes of RF&P rolling stock since the 1920s. The tables below, reprinted from 1943 and 1955 issues of the Official Railway Equipment Register, show the RF&P fleet at its height and in later days.

Item Number	A.A.R. Mech. Designation	MARKINGS AND KIND OF CARS.	NUMBERS.	INSIDE Length	INSIDE Width	INSIDE Height	OUTSIDE Length	Width At Eaves or Top of Sides or Platform	Extreme Width	To Extreme Width	To Eaves or Top of Sides or Platform	To Top of Running Board.	To Extreme Height.	Side Width of Open'g	Side Height of Open'g	End Width of Open'g	End Height of Open'g	Cubic Feet Level Full.	Pounds or Gallons.	Number of Cars.
1	FM	Flat, Steel......	554 to 556	42	9 4	1	43 8	....	10 1½			4 6						375	100000 lb.	8
2	XM	Box, Steel Underframe Steel Frame	981 to 1130	40 6	8 6	9	41 4½	9 8½	....		12 9	13 6⅞	14 1¾	6	8 7			3098	100000 lb.	145
3	SM	Stock, Steel Underf.	2267, 2282, 2300 2331, 2409, 2420 2421	40 6	8 6	9	41 4½	9 8½	....		12 9	13 6⅞	14 1¾	6	8 7			3098	80000 lb.	7
4	XM	Box, Steel Underframe Steel Frame..	2451 to 2800	40 6	8 6	9	41 4½	9 8½	....		12 9	13 6⅞	14 1¾	6	8 7			3098	100000 lb.	339
5	GB	Gond., Steel, Fixed Ends, Solid Bottom, Steel Floor...........	3001 to 3100	40	9 7	4 2	40 7½	10 2⅛			7 8¾	....	8 5½					1600	100000 lb.	83
6	GB	Gond., Steel, Fixed Ends, Solid Flat Bottom, Steel Floor.......	3101 to 3150	38 2	9 2	2 6½	40 2¼	9 7¼			6		6 9					879	100000 lb.	47
7	HM	Hopper, Self-Clearing.	3402 to 3501	30 3	9 6¾	6 0¾	31 8	9 9¾			10 1		10 1					1700	100000 lb.	84
11	HM	" Self-Clearing.	3506 to 3555	30 6	9 5½	10 8	31 11	10 0⅜			10 10		11 5					1880	110000 lb.	40
12	HM	" Steel, Self-Clearing.	3561 to 3590	30 6	9 5½	10 2	31 11	10 0⅜			10 10		11 5					1880	100000 lb.	30
13	HM	" Self-Clearing, (See Exception). ▲	6001 to 6018	30 3	9 6¾	6 0¾	31 8	9 9¾			10 1		10 1					1700	100000 lb.	18
14	GA	Gond., Steel, Drop Bot., Stl. Floor, Exception.	6007	40	9 7	4 2	40 7½	10 2⅛			7 8¾	....	8 5½					1600	"	1
15	NE	Caboose........	803 to 934																		55
		Total........																			806

Official Railway Equipment Register, April 1943

Item Number	A.A.R. Mech. Designation	MARKINGS AND KIND OF CARS.	NUMBERS.	INSIDE Length	INSIDE Width	INSIDE Height	OUTSIDE Length	Width At Eaves or Top of Sides or Platform	Extreme Width	To Extreme Width	To Eaves or Top of Sides or Platform	To Top of Running Board.	To Extreme Height.	Side Width of Open'g	Side Height of Open'g	End Width of Open'g	End Height of Open'g	Cubic Feet Level Full.	Pounds or Gallons.	Number of Cars.
1	XM	Box, Stl. Underframe Steel Frame..	981 to 1130	40 6	8 6	9	41 4½	9 8½	....		12 9	13 6⅞	14 1¾	6	8 7			3098	100000 lb.	9
2	SM	Stock, Steel Underfr.	2409	40 6	8 6	9	41 4½	9 8½	....		12 9	13 6⅞	14 1¾	6	8 7			3098	80000 lb.	1
3	XM	Box, Stl. Underframe Steel Frame.	2451 to 2800	40 6	8 6	9	41 4½	9 8½	....		12 9	13 6⅞	14 1¾	6	8 7			3098	100000 lb.	17
4	XM	"	2801 to 2900	40 6	9 2	10 6	41 10	9 5	10 4	13 7	14 5	14 11	14 11	6	9 10			3098	100000 lb.	100
5	GB	Gond., Steel, Fixed Ends, Solid Flat Bot., Stl. Fl.	3101 to 3150	38 2	9 2	2 6½	40 2¼	9 7¼			6		6 9					879	100000 lb.	88
6	GB	Gond., Stl., Solid Flat Bot., Drop Ends, Wood Fl.	3301 to 3350	52 6	9 6	2 11⅞	54 4	10 6¾			6 8⅝		6 8⅝					1491	140000 lb.	50
11	HM	Hopper, Self Clearing.	3402 to 3501	30 3	9 6¾	6 0¾	31 8	9 9¾			10 1		10 1					1700	100000 lb.	18
12	HM	"	3506 to 3555	30 6	9 5½	10 8	31 11	10 0⅜			10 10		11 5					1880	100000 lb.	48
13	HM	" Steel, Self-Clearing	3561 to 3590	30 6	9 5½	10 2	31 11	10 0⅜			10 10		11 5					1880	100000 lb.	30
14	NE	Caboose...	803 to 941																		84
		Total........																			845

Official Railway Equipment Register, October 1955

Typical of the era, No. 1001 was the first of a group of 30 stock cars acquired by RF&P in 1898.

(all) William E. Griffin Coll.

(Right and below) RF&P No. 2132 was one of the 2001-2200 series 40-ton, 37-foot, steel underframe, wooden box cars built in 1907 and retired in the late 1920s. They had corrigated steel ends and rode on Bettendorf steel frame trucks.

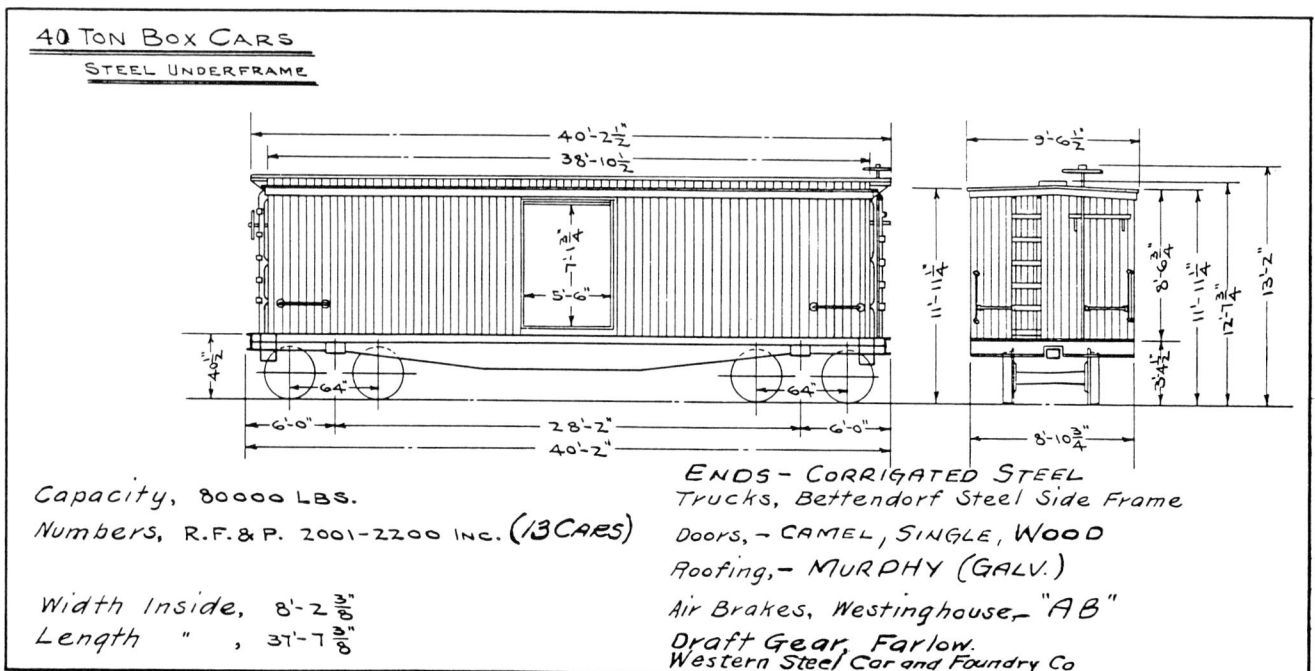

40 TON BOX CARS
STEEL UNDERFRAME

Capacity, 80000 LBS.
Numbers, R.F.&P. 2001-2200 INC. (13 CARS)

Width Inside, 8'-2 3/8"
Length   "   , 37'-7 3/8"

ENDS - CORRIGATED STEEL
Trucks, Bettendorf Steel Side Frame
Doors, - CAMEL, SINGLE, WOOD
Roofing, - MURPHY (GALV.)
Air Brakes, Westinghouse - "AB"
Draft Gear, Farlow.
Western Steel Car and Foundry Co

About as typical and standard a railroad car of the turn of the century as it is possible to find, the 40-foot, 40-ton box car, similar to these RF&P examples, populated almost every railroad in quantity.

RF&P 2719 is one of the 350 United States Railroad Administration (USRA) single-sheathed box cars (Nos. 2451-2800) that were acquired by RF&P in 1919 from American Car and Foundry. The steel-underframe, wooden cars had a capacity of 100,000 pounds. This photo was taken on July 1, 1939. While most of the cars were retired between 1947 and 1956, some were still in service in the 1960s.

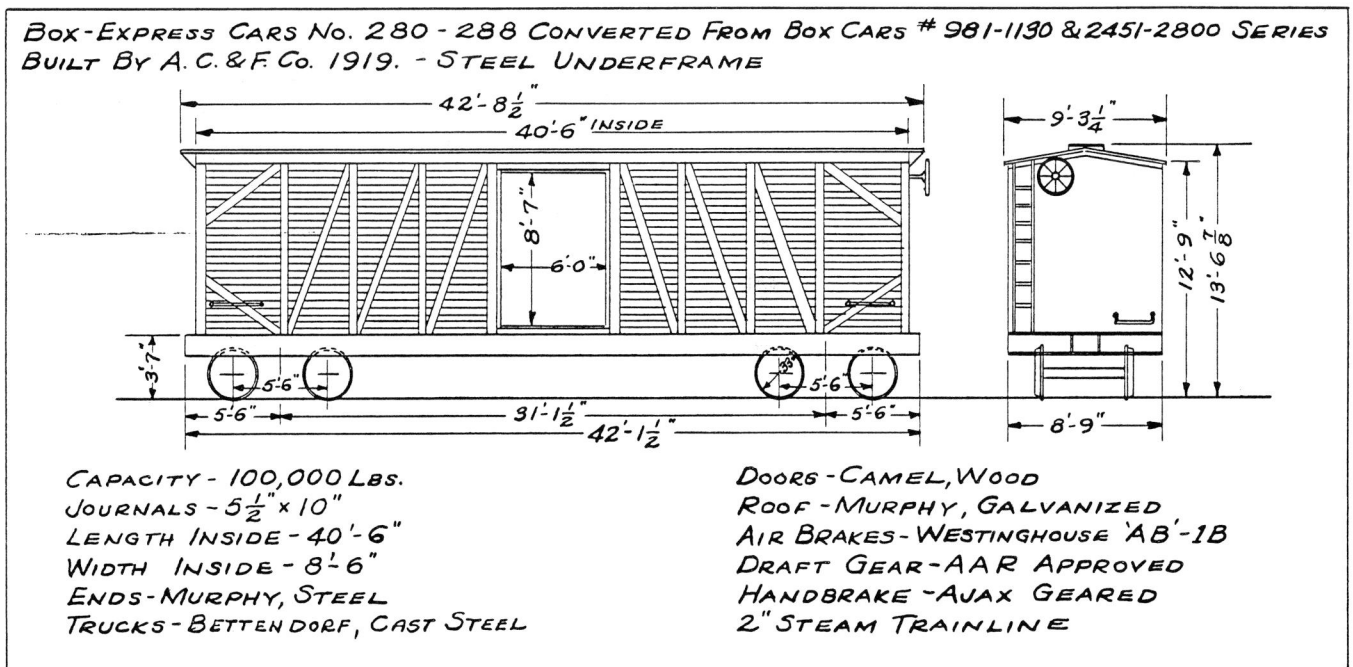

BOX-EXPRESS CARS NO. 280-288 CONVERTED FROM BOX CARS # 981-1190 & 2451-2800 SERIES BUILT BY A.C.&F. CO. 1919. - STEEL UNDERFRAME

CAPACITY - 100,000 LBS.
JOURNALS - 5½" x 10"
LENGTH INSIDE - 40'-6"
WIDTH INSIDE - 8'-6"
ENDS - MURPHY, STEEL
TRUCKS - BETTENDORF, CAST STEEL

DOORS - CAMEL, WOOD
ROOF - MURPHY, GALVANIZED
AIR BRAKES - WESTINGHOUSE 'AB'-1B
DRAFT GEAR - AAR APPROVED
HANDBRAKE - AJAX GEARED
2" STEAM TRAINLINE

As can be discerned from this diagram, some of the cars in this series were converted to box express cars for use on passenger trains and head-end cars when not enough of the regular passenger-train type express cars were available.

This 40-ton, steel-underframe, Automobile box car No. 2212 was photographed on November 24, 1936. It was one of 48 in the series 2201-2250.

No. 2598 is a 50-ton USRA box car from 1919 rebuilt in 1939 with a steel underframe and steel sheathing.

The 70-ton, 56-foot/6-inch single sheathed box cars in the 2100-2200 number series were purchased in December 1973 from the Berwick Forge and Fabricating Company.

50-ton steel underframe steel superstructure box car No. 1132 was formerly No. 2598 (see previous page), starting life on September 25, 1919. It is shown here still in service in 1968.

The RF&P acquired 100 of the 70-ton, 50-ft./6-in. PS-1 type steel cushion underframe box cars in the 2301-2400 series from Pullman-Standard in February 1963. A state-of-the-art car of its time, its extended couplers and black lettering on the door identifying it as a cushioned car, to minimize load damage. Its mechanical diagram showing major dimensions is below.

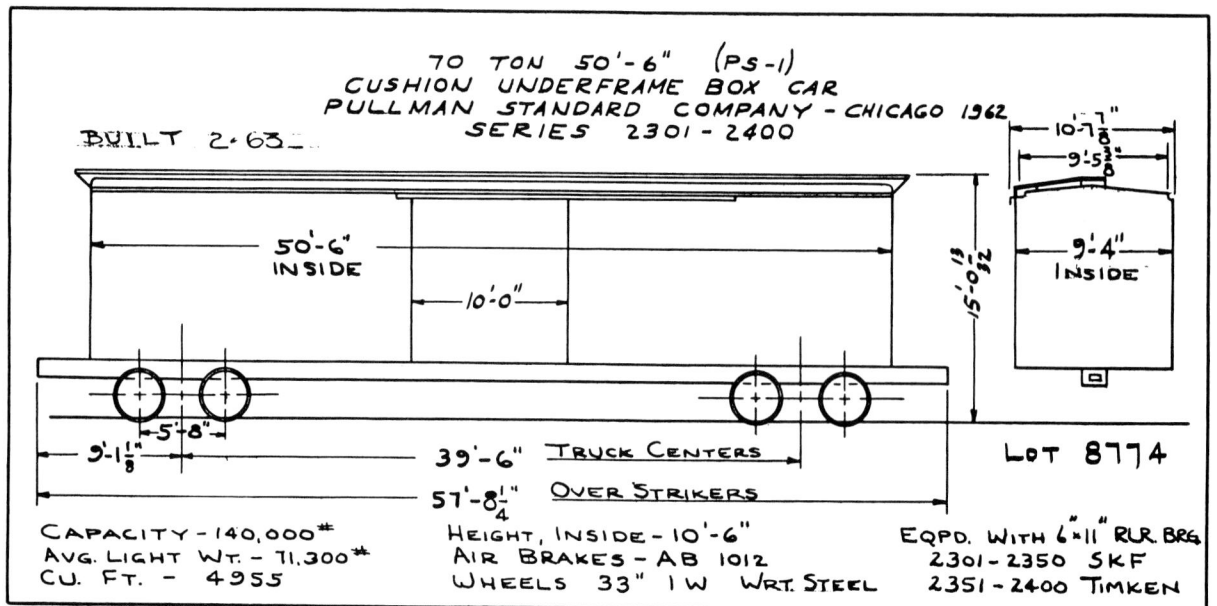

William E. Griffin

(Right) In 1969 RF&P stenciled five of its 2301-2400-series box cars to proclaim America's freedom message and to promote the sale of U. S. Savings Bonds. No. 2376 is at Acca Yard on May 20, 1969.

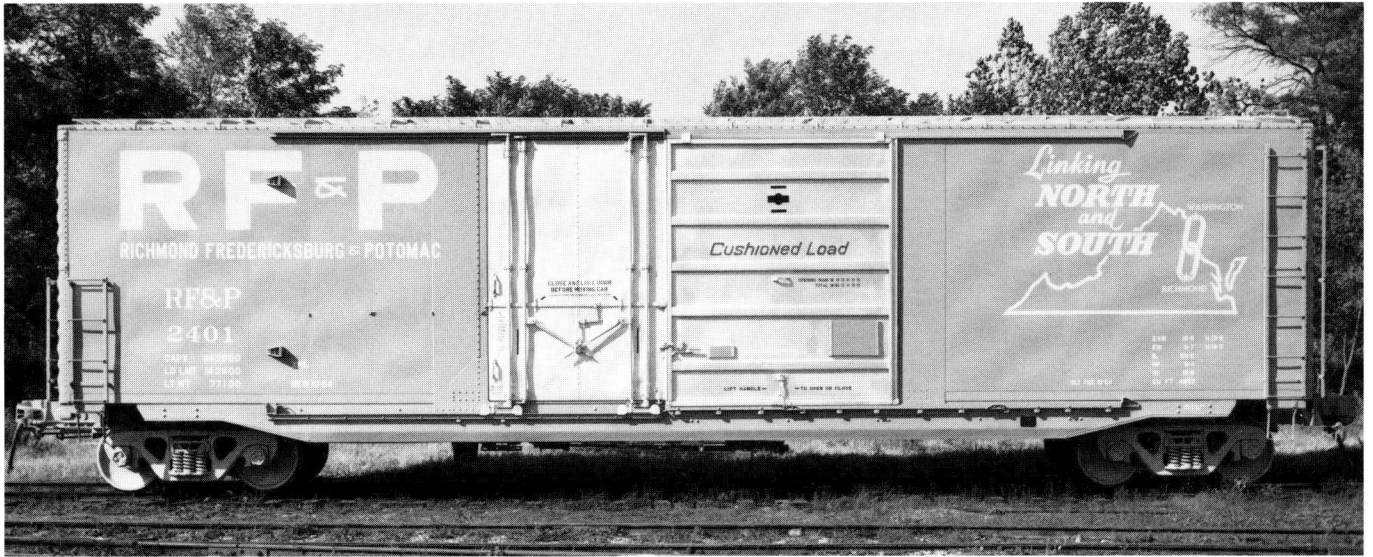

Nos. 2401-2500-series 70-ton box cars were built by Fruit Growers Express at its Alexandria shops in 1964. Here is No. 2401 with its bold lettering.

(Above) That's an unusual RF&P logo on this 40-foot, 50-ton all steel PS-1 box car No. 2880. This car was one of 99 in the series 2801-2900 that were built by Pullman-Standard in 1952.

(Right) "B" end view of 2801-2900 series box cars, showing No. 2880. These cars were built at the Pullman-Standard plant in Bessemer, Alabama, at a cost of $5,924.31 each. They were equipped with 6-foot Youngstown steel doors and Camel roller lift fixtures. Inside they had lading strap anchors located 4 at the door posts and 8 on intermediate side post Z-bars, to secure loads.

(all) William E. Griffin Coll.

No. 2920 was one of 25 box cars in the 2901-2925 series. It is a 50-ton capacity car, measuring 50-feet, 6 inches, and falls in the Pullman-Standard Car Manufacturing Company's PS-1 classification. It was built in 1960. The big "DF" stands for "Damage Free," indicating that the car is quipped with special restraining devices inside so that loads can be stabilized against shifting.

(both) William E. Griffin Coll.

In December 1960, RF&P purchased 83 of the 60-foot, 100-ton box cars numbered 6000-6082 from FMC Corporation to handle the newsprint business of the Bear Island Paper Company. Newsprint is sent from the paper mill to users in huge rolls.

No. 3301, a 70-ton, 52-foot, low-side, drop-end gondola was built by General American Transportation Co. in January 1952. It was one of 48 cars in the 3301-3350 series. RF&P characteristically has had little use for gondolas since it served few heavy industries.

(both) William E. Griffin Coll.

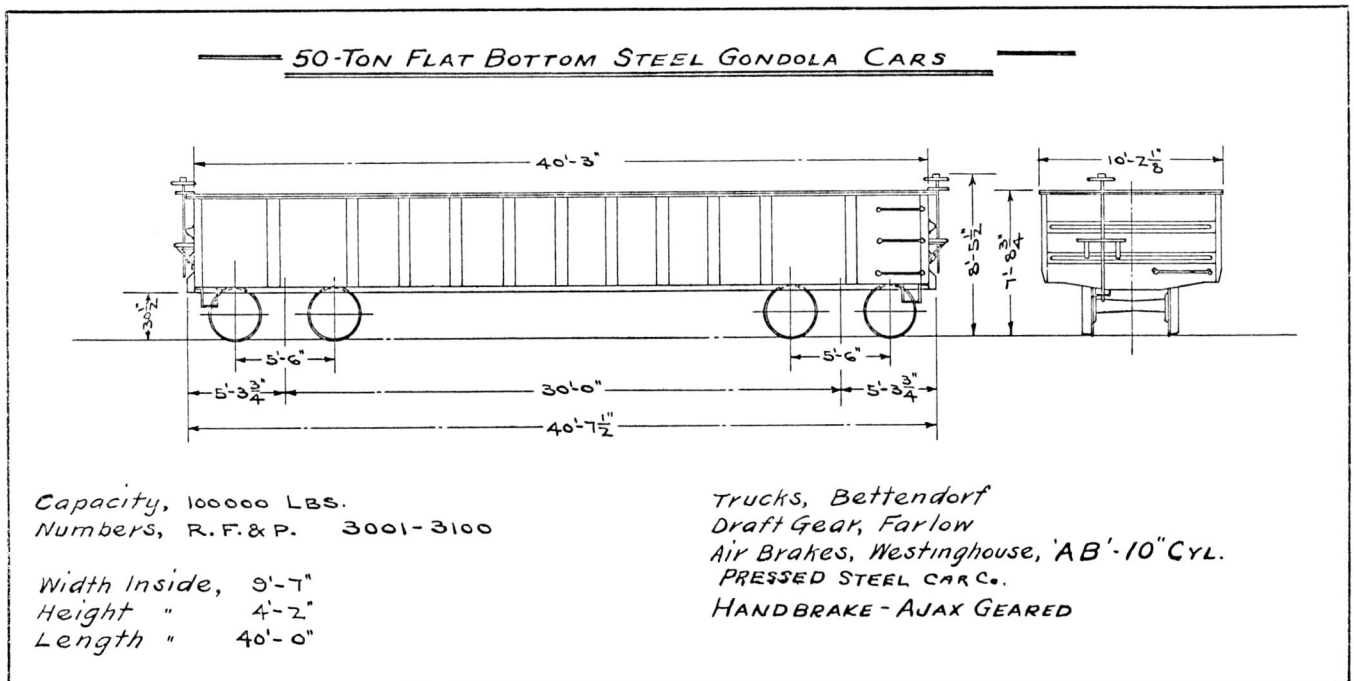

50-TON FLAT BOTTOM STEEL GONDOLA CARS

Capacity, 100000 LBS.
Numbers, R.F.& P. 3001-3100

Width Inside, 9'-7"
Height " 4'-2"
Length " 40'-0"

Trucks, Bettendorf
Draft Gear, Farlow
Air Brakes, Westinghouse, 'AB'-10"Cyl.
PRESSED STEEL CAR Co.
HANDBRAKE - AJAX GEARED

A mechanical diagram showing a more standard gondola owned by the RF&P.

O. W. Kimsey photo, John C. LaRue Coll.

55-ton covered hopper No. 7004 had a capacity of 100,000 pounds. This car was originally numbered 3573 and was built in May 1923. It was photographed at Richmond in 1968.

William E. Griffin Coll.

In April 1980 the RF&P purchased 15 covered hoppers in the series 9000-9014. The 100-ton, 4750-cubic feet capacity cars had round hatches and interior lining and were built by Thrall Car Manufacturing Company.

Hopper cars 7001-7062 were built by Bessemer Company in 1946 and were acquired by RF&P in 1972. They had a capacity of 154,000 pounds and were equipped with two hopper bays.

(Left & right) End views of the two hopper cars at top and bottom of this page.

(all) William E. Griffin Coll.

(Right) Hopper car No. 3601 was the first in a series of 72 cars numbered 3601-3685. These 50-ton steel hoppers with 100,000-pound capacity, were built by Bethlehem Steel Co. in 1905 and were acquired by the RF&P 62 years later, in 1967, and rebuilt. This car was retired in 1979.

RF&P owned 50 LC-class woodrack cars Nos. 3801-3850. These 70-capacity cars were built by Fruit Growers Express in 1965. Nos. 3801-3831 were converted to bulkhead flats in December 1977. RF&P also owned 20 SP-class 70-ton woodracks Nos. 3851-3870, built by Fruit Growers Express in 1967. Beginning in 1984, most woodrack cars were leased to Westvaco Corporation. These cars are at the Doswell pulpwood yard.

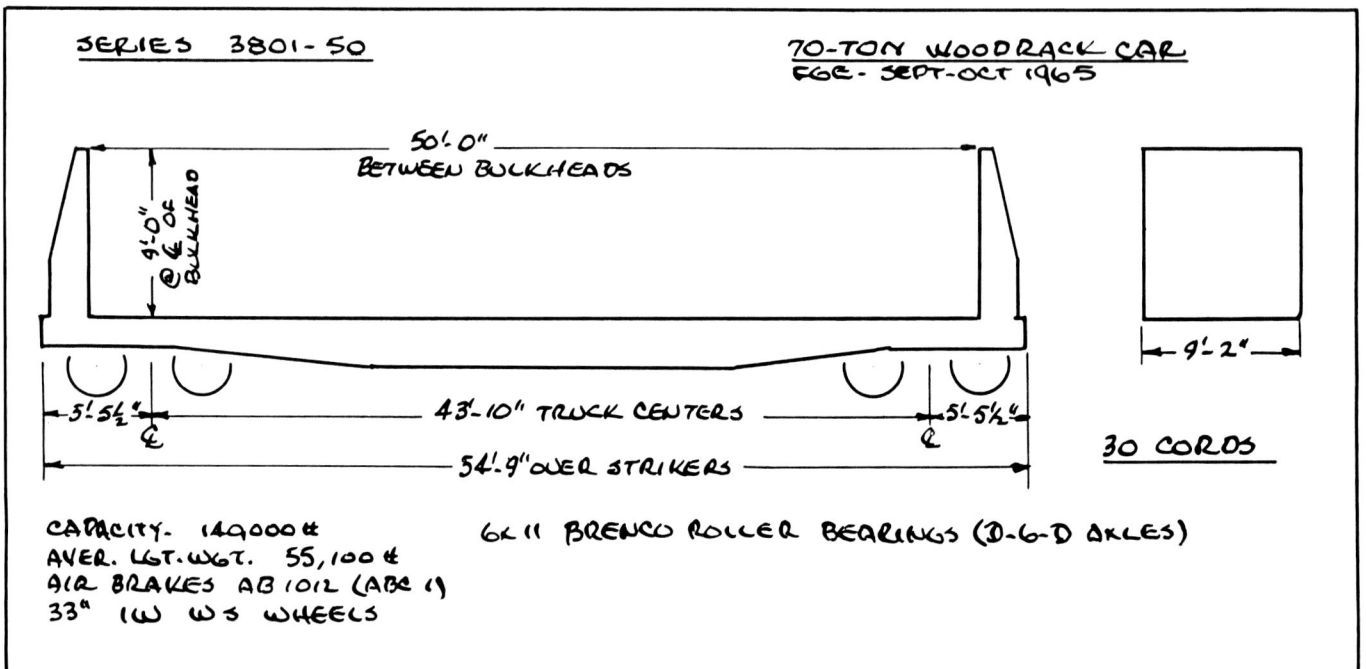

SERIES 3801-50   70-TON WOODRACK CAR
                                                   FGE - SEPT-OCT 1965

50'-0"
BETWEEN BULKHEADS

9'-0"
@ ℄ OF
BULKHEAD

43'-10" TRUCK CENTERS   5'-5½"
5'-5½"   9'-2"

54'-9" OVER STRIKERS   30 CORDS

CAPACITY. 140000#   6K11 BRENCO ROLLER BEARINGS (D-6-D AXLES)
AVER. LGT. WGT. 55,100#
AIR BRAKES AB 1012 (ABC 1)
33" IW WS WHEELS

(both) William E. Griffin Coll.

Mechanical diagram for the 3801-3850-series woodrack cars shows a 54-foot/9-inch car with a capacity of 140,000 pounds and light weight of 55,100 pounds. Pulpwood was brought by local cutters by truck to wood yards either owned by the railroad or a major paper company, where the wood was purchased and stored, then shipped by rail to the appropriate mill. Today most of the wood is taken directly to the mill by truck.

RF&P leased 15 Bi-level Automobile Rack Cars from Trailer Train Company in October 1966 in the Trailer Train series BTTX 904782-904799, and added its logos and name to the racks. By the late 1950s, transportation of new automobiles by box car, which had been the norm since the beginnning of the business, had shifted to rack-trucks over the highway, but for long distance transportation the railroads began to develop the automobile rack car like this one.

A more modern auto rack car is this TTBX bi-level No. 802129 built in July 1974. Totally enclosed, these cars were designed to prevent vandalism that could occur with the open-rack cars.

(all) William E. Griffin Coll.

RF&P might have relied on its connecting roads to provide most of the cars in its freight trains, but the railroad had its own caboose on each one while making the Richmond-Washingon trip, and for its own local freights. Caboose No. 822, shown in June 1944, was built in 1904 and sold by the RF&P in 1950 to the Pacific Electric Railway.

The 41-foot, steel-underframe wooden cabooses in the 932-941 series illustrated on this page were converted from stock cars by RF&P mechanical forces in 1943-44. No. 941 is shown at Fredericksburg on July 12, 1952.

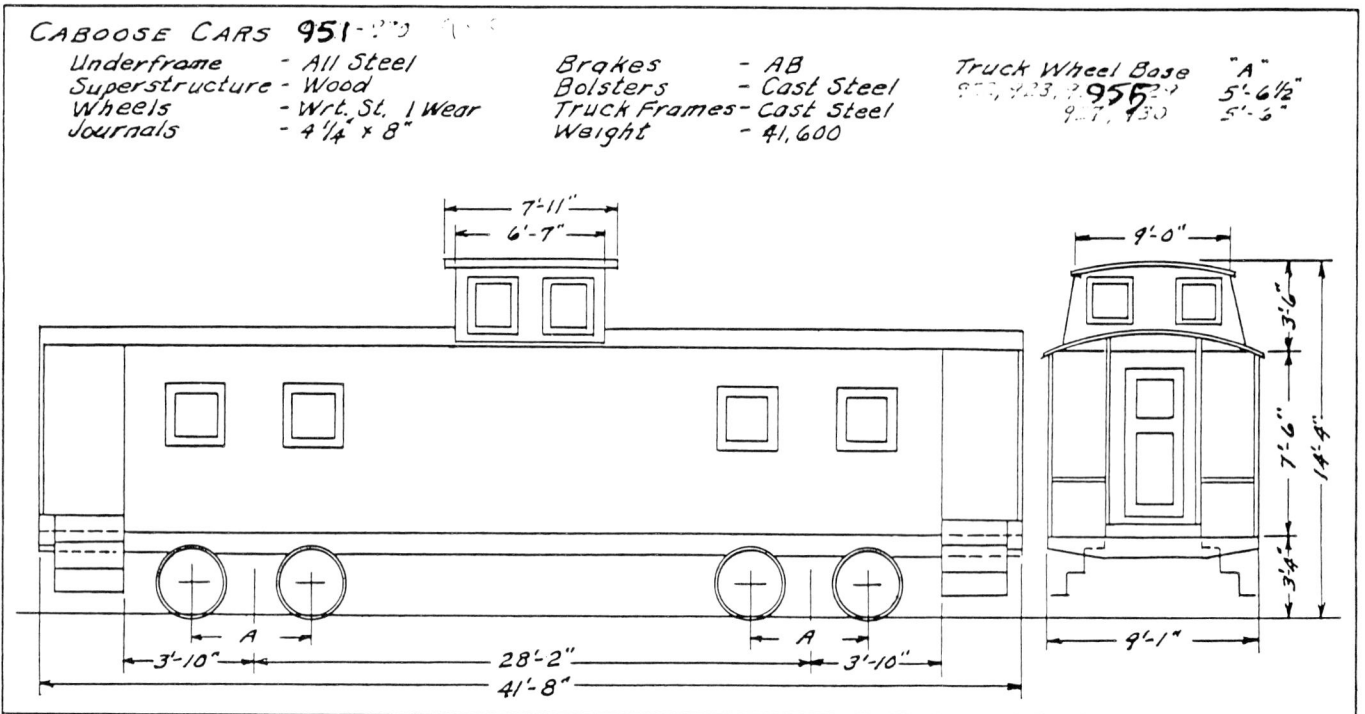

CABOOSE CARS 951-

Underframe	- All Steel	Brakes	- AB	Truck Wheel Base	"A"	
Superstructure	- Wood	Bolsters	- Cast Steel	955, 923, 2 **955**	5'-6½"	
Wheels	- Wrt. St. 1 Wear	Truck Frames	- Cast Steel	9 , 930	5'- 6	
Journals	- 4¼" x 8"	Weight	- 41,600			

(Above) Mechanical diagram for the converted cabooses, some of which were later renumbered.

(Right) No. 935 at Potomac Yard August 18, 1957, wearing the fairly uncommon round RF&P herald.

Photos and drawings on this page show RF&P cabooses in the 801-845 series. At right No. 839 awaits another assignment at Potomac Yard on May 2, 1937.

L. W. Rice photo, T. W. Dixon Coll.

No. 817, built in 1917, is shown here at Acca Yard in 1969. It was retired in 1970.

(both) William E. Griffin Coll.

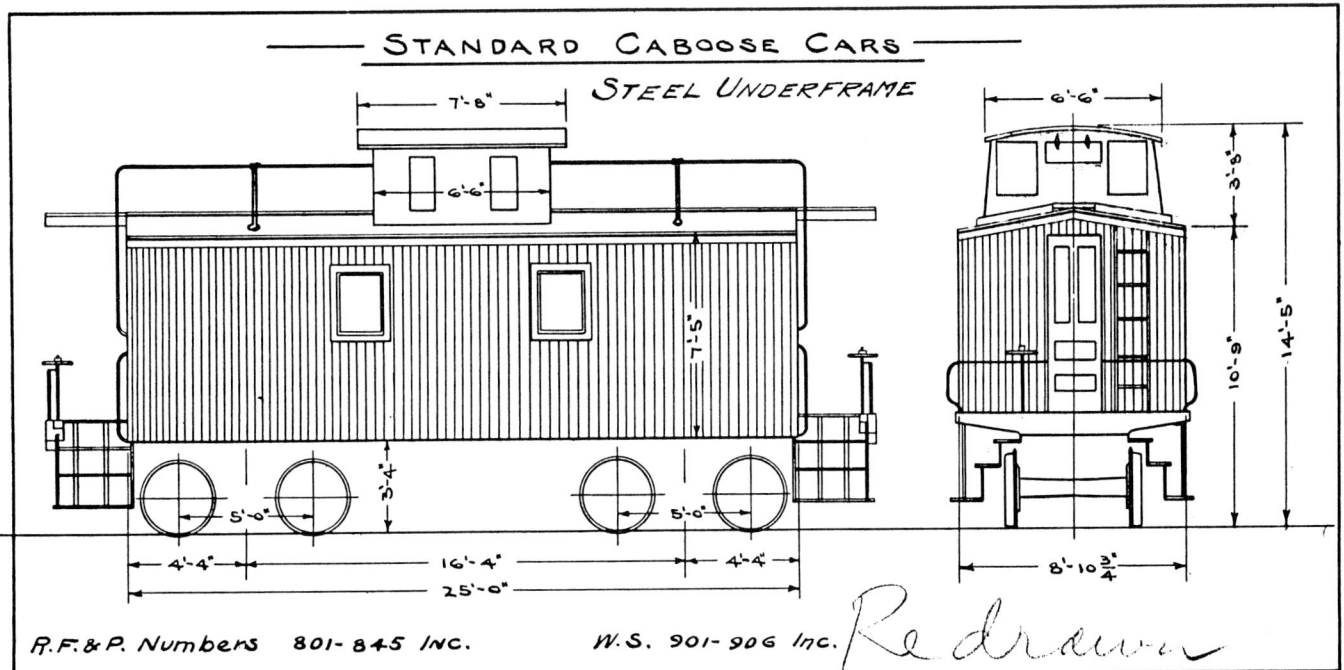

STANDARD CABOOSE CARS
STEEL UNDERFRAME

R.F.&P. Numbers 801-845 Inc.   W.S. 901-906 Inc.   Redrawn

Diagram of the 801-845 series shows a different looking car. They were modified through a long life to look more like those in the photos on this page.

Steel-underframe wooden caboose No. 954 was built in 1942 and was formerly No. 920 until renumbered in 1971. It is shown here at Acca Yard on March 9, 1973, with the "Linking North & South" logo.

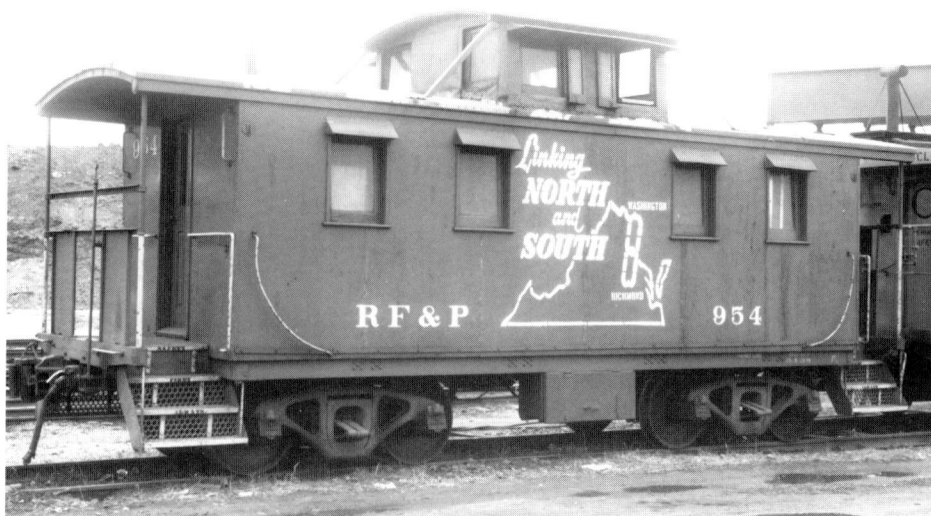

Caboose No. 933 was photographed at Richmond on May 9, 1986. The cabooses in the 921-923 and 931-933 series were built by Southern Iron and Equipment Company in 1971 and were the first all-steel cabooses owned by RF&P.

New caboose No. 905 is shown at Bryan Park Terminal on May 5, 1973 prior to its first service trip.

William E. Griffin

RF&P owned six of the "air-operated side dump" type 80,000-pound-capacity ballast cars. Nos. 681-684 were purchased from the Clark Car Co. in 1923 and were renumbered 241-244 in 1970. Cars 685 and 686 were built by Koppel Industrial Car and Equipment Co. in 1945. The cars were especially built so that ballast could be dumped easily alongside the track for maintenance work. Ordinary hoppers could be used but were much less efficient because they dumped directly under the car, fouling it.

David E. George

In 1979 RF&P purchased 20 ore cars of 60-ton capacity from Duluth, Missabe & Iron Range Railroad and had them converted for use as ballast cars. Numbered 316-355, these cars had been built by Pullman-Standard in 1943. No. 317 is pictured at Fredericksburg in 1986.

RF&P owned 15 "sides-extended" 100,000-pound-capacity ballast cars. Built by Rogers Ballast Car Co. in 1924, they were originally numbered 666-680 and later renumbered to 301-315. Note the side-opening doors, which allowed the ballast to spill out beside the track rather than under the car, similar to the side-dump cars except in a different arrangement. Although considered a fairly archaic design, Chessie System had a number of this style car built in the mid-1970s for revenue service.

Wreck train camp car No. 20037 was originally a 1900-era baggage car that was converted to company service January 16, 1940. It was retired in 1968 and sold for scrap.

Another wreck train car was No. 20041, converted from a 1910 coach in August 1947, and retired on May 15, 1968.

(three) William E. Griffin Coll.

RF&P's ancient and diminutive inspection car No. 50000 is shown here at Acca Yard on October 24, 1937. It was being used on a Railroad Enthusuiasts Washington Chapter "fantrip."

L. W. Rice photo, T. W. Dixon Coll.

Wrecking cranes were a necessity for any railroad. Pictured above is new 250-ton-capacity RF&P No. 1, built by Industrial Brownhoist Corporation and placed in service December 26, 1945. It was retired in 1980. By that date most railroads were using contractors to remove wrecks and the need for railroad-owned equipment such as this, especially those steam-powered cranes, diminished.

Another RF&P wrecker, smaller in size than No. 1 above, is pictured at Potomac Yard July 4, 1946. It was built by Bucyrus, another of the important crane manufacturers.

The car pictured on this page, RF&P No. 700 is not easily classified. It certainly is neither maintenance nor revenue equipment. It's a very unusual piece of equipment used at Potomac Yard and classified simply as a "Poling Car."

Most freight cars until about thirty years ago were built with "pole pockets" on each of their corners, so that a heavy wooden pole could be placed by a brakeman between the pocket on the car and the pocket on the pilot beam of a locomotive on an adjacent track and the car could then be pushed by the locomotive from the adjacent track. This saved additional switching moves, but was also dangerous for the brakemen handling the poles, so it was eventually banned. In 1940, when these photos were taken, the practice was still common, and this car was especially built for use on the yard. It's pole was a permanently attached beam that had a counterweight which a brakeman standing in the side door could manipulate into the pole pocket of the car, while being shoved by a switcher. This was a much safer method.

The car may be unique to the RF&P—certainly quite unusual.

(all) L. W. Rice photos, T. W. Dixon Coll.

A small RF&P "yard" or "shop" crane at Potomac Yard April 13, 1947. These cranes were common fixtures on railroads of that era, used to handle innumerable small lifting jobs around shops and in yards, and for various track maintenance duties out on the road.

The Potomac Yard wreck train on August 18, 1957, consisted of a crane, two flat cars loaded with tools and a couple of sets of freight car trucks, as well as appropriate wooden blocking material, a converted passenger car serving as a diner/sleeper for the crew, and two supply cars carrying additional tools, parts, and supplies that might be needed at a wreck site.

Steam-Era Color Chart for RF&P Locomotives & Cars

Locomotives

Cab exterior, roof, frames, running gear, wheels, cab sash	Black
Letters, numbers & striping	Gold Leaf
Smokebox	Light Gray Graphite
Boiler Jacket	Gray
Main & Side Rods	Polished & oiled
Running Boards	Imitation gold outside edge
Tenders:	
Wheels	Black with imitation gold on rims
Letters, numbers & striping	Gold Leaf
All other parts	Black

Passenger Equipment

Exterior body including: sash, steps, trucks, fronts of underbody boxes	Pullman Green
Underframe, underneath equipment, roof, hand holds, drip molding, diaphragms	Black
Lettering & numbering	Gold Leaf

Freight Equipment

Box Cars	
Underframe	Black
Sides, doors, ends, roof, running boards	Freight Car Brown
Sill steps, trucks	Black
Lettering	White
Gondola & Hopper Cars	
Underframe	Black
Floors	Not painted
Sides, ends, sill steps, trucks	Black
Lettering	White
Stock Cars	
Underframe, sill steps, trucks	Black
Sides, doors, ends, roof, running boards	Freight Car Brown
Lettering	White
Flat Cars	
Underframe, sides, ends, sill steps, trucks	Black
Lettering	White
Work Equipment	
Body	Pullman Green
Trucks , roof	Black
Lettering	Yellow
Caboose Cars	
Car body, exterior	Vermillion enamel
Roof and trucks, railing, columns, ladders	Black
Underframe, metal toolbox, hand holds (end sill)	Black
Lettering	White
Car Body, interior:	Ceiling: Gray, Side walls: yellow
Hand holds, body	Vermillion

RF&P Letter 2/3/1945, W. E. Griffin Coll.

NEED A PLANT SITE?

The RF&P has one for YOU in

VIRGINIA

WITH SOUTHERN ADVANTAGES:

- Excellent Rail Service in all Directions
- Moderate Climate
- Friendly Government
- Abundant Manpower
- Favorable Labor-Management Relations
- Reasonable Taxes & Real Estate Values
- Low Cost Power & Utilities
- Access to Major Consumer Markets
- Friendly Communities
- Outstanding Educational Facilities

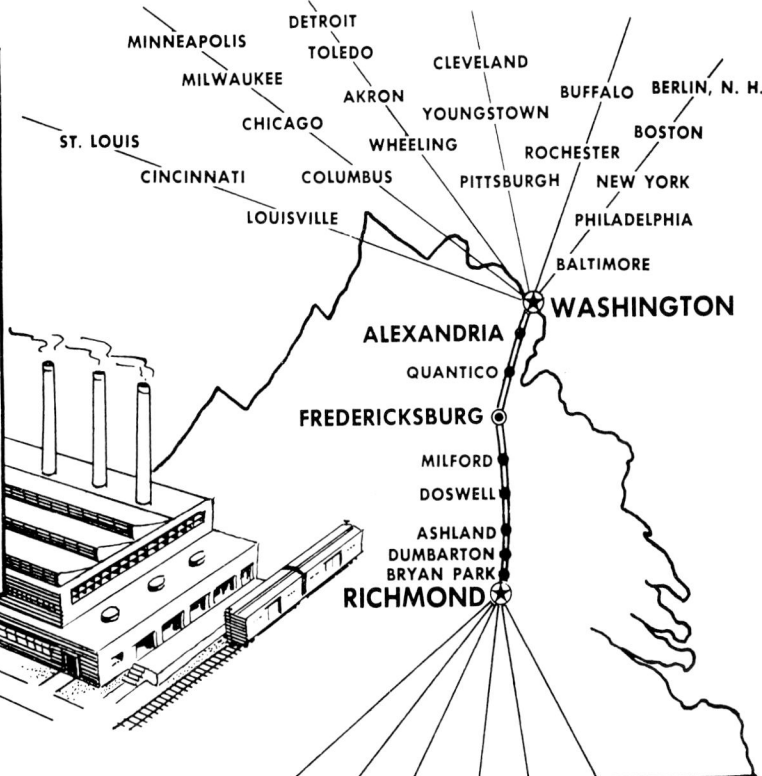

DETROIT
MINNEAPOLIS · TOLEDO · CLEVELAND
MILWAUKEE · AKRON · YOUNGSTOWN · BUFFALO · BERLIN, N. H.
CHICAGO · WHEELING · ROCHESTER · BOSTON
ST. LOUIS · COLUMBUS · PITTSBURGH · NEW YORK
CINCINNATI · LOUISVILLE · PHILADELPHIA · BALTIMORE

WASHINGTON
ALEXANDRIA
QUANTICO
FREDERICKSBURG
MILFORD
DOSWELL
ASHLAND
DUMBARTON
BRYAN PARK
RICHMOND

ATHENS · AUGUSTA · GOLDSBORO · PETERSBURG
CHATTANOOGA · MACON · WILSON · FRANKLIN
ATLANTA · MONTGOMERY · RALEIGH · SUFFOLK
BIRMINGHAM · MOBILE · TAMPA · WILMINGTON · PORTSMOUTH
NEW ORLEANS · CHARLOTTE · CHARLESTON · NEWPORT NEWS
ST. PETERSBURG · COLUMBIA · NORFOLK
MIAMI · QUINLAN · SAVANNAH
JACKSONVILLE

**Let Us Help You Find
A Profit-Making Plant Site
in VIRGINIA!**

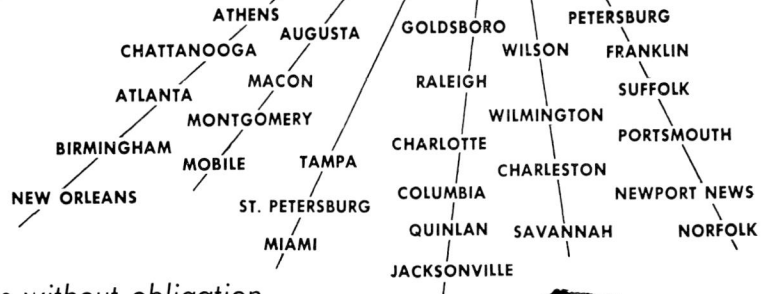

Confidential, personalized surveys without obligation

Write:

William E. Turner
Vice Pres., Traffic &
Industrial Development

C. E. Whitmore, Jr.
Manager, Real Estate &
Industrial Development

1001

William E. Griffin Coll.

RICHMOND, FREDERICKSBURG & POTOMAC RAILROAD
Broad Street Station • Richmond 20, Virginia

1834 • *134 Years of Dependable Service* • 1968

RF&P loved to use its map showing all the connections north and south in ads such as this, trying to attract new business to the area.

189

In December 1984 GP35 No. 131 rounds the curve at Daffan, just south of Potomac Creek, with southbound Train No. 171, the "Orange Blossom Special." *(William E. Griffin, Jr.)*

Chapter 9

The RF&P in Color - An Album

William E. Griffin Coll.

Northbound Train No. 92, the *West Coast Champion*, is ready to depart Broad Street Station behind RF&P E8 No. 1004. This train operated between New York and Tampa via the Pennsylvania Railroad, RF&P, and Atlantic Coast Line.

A southbound freight rolls through Gwathmey, just south of Ashland, behind an A-B-A set of F7s. No. 1106 heads up the consists in this 1953 view.

William B. Gwaltney

Freshly painted and sparkling in the morning sun, a pair of RF&P E8s with No. 1002 nearest are parked at Broad Street Station on May 24, 1970, in the last year of passenger service before the Amtrak takeover. They wear the simplified second paint scheme with the gray stripe horizontal around the nose. The initial scheme had the stripe dip in a stylish "bow wave" at the front (see previous page).

(both) Thomas W. Dixon

This view of the ready tracks at Bryan Park Terminal on January 25, 1970 shows a variety of power including two RF&P E8s.

F7A No. 1104 at Bryan Park Terminal in Richmond.

William E. Griffin Coll.

In 1986 RF&P recommissioned GP7 No. 101 to service after a painstaking restoration. Using parts taken from four locomotives the "new 101" was restored as nearly as possible to its original appearance. This photo was taken on June 19, 1986, the date of its recommissioning ceremony at Acca Yard. It was donated to the Old Dominion Chapter, NRHS and later leased to the Buckingham Branch Railroad, a shortline using a former C&O branch on the James River west of Richmond.

RF&P GP-diesels, incluidng GP40 No. 125 and GP40-2 No. 147 have been serviced at Bryan Park Terminal and are ready for the next trip north in November 1980.

William E. Griffin

The cab of an overhead Whiting 120-foot traveling bridge crane provided an excellent vantage point to photograph the locomotive section of Bryan Park Terminal, with a variety of motive power undergoing heavy repairs in 1969.

William E. Griffin Coll.

A historic photograph—GP35 No. 133 is posed in front of the paint shop at Bryan Park Terminal on July 26, 1991. This was the last RF&P diesel to be painted at the shop (which was the only building left of the old Acca Locomotive Terminal that had been built in 1924).

(both) William E. Griffin

Departing Potomac Yard, GP40-2 No. 141 leads southbound Train No. 109 past Amtrak No. 82, the northbound *Silver Star* at Alexandria Union Station in January 1984.

Fall color highlights the passage of southbound Train No. 191 in October 1985. GP35 No. 133 leads the train in a view taken from the US Route 17 overpass at Fredericksburg. *(William E. Griffin)*

Coupled to the rear of Amtrak Train No. 86, the northbound *Virginian*, RF&P Car *ONE* is ready to depart Amtrak's Greendale (Richmond) passenger station on a May 1991 morning with the RF&P President and members of his staff for a business trip to Alexandria and Potomac Yard.

(both) William E. Griffin

The table's set and as we pull through Ashland its time to sit down for breakfast on our morning trip to Alexandria aboard business car *ONE*. The table, set by the car's cook Jimmy Green, is in the grand style of private cars.

Thomas W. Dixon, Jr.

Lightweight coach 843 glistens with fresh paint at Broad Street Station on May 24, 1970, in its tastefully understated blue/gray livery with gold striping and lettering for accentuation.

William E. Griffin

GP40 No. 124 heads up the Tropicana Juice Train, shown at Hermitage Road Crossing north of Acca Yard in May 1991. RF&P participated with Conrail and SCL in handling this unit train of Tropicana Products between Bradenton, Florida and Kearney, New Jersey.

199

Slug No. S-2 and SW1500 No. 7 at the Potomac Yard engine servicing facility in August 1990. Chrome Locomotive rebuilt four of the SW1500s (including No. 7). Two slugs (No. S-1 and S-2) were purchased in 1985 for service on the new processed controlled computerized northbound hump yard.

(both) William E. Griffin

GP40 No. 125, fresh from the paint shop at Bryan Park Terminal on May 19, 1989, sports the last paint scheme applied to diesels, which included the stylized "RF&P" on the nose and rear of the long hood, the gold herald under the cab window and large number. In blue and gray it was symbolic of the North-South link.

Resplendent in light blue and white paint, RF&P Caboose No. 951, renumbered from 824 in 1971, and box car No. 2392 were photographed at the Fredericksburg freight station in July 1973.

The 70-ton, 50-foot (actually 50-feet and 6-inches long) box car No. 2530 was built by Fruit Growers Express, whose shop was next to the RF&P main line in Alexandria, in 1966.

Slug unit "A," shown at Potomac Yard in August 1984, was converted from former ALCO S-2 switcher No.62. Along with slugs "B" and "C," also converted from ALCO diesels, it was used as an auxiliary power booster unit with the 1500-horsepower diesels on the hump switching assignments.

Steel-underframe wooden caboose No. 803 was built in 1917 and was still in service when photographed in July 1970.

Steel caboose No. 906 was brand new when photographed at Bryan Park Terminal in May 1973.

(both) William E. Griffin

The last two RF&P cabooses, steel cars Nos. 903 and 907, were painted red in 1987. In this photo, No. 903 is fresh from the paint shop in February 1987.

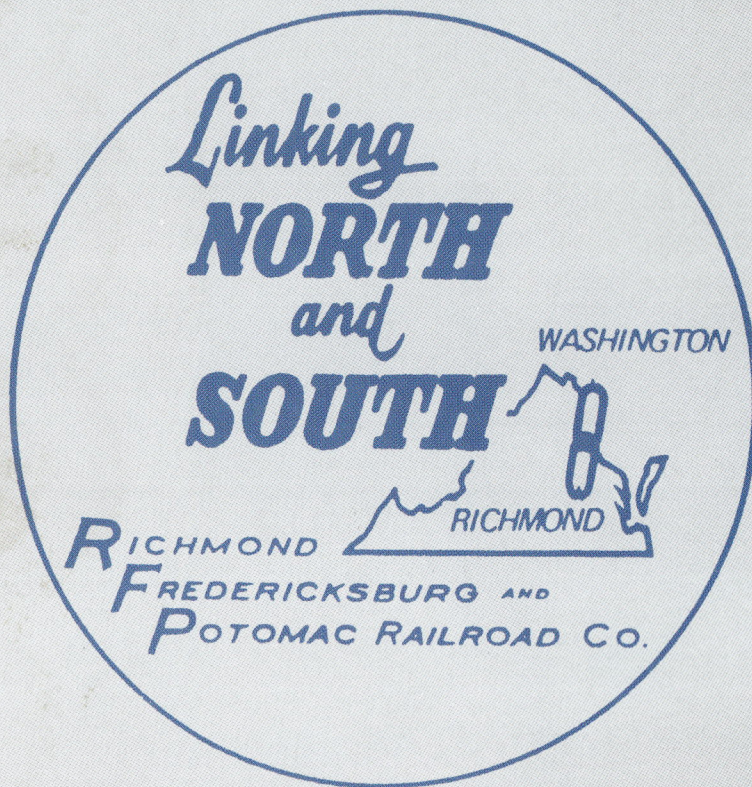

Linking
NORTH
and
SOUTH

WASHINGTON

RICHMOND

Richmond
Fredericksburg and
Potomac Railroad Co.